They Seek a Country

THE AMERICAN PRESBYTERIANS

". . . they seek a country"

HEBREWS 11:4

THE MACMILLAN COMPANY
NEW YORK • CHICAGO
DALLAS • ATLANTA • SAN FRANCISCO
LONDON • MANILA

**THE MACMILLAN COMPANY
OF CANADA, LIMITED**
TORONTO

They Seek a Country

THE AMERICAN PRESBYTERIANS

Some Aspects

GAIUS JACKSON SLOSSER, EDITOR

CONTRIBUTORS

FRANK H. CALDWELL

DAVID M. CARSON

CLIFFORD M. DRURY

JOHN H. GERSTNER, JR.

H. GORDON HAROLD

KENNETH SCOTT LATOURETTE

LEFFERTS A. LOETSCHER

JOHN A. MACKAY

WILLIAM W. MCKINNEY

JAMES HASTINGS NICHOLS

GLADYS SCHMITT

GAIUS JACKSON SLOSSER

WILLIAM WARREN SWEET

ERNEST TRICE THOMPSON

EDWARD BURGETT WELSH

The Macmillan Company, NEW YORK, 1955

Introduction

THIS volume had its inception as the result of the united action of the Presbyterian Historical Society of the Upper Ohio Valley, an Auxiliary of the Historical Society of the Presbyterian Church in the United States of America, with its headquarters and library in the Witherspoon Building of Philadelphia. On October 2–3, 1953, a notable Historical Symposium, with the editor as program chairman, was carried out with its session in the First United Presbyterian Church of Allegheny in Pittsburgh. At this Symposium the lectures behind the various chapters of this book were delivered. These lectures, with their authors, their subjects, and the chapters in which their messages are to be found, are as follows:

Ch. I ORIGINS *Gaius Jackson Slosser*
Ch. II BEGINNINGS IN THE NORTH *William W. McKinney*
Ch. III BEGINNINGS IN THE SOUTH *Ernest Trice Thompson*
Ch. IV THE UNITED PRESBYTERIAN CHURCH
John H. Gerstner, Jr.
Ch. V THE REFORMED PRESBYTERIAN CHURCH IN AMERICA
David M. Carson
Ch. VI THE FOUNDING OF EDUCATIONAL INSTITUTIONS
William Warren Sweet
Ch. VII SERVICE IN FOUNDING AND PRESERVING THE NATION
H. Gordon Harold
Ch. VIII MISSIONARY EXPANSION AT HOME *Clifford M. Drury*
Ch. IX SERVING OVERSEAS *Kenneth Scott Latourette*

Ch. X WRESTLING WITH HUMAN VALUES: THE SLAVERY YEARS
Edward Burgett Welsh

Ch. XI EVENTS AND TRENDS—EARLY NINETEENTH CENTURY
James Hastings Nichols

Ch. XII SOME TRENDS AND EVENTS SINCE 1869
Lefferts A. Loetscher

Ch. XIII TODAY AND TOMORROW: THE ROAD AHEAD
Gladys Schmitt, Frank H. Caldwell, John A. Mackay

All of the foregoing lectures, with a minimum of editing, have been brought together to present what is believed to be a much needed and up-to-date sketch of one of America's Christian communions. A complete narrative history has not been attempted. But it is believed that the chronological arrangement, together with the cross references, make for a unity of treatment that possesses the added value of having been produced with inclusive viewpoints.

At the Symposium the Western Theological Seminary of the Presbyterian Church in the U.S.A. and the Pittsburgh-Xenia Theological Seminary of the United Presbyterian Church of North America cooperated by suspending all classes for the two days, so that the faculties and student bodies could be present.

Special recognition must be given to the following, who performed invaluable service in connection with the Symposium and with the consequent production of this volume:

All of the lecturers as listed; the officers and members of the local Presbyterian Historical Society; my colleagues on the faculty of Western Theological Seminary, Dr. J. Carter Swaim and Dr. Ralph G. Turnbull; Dr. Charles A. Anderson, Executive of the Presbyterian Historical Society; my pupils William D. Bair and especially Roland William Gorton, the latter giving expert assistance in the preparation of the manuscript, the bibliography, and index; John J. Bates, George W. Kiehl, William G. Rusch, and David M. Thompson for numerous helps; President Clifford Barbour for allocating the Elliot Lecture Fund of Western Theological Seminary for Dr. Latourette's address; the faculties both of Western and of the Pittsburgh-Xenia Theological seminaries for cooperation with the Symposium; the Ruling Elders Association of the Presbytery of Pittsburgh; the Pitcairn-Crabbe Foundation; and the following outstanding lay leaders of Presbyterianism: Wilson A. Campbell, Lynn A. Carson, Allen S. Davison, Mrs. J. Harry Gorley, Lewis W. Hicks, Ernest K. Hoge, T. Lamar Jackson, Esq., the Honorable Edward Martin, Samuel Chalmers McConahey, Samuel W. Miller, Esq., John J. Paull, Alexander C. Robinson, William M. Robinson, and Mrs. Samuel Warden. These latter are examples of the laity without whom the visible church of Christ, in any age, could not live and serve.

Certain major groups of American Presbyterians, such as the continuing Cumberland Presbyterian Church, in their developments of nearly the last half-century, are not included in this story. Because this volume is adorned and greatly enhanced in value by its illustrations and because its title includes the term "aspects," the editor has constructed a "Who's Who" which admittedly includes many not found in the illustrations and some not mentioned in the text.

The Appendix, "Educational Institutions . . . and Theological Seminaries," has been added for the same reasons. Its contents are believed to be of great importance for the presentation of a major aspect. To have set forth the whole picture would have required volumes. Hence the chronological method, which we hope expresses the most in the fewest words. To fulfill the scheme of the treatise, there have been certain omissions, additions, and changes with respect to the lectures as actually delivered. The editor promises to refer all comments to the proper source, whether in praise or blame.

GAIUS JACKSON SLOSSER

203 SUMMIT AVENUE
BELLEVUE, PITTSBURGH, PA.
NEW YEAR'S DAY, 1955

Contents

INTRODUCTION   v

CHAPTER I *Origins*   1

The three groups in early American Presbyterianism.—Subsequent broadening influences.—Graphs setting forth origins.—Protestant beginnings in northern Ireland.—Convictions and doctrines brought to America.—Calvinism, its origin, analysis, main features, and basic principles.—How Calvinism was brought to America.—The origin and nature of departures from "Orthodoxy".—Rise and influence of Marrowism.—Marrowism and other trends in the background of United Presbyterianism.—Sabbatarianism.—The Ulster-Scotch take a prominent part in the American struggle.—Psalmody and its origins.—Presbyterianism through the centuries.—Strictness in godly character.

CHAPTER II *Beginnings in the North*   27

General appraisal of early American Presbyterianism.—The nature and expansion of Puritan presbyterianism.—Francis Makemie and beginnings of Ulster-Scotch and Scotch Presbyterianism.—The first Presbytery.—Inter-Colonialism promoted by Presbyterianism.—Makemie's trial before Governor Cornbury.—Missionary passion and policy.—Synod of Philadelphia.—Adoption of the Westminster standards with modified subscription.—New Presbyteries formed.—Ulster-Scotch migration.—Assignments for missions work.—The Great Awakening.—Jonathan Edwards.—T. J. Frelinghuysen, Jonathan Dickinson, William and Gilbert Tennent, George Whitefield.—Old Side and New Side schism.—Growth of the united church.

CHAPTER III *Beginnings in the South*   60

Modes of existence, not geography, the key.—The Chesapeake Society.—Alexander Whitaker and Puritan presbyterianism in Virginia.—Francis

ix

Makemie and other leaders.—The first Presbytery and Synod.—The
Carolina Society.—The Back Country-Shenandoah Valley Presbyterianism.—The coming of the Ulster-Scots.—Missionary itineration.—Toleration obtained.—The four earliest pastors in the Valley.—Old Side-New
Side schism.—The Hanover Revival; Samuel Davies.—In the western
Carolinas.—Presbytery of Orange.—Additional Presbyteries.—Comparative failure.—Compensations to an ordered society, to religious liberty,
to political freedom, to education.

CHAPTER IV *The United Presbyterian Church*   86

Scottish origins.—Ebenezer Erskine.—The Secession of 1733.—The
patronage issue, moderatism, Marrowism.—Inner development.—Attachment to the Reformed theology with Calvinistic emphasis.—The Confessional Statement of 1925.—Eight particular emphases of the United
Presbyterians.—Slavery attitudes.—Outer development.—The union of
1782 and subsequent events.—Union of 1858 and growth following.
—Benevolence giving, missions.—Theological education.—Colleges.—
Progress of catholicity.

CHAPTER V *The Reformed Presbyterian Church
in America*   102

Beginnings of covenanting in Scotland.—The National and the Solemn
League and Covenant.—Early names of Covenanters.—Migration to
America.—Alexander Craighead.—Coming of the Cameronians.—John
Cuthbertson.—First Reformed Presbytery.—Foreign missions.—Educa-
tional institutions.—The maintenance of identity.—Adult education.—
Exercise of discipline.—The Society Meeting.—Practice of covenanting.
—Sovereignty of Christ in the Constitution.—For the abolition of
slavery.

CHAPTER VI *The Founding of Educational
Institutions*   127

Calvinists, including several denominations, lead in founding early colleges and universities.—Explanation of this fact.—The earliest colleges
in America.—Princeton University's founding, the Log College, the College of New Jersey.—Princeton, interdenominational, international.—
Other factors leading to the founding of church colleges.—Principle of
separation of church and state.—Dartmouth College case.—Second
Great Awakening.—The challenge of the Frontier.—Presbyterians and
Congregationalists in Plan of Union of 1801.—Methodists and Baptists.

—Presbyterians and Log Colleges.—John McMillan.—Earliest colleges of western Pennsylvania, Kentucky, Tennessee, Ohio.—Covenanters and United Presbyterians.—Presbyterians lead in founding colleges.—Motives in college founding.—By-products.—The beginning of theological schools.

CHAPTER VII *Service in Founding and Preserving the Nation* 150

Calvinism, the theology of colonial churchmen.—"John Calvin, Founder of America".—Calvinism's influence.—Factors promoting independence. —The Mecklenburg Resolves, 1775.—Presbyterians in the Revolutionary War.—The Preservation of the nation.—Sociological and spiritual service.

CHAPTER VIII *Missionary Expansion at Home* 165

Expansion by migration and maintenance of institutional loyalties.— Early missionary techniques.—Eighteenth century church membership proportionately low.—The period of experimentation and growth, 1802–1837.—Plan of Union of 1801.—The whole church becoming a missionary society.—Why the Presbyterians trailed the Methodists and the Baptists.—The founding of theological seminaries and colleges.—The period of division, 1837–1869.—Continued growth, 1870–1952.—Factors effecting growth evaluated.

CHAPTER IX *Serving Overseas* 191

Adequate treatment difficult.—Early participation in work of American Board.—Missions in many countries.—Spanish America.—Africa, the Moslem World.—Southeastern Asia.—China.—Korea.—Are characteristic patterns discernible?—Colleges and universities.—Educational, language, and other problems.—Participation in union enterprises.—The purpose of true unity.

CHAPTER X *Wrestling with Human Values: The Slavery Years* 210

Moral versus theological struggles.—An infant evil grows into a giant curse.—Seven steps which led to open conflict.—The background and setting of this drama.—The economic complications of this moral problem.—Various church court actions cited.—Resolutions of 1787, 1793,

1795, 1815, 1818.—Proof of loss of power to discern evil.—New School
Assembly actions.—Origins of the Free Church.

CHAPTER XI *Events and Trends—Early Nineteenth
Century*   234

Ulster-Scotch Presbyterian migration to points in western New York,
Pennsylvania, Ohio, western Virginia, and Kentucky after the Revolution.—Strict conservatism brings troubles.—The Plan of Union of 1801
and resulting schism.—The Auburn Affirmation.—The Mercersburg
Movement.—John W. Nevin and Philip Schaff, their views relative to
the church, the sacraments, and related themes.—Charles Hodge and
the same themes.—What may be anticipated.

CHAPTER XII *Some Trends and Events Since 1869*   251

Expansion at home and abroad.—Educational advances.—Social concern.—Problems of peace and war.—Organization and promotion.—
Theological changes.—Public worship.—Interdenominational cooperation.—Toward a universal church.

CHAPTER XIII *Today and Tomorrow: The Road
Ahead*   267

GLADYS SCHMITT   267
Need of spiritual revival.—Situation today not so different from that of
the early church.—Current literature and cinema tawdry.—Biblical history and themes deserve greater literature and finer art.—Terrible honesty
and self-discipline needed to set forth adequately the Christian mes-
sage.—This century yearns for truly great Christian drama.

FRANK H. CALDWELL   271
A way backward to go forward.—The evils of church division.—A way
to renewed vitality as the fellowship of redemption.—The Word of
God in persons who are a renewed creation by and in the Spirit of God.
—Such persons must be dedicated in full allegiance including thought,
affection, and volition.—Christ's peace, not mere earthly peace.

JOHN A. MACKAY   279
Presbyterianism as theological outlook: emphasizes that God should be
loved with the mind.—The church is Biblical; it is the instrument of
God's glory to be the witness to His truth, to execute His redemptive

will; it must permit no rival to Deity.—The majesty of truth; truth must not become subordinate to propaganda; it must become incarnate.

The Reformed heritage emphasizes the vocation of man.—Man's chief end.—Jesus, the clue to man's calling.—Man is truly man when he is God's man.

The sovereign rule of God involves the unveiling of the inner meaning of God's order.—The following affirmations stand forth: (1) Every human individual is sacred; (2) It never pays to be vindictive; (3) Ideas can not be dealt with by the police or the military; (4) Conference must never be refused; grace must be exercised even with those who are evil.

Presbyterianism involves ecclesiastical structure.—The World Presbyterian Alliance.—The pending union between three Presbyterian denominations examined and observations made.—Reasons why this proposed union should be consummated.—Objections answered.—The Alliance should lead its members out of narrow nationalism and racialism.—Presbyterianism and the ecumenical movement.—"The Communion of Saints" is taken seriously.—Opposed to making any structural form absolute, also to creation of a super-church.—Unity must be in the Saviourhood and Lordship of Jesus Christ.—Conclusion.

WHO'S WHO   Sketches of Notable Presbyterians   292

APPENDIX   Educational Institutions . . . and Theological Seminaries   302

NOTES   308

BIBLIOGRAPHY   322

INDEX   325

GRAPHS   of Scottish and American Presbyterianism   331

Illustrations

BETWEEN PAGES 14–15

FOUNDERS: John Calvin, John Knox, Ebenezer Erskine, Francis Makemie

FOUNDERS: John Witherspoon, Jonathan Dickinson, Elisha Swift, Ashbel Green

PREACHER-EVANGELISTS: Gilbert Tennent, Charles G. Finney, George Whitefield, Toyohiko Kagawa, Samuel Davies

COLLEGE BEGINNINGS: The Log College, Nassau Hall

78–79

MISSIONARIES: Hunter Corbett, William H. Sheppard, J. C. R. Ewing, W. A. P. Martin, W. M. Morrison

MISSIONARIES: Sheldon Jackson, A. P. Happer, Daniel Baker, Mrs. A. R. McFarland, Sam Higginbottom

MISSIONS ADMINISTRATORS: Robert E. Speer, John Leighton Wilson, Charles R. Watson

MISSIONS ADMINISTRATORS: Henry Kendall, A. J. Brown, Hermann N. Morse, John A. Mackay

142–143

EDUCATIONAL FOUNDERS: John McMillan, William Graham, Philip Lindsley, Isaac Ketler, John Holt Rice

SUPPORTERS OF EDUCATION: Robert Dollar, L. H. Severance, Charles C. Beatty, Cyrus H. McCormick

PREACHERS: Jonathan Edwards, Lyman Beecher, Moses Drury Hoge, William S. Plumer

PREACHERS: Henry Sloane Coffin, Henry van Dyke, Albert Barnes, Hugh T. Kerr, George A. Buttrick

206–207

LAYMEN: Harriet Beecher Stowe, Stonewall Jackson, Robert Field Stockton, John Wanamaker

LAYMEN: Henry J. Heinz, Andrew Carnegie, Mrs. W. C. Winsborough, Marcus Whitman, Mildred McAfee Horton

SCHOLARS: Philip Schaff, Charles A. Briggs, James Woodrow, John W. Nevin, Elias Compton

SCHOLARS: Archibald Alexander, John T. Pressly, Charles Hodge, Henry Ruffner, William J. Holland

270–271

MOLDERS OF THOUGHT: Charles Stelzle, James D. Moffatt, John McNaugher, James A. Kelso, Eugene C. Caldwell

STATESMEN-PATRIOTS: Benjamin Rush, John Hay, Elias Boudinot, Henry L. Stimson, John Foster Dulles

PRESIDENTS: Andrew Jackson, James Buchanan, Woodrow Wilson

PRESIDENTS: Grover Cleveland, Benjamin Harrison, Dwight David Eisenhower

They Seek a Country

THE AMERICAN PRESBYTERIANS

CHAPTER I

Origins

AMERICAN Presbyterianism, at the time of the formation of
the Constitution, was composed of three rather clearly defined
groups. The first group had its rise with the beginnings of Puritanism in England. The second group had its rise in Scotland and
the northern parts of Ireland either in connection with schisms
from the main body of the Presbyterian Church in these areas, or
was made up of emigrants from that main body and the schisms
—these and their successors in America who took no part in the
Great Awakening of 1725–1745. The third group included those of
English Puritan and those of Scotch or of Ulster-Scotch origins who
took active part in the Great Awakening and led in the founding
of the Log College on the Neshaminy (1728) and in the founding
of the College of New Jersey (1746), now Princeton University.

The earliest leaders of the first and third groups came in ships
that were noted in American colonial history. To Salem, Massachusetts, on June 29, 1629, on the good ship *Talbot*, came the
Reverend Francis Higginson and the Reverend Samuel Skelton
with 406 Puritans, presbyterian Anglicans all. To Boston (later to
Roxbury), Massachusetts, on November 3, 1631, came the Reverend John Eliot, presbyterian Puritan. Already there had served for
six years (1611–1617) at Henricopolis and Bermuda Hundreds, on
the James River, Virginia, that notable presbyterian Puritan Alex-

ander Whitaker, son of the founder of English presbyterian puritanism William Whitaker, Regius Professor of Divinity at the University of Cambridge.

To Plymouth in the *Mayflower* in 1620 had come Elder (presbyter) William Brewster.[1] In his library Calvin's *Institutes of the Christian Religion* and a metrical version of the Psalms were working guides to the understanding of the Scriptures from whence, as Pastor Robinson prayed when the Pilgrims left Holland, it was believed that more light would come.

This presbyterian puritanism and independency culminated in the presbyterian-congregationalism of the Saybrook Platform and in producing such a man as Jonathan Dickinson, the leader in non-strict subscription to the Westminster Standards and first president of the College of New Jersey.

Representatives of the second group attempted to reach America by sailing for the shores of the Merrimac River, in Massachusetts, leaving Groomsport, Ireland, on September 9, 1636, in the ship *Eagle's Wing*. Aboard were 140 subscribers to the Scottish Confession of Faith, the product of John Knox. But, in the providence of God, a purely Ulster-Scotch Presbyterianism was not to have formal beginnings in America thus early. A terrible storm at sea forced the ship to turn back when in the middle of the Atlantic.[2]

In subsequent years, preceding the mass migration from northern Ireland which began in the second quarter of the eighteenth century, there were numerous instances of comparatively small companies of Ulster-Scotch and Scotch Presbyterian churchmen taking up residence in the colonies.

However, the representatives of this second group were here in sufficient numbers by 1706, so that the first Presbytery of what are now the U.S.A. and the U.S. churches was organized in Philadelphia; by 1753 the first Associate Presbytery of the Reformed and United Presbyterian Churches was organized at or near Pequea, Pennsylvania. The first Reformed Presbytery also in the ancestry of the United Presbyterian and the Reformed Churches was organized at Paxtang, near Harrisburg, Pennsylvania, in 1774.

As for the third group—the non-strict subscriptionists—those who stood as they believed for New Testament presbyterianism, including freedom within evangelical catholic bounds—came out of "liberal" (they would now be rated "conservative") backgrounds in Scotland, Ireland, and England, and appeared in a distinct role at the time American Presbyterians faced the issue of subscription to the Westminster Standards in 1729. With the founding of the Log College and Princeton University they came, not without opposition, to full bloom.

I have thus characterized the Presbyterianism of America as it existed at the time of the formation of the United States Constitution. Since then this communion, particularly the northern branch later to be known as the Presbyterian Church in the U.S.A., has become increasingly cosmopolitan in its make-up, having taken into membership those who either directly or indirectly have come from other denominations, such as the French Huguenot, Swiss Reformed, Dutch and German Reformed, Protestant Episcopal, Methodist, Baptist, Lutheran, Congregational, and Roman Catholic. During the nineteenth and twentieth centuries, American Presbyterianism has been greatly enriched by persons coming principally from Scotland, whose attitudes have been broadened by the scholarship of the great Scottish universities. These have helped to remove some of the clannishness and provincialism, racial, national, doctrinal, and Biblical, which led to much of the bitterness of the schisms of 1741–1758 and 1837–1870 and also between the United Presbyterians and Presbyterians resident in the same areas. Having paid tribute to the liberalizing influences coming from Scotland in more recent years, it must be stated that within every branch of American Presbyterianism, beginning with men like Philip Schaff and Charles A. Briggs, there has been, and is now, taking place a broadening process as a result of the influence gained by fearless and catholic evangelical Christian scholarly leadership.

GRAPHS SETTING FORTH ORIGINS *

With this brief over-all survey of American Presbyterian origins up to quite recent times, let us return to an examination, in greater detail, of the origins prior to 1787. For this purpose I have included certain graphs, one labeled "Explanation of Scottish Presbyterian Schisms and Unions, also Unions with the Church of England," [3] and the other "Presbyterian Family Connection." In the former, take special note of the chronology appearing at the top and bottom. Within the period 1608–1824 there are graphed, so far as Presbyterian denominations are concerned, the following: (1) the Church of Scotland; (2) the "Societies," later the "Reformed Presbytery," still later, the "Reformed Presbyterian Church" —this the Covenanter Church, 1663; (3) the Associate Presbytery, Secession Church, 1733, which divided in 1747 into the Anti-Burghers and the Burghers, the latter in 1799 dividing into the Old Light and New Light, the former in 1804 similarly dividing; (4) the Presbytery of Relief, 1752. Note also the union of 1820 forming the United Secession Church and the union of 1847 forming the United Presbyterian Church. Among the Ulster-Scotch Presbyterians of northern Ireland there were similar splits from the parent church (which was really the Scottish Presbyterian Church in Ireland) even though these Ulster Presbyterians had few specific reasons for such schisms as had those of Scotland. More about that later.

Now notice the second graph, "Presbyterian Family Connection."

The Presbyterian Church in the U.S.A. and the Presbyterian Church in the U.S. had their beginnings: (1) (not indicated on the graph) from the early presbyterian Puritans from England;

* See chart at end of volume.—ED.

(2) as the result of Scotch and Ulster-Scotch Presbyterians migrating from Scotland and northern Ireland—practically all coming from the undivided Presbyterianism of Scotland and Ireland; (3) (not shown) as the result of the coming of those French Huguenots, French, Dutch, and German Reformed, and so on, who did not form churches of their own denominations here.

Note the United Presbyterian Church of North America, the result of a union in 1858 of the Associate Reformed and the Associate Synod—both of which, with their antecedents, were made up of colonists who came to America from those churches in Scotland and Ireland which were in schism from the parent church, namely the Seceders (Associate) and the Reformed.

The Reformed Presbyterian Churches (Covenanters) here in America had as their founders the Reformed of Scotland and the most conservative of the Secession groups, such as the Old Light Anti-Burghers of northern Ireland.

PROTESTANT BEGINNINGS IN NORTHERN IRELAND

For our purposes we need to consider the circumstances by which the Protestant Church came to be in northern Ireland. The chief facts relative to this establishment furnish necessary help for the understanding of the attitudes and viewpoints of the Ulster-Scotch Presbyterian churchmen who later migrated to America. Under James I, who had been James VI in Scotland, after rebellious wars on the part of the Irish had laid waste northern Ireland, there was instituted and carried out in the name of peace and for purposes of national unity a resettlement of Ulster partly by English but mainly by Scots from the lowlands of Scotland. Already, there were some of each in the area. A very few of the native Irish were allowed to occupy the less desirable districts. There is abundant proof that between the Scotch emigrants and the native Irish an impenetrable wall was fixed both as to religion and as to intermarriage. Those whom we in America term the Scotch-Irish of this period were really Ulster Scots. And between the English and the native Irish the same separateness was well nigh perfectly maintained.

From the first the English, as Anglicans, took control ecclesiastically. This they did by controlling the Irish Parliament, with its seat in Dublin. The Anglican archbishop, a very great Christian, who had received his education at the feet of two leaders of the Reformed Church, was James Ussher. He recognized the validity of Presbyterian orders in theory, and even beyond the letter of the civil law in practice. But the Anglican leaders who were his contemporaries and successors were neither as broadminded nor as kindhearted as he. Being in control of the Parliament in Dublin, they heaped disabilities upon both the Presbyterians and the Roman Catholics. Finally in 1641 the Roman Catholics broke forth in rebellion. This resulted in the wholesale slaughter of a large number of the Anglicans and of a lesser number of the Presbyterians. Many of the Presbyterian clergy escaped to Scotland, soon to return and lead in the revival of their church in Ulster. During the remainder of the Cromwellian era this northern Ireland Presbyterianism grew steadily. It suffered all sorts of hardships in the reigns of Charles II (1660–1685) and of James II (1685–1689). The latter's invading Roman Catholic army was defeated as it laid siege to Londonderry (1689). Under William and Mary (1689–1702) this Presbyterianism prospered. In the reign of Anne (1702–1714) the Presbyterianism of both Scotland and northern Ireland was overtaken by grievous difficulties.

The first and chief trouble came in the form of the Test Act of 1704. By the Act the Presbyterian Church in Ireland was declared to be without legal recognition in many important respects. Its clergy were forbidden to unite couples in marriage. Any married by them would be living in fornication. No Presbyterian in Ulster could thereafter hold a position in the Army or Navy, in the customs, excise, or post office, in any court of law or in the magistracy, without first conforming to the Anglican Church. In Londonderry, for example, ten of the twelve aldermen and fourteen of the twenty-four burgesses, being Presbyterians, were turned out of office, notwithstanding that all these had valiantly assisted their city in opposing the famous siege of 1689 by the Roman Catholic forces of James II.

Here follow the words of James Froude, who is describing what followed the passage of the Test Act:

And now recommenced the Protestant emigration, which robbed Ireland of the bravest defenders of the English interests, and peopled the American seaboard with fresh flights of Puritans. Twenty thousand left Ulster on the destruction of the woolen trade. Many more were driven away by the first passage of the Test Act. The stream had slackened, in the hope that the law would be altered. When the prospect was finally closed, men of spirit and energy refused to remain in a country where they were held unfit to receive the rights of citizens; and thenceforward, until the spell of tyranny was broken in 1782, annual shiploads of families poured themselves out from Belfast and Londonderry. The resentment which they carried with them continued to burn in their new homes; and, in the War of Independence, England had no fiercer enemies than the grandsons and great-grandsons of the Presbyterians who had held Ulster against Tyrconnell.

And so the emigration continued. The young, the courageous, the earnest, those alone among her colonists who, if Ireland was ever to be a Protestant country, could be effective missionaries, were torn up by the roots, flung out, and bid find a home elsewhere; and they found a home to which England fifty years later had to regret that she had allowed them to be driven.[4]

The second trouble which beset British Presbyterianism, in Scotland directly, in Ireland indirectly, was the reenactment of the laws of lay patronage. By these laws the choice of a pastor for a local church could not be made by the current membership but was wholly within the power of a lay patron, or his designated successors, as indicated in the original will providing for the endowment. This imposition of the dead hand of the past upon the present was a principal cause for the schism from the Church of Scotland in 1733, 1751, and 1843.

These two troubles, together with many others, were brought to a head by discriminating tariffs against Ireland's farm products and industries in favor of English. In 1741 there was a failure of crops with a resultant famine. Is it necessary to state that further residence in northern Ireland became intolerable for the Ulster-Scotch Presbyterians? Those whose health and age would permit (as well as many who did not thus qualify) migrated to America. Between 1731 and 1768 one-third of the Protestant population of Ireland journeyed to a new home across the Atlantic. In all, over two hundred thousand joined the trek. Following the first famine year of 1741, for several years some twelve thousand left annually for America. In the years 1771–1773 it is estimated that thirty thousand migrated, of whom ten thousand were weavers. All of this means that the more desirable, the more enterprising of the younger generation of Ulster, by their leaving, impoverished Ireland and enriched the new homeland.

CONVICTIONS AND DOCTRINES BROUGHT TO AMERICA

We have been taking special note of the more personal origins of early American Ulster-Scotch Presbyterianism. But human beings, alone, do not constitute the necessary materials for the founding of churches or a church denomination. With the people must come certain theological and ecclesiastical convictions with all their accompanying items of thought and attitude.

To begin with, what was the general theological conviction held by the migrating Presbyterians, whether from England, Scotland, Ireland, or the Reformed group of continental Europe? The answer is, Calvinistic.

Not all will understand what is meant when it is stated that generally the theological background and the presently practiced faith of the founders of American Presbyterianism were Calvinistic. What were the outstanding features of this Calvinism and what were the origins of it?

l other influences which caused John Calvin to think
e as he did were: (1) his acceptance of the aims of the
f the Renaissance, which primarily struck out for the
the individual from the shackles of medievalism, in
of human thought and practical interest; (2) the
nt return to the study of the Scriptures in the original
nd the placing of the Scriptures in the seat of supreme
in Christian religious, moral, and political guidance;
which logically followed, (3) the revamping of theological
thought.

In many respects John Calvin was of the second generation of
Protestant reformers. The Calvinism which came to have outstanding influence was that found in the last editions of his *Institutes*, appearing in 1559, and in his exegetical works. His pred-
ecessors, his contemporaries, and he himself were profoundly
influenced by Augustine and such of the latter's disciples as John
Wiclif, Guillaume Farel, Martin Bucer, Huldreich Zwingli, and
Martin Luther, and others of that day. Luther must have added
to Calvin's determination that reform was needed. Both men held
to the doctrine of the predestination of the elect to salvation. Calvin
also included the predestination of the non-elect to damnation.
Luther built his system by starting with the justification of the
sinner by faith in Christ. Calvin's foundation doctrine was the
absolute and uncompromised sovereignty of God.

The resultant Calvinism, to characterize its main features briefly:
(1) substituted the sovereignty of God for the Roman Catholic
sovereignty of the visible church; (2) set forth the teaching that
the truly elect are certain to persevere, this to take the place of
the assurance expressed by the priest in the confessional; (3) emphasized divine predestination so as to take away the egotistic pride
of such as the Pelagians, who claimed that human capabilities were
life's chief determining factors; (4) included the doctrine that
all elect heathen and infants are heirs to eternal life—this a much
less severe doctrine than that of the medieval Latin Church as

popularly understood; namely, that only baptized
heathen will be saved.[5]

Calvinism when fully developed, including the ac
social, economic, educational, and governmental theo
tion to its distinctly religious teachings, constituted t
portion of the more precious theories which guided, for
the founding of the United States. Let us be reminded th
Calvinism here being depicted was not the exclusive possession
Presbyterianism. In the seventeenth and eighteenth centuries,
Calvinism was in the possession of the puritan Anglicans, the
separatist Congregationalists, the Baptists, the Calvinistic Methodists, the French Huguenots, and French and German Reformed.
With these acknowledgments, the fundamental principles generally
held by the Calvinistic family and brought by it to America may
be stated as follows, except that the groups just named who were
extreme independents in church polity did not subscribe to Principle 3 below:

1. Every child has the inherent right to the highest type of Christian
cultural education, this being the responsibility of all adults as Christian stewards.[6]
2. The moral welfare of the whole population is the joint responsibility of both Church and State working separately yet co-operatively.
3. The visible Church shall be so organized as to provide an ascending
series of courts as, e.g., the session, presbytery, synod and general assembly. In this polity there shall be every provision made for ruling elders
(laymen) to be joined with minister-elders in the membership of each of
these courts.
4. The visible Church and State shall be separate, but mutually cooperative. In all matters of conscience and religion, God, through His
Church, is the supreme Administrator as well as Teacher.[7]
5. In the Lord's Supper, Christ's body and blood are present "really,
but spiritually, to the faith of believers" partaking.
6. God alone is Lord of the conscience. Freedom of conscience is an
inalienable right under laws and constitutions democratically created
and imposed.
7. God, by His Holy Spirit, working in and through the qualified
leadership of His Church, makes known His Word as found in the

...ures. His Word thus made known constitutes the supreme basis
authority in the visible Church.

8. God, the Father, Son and Holy Spirit is the supreme Sovereign.
As He is revealed in His Word, so every theory and practice that has
to do with man or men is to be shaped or ordered accordingly.[8]

Taken singly or collectively, the foregoing principles or teachings
constituted a boon to this nation and to the whole world.

The distinctly religious teachings of Calvinism that were brought
to America in printed matter by those who were to constitute
American Presbyterianism were in the Reformed and Presbyterian
creeds and confessions. Sooner or later, it is safe to assume, they
reached these shores in someone's library or by virtue of some
person here asking that they be sent to him. The earlier clergymen
were graduates of English, Scottish, Irish, and European universities whose theological courses were solidly Augustinian-Calvin-
istic. Here in America the publications which came to be distributed
generally, and which beyond all others contained modified forms
of Calvinism, were the Shorter Catechism of the Westminster
Standards, the Larger Catechism and the Confession of Faith
(from the same source), and the Heidelberg Catechism. It was the
Shorter Catechism which in many respects, even as late as the
first quarter of the nineteenth century, became the controlling
religious text (aside from the Bible and the various metrical versions
of the Psalms) among those religiously inclined. This took place
through the *New England Primer*, a school and home text (religious and secular) in which the Shorter Catechism was incorporated. This primer attained a circulation and use that on a
proportionate population basis is without parallel in American
educational history.

In the early years of this nation the clergy held outstanding
positions. As they were learned and mildly or strongly Calvinistic,
and their congregations were schooled in the rudiments of the
same interpretation of the Christian faith, it will be understood
why the faith of Geneva by way of Puritan, Scotch, Ulster-Scotch,

continental Reformed and, *particularly,* Westminster Assembly way stations exerci*sed such* a controlling influence here. We know that the *total* church membership (that is, those who could and *did qualify* to commune) in our colonial days as well as in the early years of our life as a nation was pitifully low. A controlling influence was the recognition of the clergy and of certain outstanding lay churchmen in councils of state.

The Origin and Nature of Departures from "Orthodoxy"

Returning now to the more restricted theme of Presbyterian origins, it is necessary to take note of the non-strict subscription attitudes among the earliest Presbyterians in America and to record their origin. These attitudes first showed in marked form in 1729 in connection with the adoption of the Westminster Standards for any sort of directive. We may anticipate a bit by noting that strict subscription under the leadership of those who either would not participate in the Great Awakening of 1725–1740 or were actively opposed to it came to a climax in 1741, forcing the first schism in American Presbyterianism into Old Side, New Side groups, a schism which continued until 1758. Within the New Side group were those tendencies and persons which led to the founding of the Log College on the Neshaminy (1728) and of the College of New Jersey (1746), now Princeton University. The New Side were non-strict subscriptionists. They held to freedom within recognized evangelical bounds. Whence this attitude of disciplined freedom as in relation to man-made creeds and confessions?

Calvinism in its pure forms, aside from those statements and treatises which were the product of Calvin himself, never had an absolutely controlling place in any part of Presbyterianism, whether in Scotland, Ireland, or America. The Confessions and Creeds, beginning with John Knox's Scottish Confession of Faith and ending with the Westminster Standards, were modified forms of

Calvinism. Within the text of the latter it is stated that "God alone is the Lord of the conscience" (Chap. XXI. 2) and that "all synods and councils . . . may err, and many have erred; therefore they are not to be made the rule of faith and practice, but to be used as a help in both" (Chap. XXXI. 3). Before the formulation of the Standards by the Westminster fathers, these same leaders, as they set about to revise the Thirty-nine Articles of Religion of the Church of England, voted to omit Article VIII altogether because they were determined that no man-made creed should take precedence over the Scriptures as the supreme source of authority. From this it may be inferred that they certainly never expected that the Westminster Standards would be regarded as sacrosanct touch-them-not oracles from God.

The English presbyterians (some spelled with a capital P) of the Westminster Assembly generation never did formally adopt the Standards, the product of their own leaders. Certain historians single out this failure to adopt the Standards as the chief reason English Presbyterianism drifted into Socinianism and Unitarianism.

When and under what circumstances did the tendency and practice of non-strict subscription to any formulated Confession arise in northern Ireland from whence so many founders of American Presbyterianism came? Before 1719 the Presbyterian Church of Plantation Ulster was in strict conformity to the parent church in Scotland. Beginning in 1705, at the formation of "The Belfast Society" (an association of ministers allegedly for theological improvement), with the Reverend John Abernethy as the founder, there began to be certain deviations from Scottish Presbyterian orthodoxy. This society began openly to show hostility to strict subscription to the accepted interpretations of the Westminster Standards. They led in the installation of the Reverend Samuel Haliday, who had refused to subscribe to a formal Confession. This, of course, aroused a furor. By 1726 the Ulster Synod took action, excluding non-subscribers from ministerial communion in church judicatories.

RISE AND INFLUENCE OF MARROWISM

In Scotland the first rumblings of storm as against the calm of a smug orthodoxy began in 1714. In this year the Reverend James Webster of Edinburgh began to find fault with the Reverend Doctor John Simpson, Professor of Divinity at the University of Edinburgh. The latter, like Socrates of the Greeks and like Abélard of the medieval church, aroused thought by means of disturbing questions without seemingly furnishing solid bases for faith. In 1717 the Reverend James Hog of Carnock republished *The Marrow of Modern Divinity*,[9] first published in 1646 by Edward Fisher, M.A. (Oxford).

What teachings of this book were destined to play so significant a part in Scottish, Ulster-Scotch, and early American Presbyterian history, especially the portions which finally became our United Presbyterian Church? Briefly, it was a skillful compendium of interwoven quotations from numerous Christian authors designed to show that essential Christianity really demands the omission of certain extreme forms of Calvinism and the inclusion of certain forms of Arminianism, especially following the example of that saintly divine, the Puritan Richard Baxter. It included teaching that "the atonement of Christ is universal" and may be made so in actuality following repentance by any person. To such heterodoxy, the strict Calvinists were aroused in determined opposition. The Marrow Men, that is, those who accepted the views set forth in this book, were characterized by deep spirituality, by zealous morality, and by a crusading zeal in opposition to the "moderateness" then paralyzing, as they believed, the church life in Scotland.

This "moderateness" was contemporaneous with the reinstitution of the scheme of lay patronage in the church life of Scotland. In the providence of God the best of "Marrowism" and the more intelligent aspects of the opposition to lay patronage were combined in the great Ebenezer Erskine (1680–1754). In his sermon preached in 1732 in his capacity as Moderator of the Synod of Perth and

John Calvin

John Knox

Ebenezer Erskine

Francis Makemie

FOUNDERS

John Witherspoon

Jonathan Dickinson

Elisha Swift

Ashbel Green

PREACHER-EVANGELISTS

Gilbert Tennent

Charles G. Finney

George Whitefield

Toyohiko Kagawa

Samuel Davies

The Log College on the Neshaminy, 1728–1746

Nassau Hall, 1754, College of New Jersey (Princeton), 1746

Stirling, he struck out against the evils resulting from the Lay Patronage Act and against the moderateness, the spiritual deadness, and moral flabbiness which would cause in any part of the Scottish Church the evils then so evidently rampant. He chose as his text Psalm 118:22. He lashed out against the leading rulers of the church, declaring Jesus the Christ to be its sole and rightful Lord. His Synod rebuked him. He appealed to the next Assembly in 1733. This Assembly sustained the rebuke of the preceding year. Erskine, joined by Alexander Moncrief, William Wilson, and James Fisher, entered protest. Their enemies magnified this protest by terming it treason. Pressing such a charge, they succeeded in getting a commission especially created which expelled these four men from the ministry. The Assembly of 1734 released the men from the commission's sentence of explusion. But they, being released from—as they believed—the hidebound literalism and the lack of moral discernment and zeal of the then Scottish Presbyterian Church, chose to stay out. They met in that same year and formed the Associate Presbytery. In 1747 this group divided into the Burgher and Anti-Burgher churches over a dispute whether a true Christian could conscientiously take the Burgher oath which some thought required sanction of the current politico-ecclesiastical regime.[10]

Marrowism and Other Trends in the Background of United Presbyterianism

Beginning with Erskine and his associates, an aloofness coupled with closed-communion developed. This is explainable not as the result of the non-strict subscription attitudes of Marrowism but as the result of moral zeal which chose to cast itself into increasingly exclusive channels as a rebuke to moderatism. The moderatism which they so detested included a compound, as they believed, of the heresy of Pelagianism, the abuses of Erastianism, and a surrender of the Headship of the church to some person or instrument other than Christ. These characteristics, which developed first in Scotland, spread to corresponding church groups in Scottish Ulster, and came from both of those areas to America. Here they formed the beginnings of the Reformed Presbyterian and the United Presbyterian churches.

In line with this observation, I quote from the historian Thomas M'Crie:

. . . . In their extreme aversion to incur the charge of schism, they were led into that course of narrowness and exclusiveness for which they were blamed from the commencement of their history. On the same principle they condemned the practice of what was called "occasional hearing," or joining in the acts of worship with other churches. To this may be added the practice of renewing in some of their congregations, the national covenants, "in a bond suited to their circumstances."

The attempt thus made to re-enact on a diminutive scale these national deeds failed to resuscitate the vitality or even to revive the memory of the departed past, to which it bore no shadow of resemblance. But for these peculiarities, which the early Seceders considered essential to identify them with the Church of the first and second Reformations, many might have adjoined themselves to a society which contended for the honour due to the supreme Head of the Church, for the liberties of his people, and for the purity of that gospel which "liveth and abideth for ever."

From its commencement the Secession was an evangelical movement. The absence of a faithful discipline in the Establishment, which was becoming more and more lax and careless in administration, was amply compensated by the "wholesome rigour in the main" practiced by the Seceders in maintaining purity of communion; and in many parts of the country, during the dark reign of Moderatism, the lamp of gospel truth was kept alive by their ministrations. Although the Marrow controversy cannot be said to have originated the Secession, there can be no doubt that the truths involved in it were uniformly held and faithfully preached in her pulpits. There is no part of the Secession testimony on which we dwell with more unmixed satisfaction than on that bearing the unpromising title of "Act concerning the Doctrine of Grace," which we owe to the united labour of Ebenezer Erskine and Alexander Moncrief, which formed an enlargement of their testimony with respect to injuries done to the doctrine on grace by several acts of Assembly, relative to the book entitled the *Marrow of Modern Divinity*. It is equally worthy of remark that to Messrs. Erskine and Fisher we are indebted for the well-known work called *Fisher's Catechism*, which was very generally employed by ministers as their text-book at the public examinations of their people, when both old and young were duly catechised; this was, in fact, a profound system of divinity, and was specially devoted to an explanation of the "Marrow doctrines." [11]

Besides the modifications of Calvinism and the tendencies against strict subscription to any formulated Confessions such as have just been set forth, certain additional trends and tendencies were brought under Presbyterian (official and unofficial) auspices to America. One was what came to be termed the "federal theology," incorporated in the Westminster Confession, Chapter VII. This consisted in the creation of a theory, believed to be Biblically based, that the relations between men and God in both the Old and New Testaments' dispensations are expressed in covenants, the Old Testament being that of works, the New Testament being that of grace. In each dispensation God keeps his end of the covenant, man breaks his. Hence the men who go to perdition are fully responsible; God is not responsible. This line of reasoning was believed to soften the decrees of God in the estimation of those disposed to characterize the damnatory decrees, especially, as "horrible." The originators of this "federal theology" were Henry Bullinger and Caspar Olevianus on the Continent, Pollock, John Howie and Edward Fisher (the author of *The Marrow*) in Scotland, and Thomas Cartwright, William Ames, and John Ball in England. In 1648 John Coccejus (Cook) of Holland published a notable treatise supporting these views; this very likely appeared too late to influence the fathers of the Westminster Assembly.

Sabbatarianism

Another very pronounced attitude and practice brought by the Puritan and Presbyterian forefathers to these shores was that which came to be called "Sabbatarianism," that is, a very strict, painfully

strict, observance of the Sabbath Day to keep it holy. Nicholas
Bownd is believed to have been the first literary supporter of this
emphasis (in 1595). It will be recalled that John Calvin was a
comparative liberal concerning the use of Sunday. He believed
the Christian Church of his time was plagued with too many
"holy days," and with too much of a tendency to be unholy in
the in-between time. He believed the more wholesome attitude
and practice would be to dedicate all days to God, all being in
his plan for the service of man. But the British children of Calvin
became so intent upon the "keeping" of the Sabbath that Puritanism and painful Sabbatarianism became synonymous. For James I,
who as James VI of Scotland had had no end of troubles with
Presbyters, the realization that in England the presbyterially inclined were the Puritans helped convince him that whatever he
could do to get even with his annoyers would be interesting, to say
the least. Accordingly, among other devices, he issued, on May
24, 1618, *The Book of Sports*, which his successor, Charles I, re-
issued on October 18, 1633. In each case the publication had the
force of a royal command to engage in sports on Sunday. The
result was the confirmation of the Puritans in the correctness of
their stand and increase in strictness of observance. The Presbyterians of both Scotland and Ireland following their leaders, Chapter XXI of the Westminster Confession, and questions with
answers 57–66 of the Shorter and 115–121 of the Larger Catechism
were the to-be-expected result. Out of such backgrounds came the
"Puritan Sabbath" with the founding of the American Presbyterianism.

THE ULSTER-SCOTCH TAKE A PROMINENT PART
IN THE AMERICAN STRUGGLE

Recognizing that religion and politics are seldom if ever contained in absolutely separate compartments, it should be made
plain that Presbyterianism brought to America very pronounced

doctrines as to the nature of church and state and the relation of each to the other. I have already indicated something of these doctrines. The Ulster-Scotch Presbyterians, finding life intolerable in Ireland, came to America by the thousands, here to realize their principles as over against the various English tyrannies and injustices. Comparatively, the Scotch Presbyterians of Scotland came in smaller numbers. They chose to remain in Scotland and there win through to the same desired goals.

PSALMODY AND ITS ORIGINS

Whence the Psalmody which the founders of American Presbyterianism brought with them?

The whole of it stems from the musical portions of worship in the church of the Old Testament. Certain hymns or chants created or developed through the first fifteen centuries of Christian history found their place in the Psalters of the Presbyterians. The birth of modern hymnody took place under the Hussite and Lutheran branches of the Protestant Reformation, with Luther as the leader. The origin of Reformed and Presbyterian Psalmody includes a larger number of leaders and covers a more extended area.

To state the origins briefly, Psalmody began in France and Switzerland with Clément Marot, Theodorus Beza, and John Calvin; in England, with Thomas Sternhold, John Hopkins, Francis Tate, Nicholas Brady, William Kethe, and Francis Rous; in Scotland, with James, John, and Robert Wedderburn, Robert Pont and John Craig. Behind all this was the conviction that the praise of God should be chanted or sung only in the paraphrased language of the inspired Word of God; the Psalms were practically the only portion of the Bible which had originally been thus used.

At Geneva the Psalter, with metrical paraphrases by Calvin, Marot, and Beza, was complete by 1562. In that same year another Psalter, originated by Thomas Sternhold and added to by John

Hopkins, appeared in its final complete form in England. This came to be referred to as the "Old Version," or as the "Day Psalter," after the name of the publisher. After 134 years the Old Version was supplanted, especially in New England, by a new version, the Tate and Brady Psalter. These two, the "Old" and the "New" versions, were among the Psalters of the Puritans, who soon, however, had one of their own; namely, the *Bay Psalm Book.* It was printed in 1640 in the home of Henry Dunston, the first president of Harvard College. This book, which was the first one of any kind to be printed here in America, included selections from the "versions" to which additions were made. Originating here, it came to have very wide circulation in both England and Scotland and was brought to America by those who sought this land as their new home.

As for Psalmody in Scotland, the story, in part, is as follows. In 1550 the first edition of the Sternhold and Hopkins Psalter appeared there. In 1556–1557 a Book of Order which included paraphrases by Sternhold and Hopkins was used by the English refugees at Geneva. The year 1560 marked the end of the Anglo-Genevan Church and the meeting of the first General Assembly of the Protestant Church of Scotland. John Knox having been an exile resident in Geneva, the Geneva Book of Order with its paraphrased Psalms under Knox's influence received official sanction in the Scottish Church. By 1564 the Scottish Psalter was completed. To the paraphrases used at Geneva, had been added twenty-five by William Kethe, and some, notably the Twenty-third Psalm, by William Whittingham, who is credited with the chief responsibility in the making of the famous Geneva Bible. The Scottish Psalter was brought to America not so much in its edition of 1564 as in the form of a new Scottish Psalter which evolved out of the action of the Scottish Church as it revised Francis Rous's Paraphrase (2nd ed.) officially sanctioned by the Westminster Assembly.

In 1641, on the eve of the Westminster Assembly, the English

Committee of Peers, lay and spiritual, created to report on religion, recommended that "the meter in the Psalms should be corrected and allowed publicly." Francis Rous (1579–1659), English Puritan, graduate of Oxford, member of Parliament from 1625 to his death, and provost of Eton College under the Commonwealth, acting on Parliament's recommendation, produced a metrical version of the Psalms which in its second edition (1643) was ordered to be printed on recommendation of the Westminster Assembly. But the Scots, suspecting Rous, who had changed from Presbyterianism to Independency, issued a new Scottish Psalter in 1650. However, here in America, among the Ulster-Scotch Presbyterian immigrants and their descendants, Rous's version came into almost general use. In 1707 Isaac Watts's volume of "original hymns adapted to Psalm meters" appeared. Gradually this began to supplant Rous, but at the expense of dissensions between "Rous" and "Watts" advocates in many a local Presbyterian church, especially among the Seceders and the Covenanters.

PRESBYTERIANISM THROUGH THE CENTURIES

This chapter would be most incomplete—it would be contrary to fact—if the impression were given that American Presbyterianism had its origins in British and European church life, and let the story end there.

In tracing the origins and continuing life of historic institutions, there are at least two different schools of thought among historians. One school makes history consist of a record of empirically discovered or discoverable facts in connection with which succession and only succession may be confidently asserted. This school holds that divine causality and purpose, the determined terrestrial or cosmic pattern which may be believed to lead to some goal, are really not in history and the historian must refrain from reading them into his narrative. The other school, in varying degrees and by varying ways, finds meaning in history, finds inherent connectionalism, finds persistence in change, finds intelligent purpose and willed causality. It refrains from holding such convictions as determining biases. Exercising all the scientific methods of the historical critical approach and setting down all the facts discovered empirically and intuitively (also remembering that much history takes place as the result of the deeper impulses of the spirit), the historian of this second school, as he writes history, produces a narrative which comes, so this author believes, very much nearer to the exact and whole truth. As one who humbly identifies himself with the latter school, I now proceed.

The Church of God in its visible forms as an institution in history had its beginnings in Old Testament times. It is a basic error to hold that it was born at Pentecost. It received the gift of the continuing presence of the Holy Spirit at Pentecost. This gift, thus received, abides in the visible church so long as it is truly the fellowship of God's spiritual children, so long as it truthfully said that Christ is in its midst. The name "Christian" arose after Pentecost. All of the various church denominations now existent in the world today, in so far as they are truly Christian, have their roots in the New Testament, in the Old Testament, and in God Himself. The Presbyterian Church, in so far as it is genuinely Christian, goes back thus to the beginning. From the standpoint of its polity, especially the place of the elders in its rule and spiritual leadership, this church has no difficulty in finding its counterparts in the Old Testament ecclesia. Presbyterianism, including the episcopal features of the Reformed Church in Hungary, has uniformly held that there is but one order in the ministry; namely, that of the presbyter to whom Paul, when he addressed the "elders" of the church in Ephesus, also gave the names of "bishops" or "overseers." Most New Testament scholars—indeed, most historians of the early Christian Church—hold the "bishop" in all of the narratives was never more than "first among equals"; he was a pastor-bishop. This appears to have been true up to and including Ignatius and his seven authentic letters, all written before 118 A.D.

Associated with Presbyterian polity, though not definitely integral with it, Calvinism of varying degrees has come to be identified with it. Such Calvinism, it is generally conceded, carries with it a goodly portion of Biblical teaching. Its sectarian valiants have been quite ready to argue that Presbytery is the only type of church clearly established by divine right. In modern times this conviction was formulated in Scotland by Andrew Melville, the successor to John Knox. As a result, certain Anglican leaders argued that episcopacy, and episcopacy only, is the form of church government sanctioned by divine right. There have been those who have insisted that congregationalism, and that alone, is by divine right. In more recent years, the abler historians, including Biblical exegetes, find elements of all three of the above-mentioned types in the Biblical narratives. They also find in James, who presided at the Council of Jerusalem, a type of archbishop or caliph. The various research studies carried on in connection with the Ecumenical movement, especially since 1910, have allayed forever, this author hopes, the tendency for any denomination to have a spirit akin to chauvinism in place of legitimate patriotism. It is with the spirit hinted at by these observations that I have drawn attention to the fact that our American Presbyterianism has had a fair share in the very earliest historical beginnings of the visible Church of God.

In the centuries between New Testament times and the Protestant Reformation of the sixteenth century, there were numerous outcroppings of presbyterian polity. The organic life of the church through all the centuries, both as an empirical and as a spiritual institution in the midst of whose life was and is God the Father, Son, and Holy Spirit, may well be pictured as a great tree. In a great tree there is a major portion of its support and substance not visible to the eye, not discoverable by the superficial historian who can see only that which is perceivable by the eye of flesh. Presbyterianism and Congregationalism, the evangelical catholic Christian gospel, and whatever else may constitute essential Christianity, in many of the years were hidden within the tree. Only now and again did such appear in visible history. To enumerate instances when forms of presbyterian polity were actually visibly instituted in various centuries is to indulge in a meaningless effort to establish an unbroken tactual line of descendance of visible institutional life from Biblical times. No present-day church, not even the Roman Catholic or the Eastern Orthodox, can do this.

As the Protestant Reformation leading to the founding of the Lutheran and Reformed churches advanced, the chief determinant which forced the overthrow of the episcopacy as then found was the doctrine that the episcopacy was the *esse*, or being, of the church, not its *bene esse*, that is, its well-being. A second and very important determinant leading to the elimination of the medieval episcopacy was that most, if not all, of the individual bishops violently opposed reform. Careful study of Reformed and Presbyterian beginnings (preceding, for example, Andrew Melville in Scotland) will indicate that such as John Calvin and John Knox were quite ready to accommodate themselves to the episcopacy when it was demonstrably for the well-being of the church. Keeping this in mind, it can be stated that if all Presbyterians had the breadth of view of Calvin, Knox, and the founders of the Reformed Church of Hungary, presbyterianism as they lived it and taught it did actually appear visibly in every century of Christian history.[12]

STRICTNESS IN GODLY CHARACTER

I now return to the consideration of the practices and tendencies of the Scotch Presbyterians and of the Ulster-Scotch Presbyterians, practices and tendencies which they brought to America resulting in the strengthening of the foundations of the republic about to be born. The Calvinistic Puritans, most of whom became Congregationalists, and the Calvinistic Baptists joined with the early Presbyterians in contributing these elements of strength. I refer to what I would term rigidity, even severity, of godly character in individual, family, and public life. This showed in their practice of family worship, in the persistent instruction of their children in the Bible with the use of catechisms, in their strict observance of the Sabbath, in their exaltation of the person and office of the Christian minister, in the maintenance of an educated ministry leading to the founding of our earliest colleges and universities.

It is not for the historian to engage in lengthy discussion as to the pros and cons of a strictly enforced puritanical regime. It is conceded that it is preferable to reach desirable ends by voluntary action arising out of Christianized inner life. But this does not argue that there is no need for restraining and disciplinary laws which should be firmly and fairly imposed on those who would flout all social responsibilities.

Coupled with the rigidity of godly character, the Ulster-Scots especially had a deep-seated hate against all forms of tyranny arising out of the notion of the divine right of kings and of an ecclesiasticism imposed by such a tyranny. We know that the religious and patriotic zeal which resulted was marred by all sorts of inconsistencies. We know that there were large parts of the population who took no interest in church life because of the forbidding aspects of an unlovely religiosity. Having made due allowances for the negative side of the picture, this author firmly believes that the total service rendered by the godly Calvinists, including the Presbyterian forefathers, tipped the balance very heavily on the positive side.

Consider the classical description of family worship as given by Robert Burns in "The Cotter's Saturday Night." Reflect upon William Wordsworth's description of Scottish home life:

A virtuous household, though exceeding poor!
Pure livers were they all, austere and grave,
And fearing God; the very children taught
Stern self-respect, a reverence for God's Word,
And an habitual piety, maintained
With strictness scarcely known on English ground.

With humility we recognize that some of the founders of our American Presbyterianism fell far short of fully exemplifying the best features of reverential, Biblically based, godly piety in personal and family life. But the majority of them did measure up.

In any day in a nation's life, whether on its natal day or on some later day,

> Ill fares the land, to hastening ills a prey,
> Where wealth accumulates, and men decay.

With apologies to Dudley Faulke:

> What makes a nation great? Huge stores of material wealth
> Massed skyward? Great multitudes who dwell
> Within white marble halls? Materials and stores
> With debts past the power of man to ken,
> To purchase awe? Nay, these are baubles, shams.
> True greatness lies where great love is won,
> Where godly men, Christian men upon the cross
> Serve humbly, think nobly, dare truly;
> That nation's loyal sons.

CHAPTER II

Beginnings in the North

THE Presbyterian Church in America is distinctly an American institution. It is the ecclesiastical product of the spirit of brotherhood and compromise which merged into a gradually developing organization of separate groups of Calvinistic refugees from various European countries where religious persecution and economic misfortunes had made an American adventure appear to be the only hope for freedom and prosperity. From the German Palatinate and Huguenot France, from the Netherlands, from England and Wales, and especially from northern Ireland and Scotland, these harassed refugees came to the American wilderness to achieve a new destiny in an undeveloped country where they might be free to worship God according to their Presbyterian modes of thought and practice and be free, also, to reap the material harvest of their creative labors. They sought to escape the religious and economic hardships which had made life a burden in their native lands.

They brought with them a resulting hatred of political and religious tyranny which manifested itself in hostility both to monarchy and prelacy. All who shared their persecution-tested convictions were welcomed to their services of worship regardless of national background. This tolerance and unity of theological certainty made possible a new and distinctive form of Presbyterian polity that was the product of frontier conditions. The nascent

27

Presbyterian Church was to be a merging of diverse presbyterian traditions, chiefly Puritan and Ulster-Scotch, not a mere continuance on American soil of any one form of European Presbyterianism.[1]

These searchers for freedom together formed a native Presbyterian Church, an independent, self-sustaining, and self-directing body of American Presbyterians. In Europe they had revolted against the control of the church by the state. In America they were scattered too widely to become the established church in any colony. Everywhere they were uncompromising advocates of the separation of church and state.

The rise of Presbyterianism in the northern United States is a story of religious activities which began with the Puritans in New England, moved south into the Middle Colonies, and gained tremendous momentum from the Ulster-Scotch migration as increasing members moved westward, especially into Pennsylvania. The story of this western expansion closes with the organization in 1781 of the Redstone Presbytery, the mother presbytery of the entire upper Ohio Valley Presbyterianism which, in its original organizational vastness, covered the broad area bounded "on the east by the Allegheny Mountains, on the north by Lake Erie, on the south by Virginia and on the west by the setting sun."[2]

The stony soil of New England was the scene of the first efforts to plant Presbyterianism north of Mason and Dixon's line. Here the Pilgrim and Puritan Fathers had landed with strong Calvinistic convictions, but with rather diverse views of the church and church government. Puritanism, in its original impetus, was an attempt to purify the religious life of England and was not planned as a seceder movement.[3] Some among the Puritans who braved the long voyage to the New England shores preferred the presbyterian practices in church government. Others would have retained the episcopalian forms. The majority favored an independent or congregational structure. The necessity for unity resulted in the establishment of the congregational type of polity in the earliest Massachusetts settlements, with the adoption of the eldership as a concession to the wishes of those presbyterially minded.[4]

The subsequent tide of immigration brought many additional Puritan Presbyterians to the expanding Massachusetts and Connecticut colonies. Among their Presbyterian preachers were Thomas Parker and James Noyes, who landed at Newbury, Massachusetts, in 1634. They served respectively as pastor and teacher for several years, but their presbyterian views resulted in considerable turmoil. Other Puritan preachers of presbyterian convictions included the Reverend Peter Hobart of Hingham and the famous John Eliot who left his congregation at Roxbury for a wider ministry among the Indians.[5] Cotton Mather reported that at least 4,000 Presbyterians were included among the 21,000 Puritans who landed in New England between 1620 and 1640.[6] It is doubtful that this famous divine could be correct in his estimate that one-fifth of the Puritans were "Presbyterians" by choice or heritage. Whatever might be their exact numbers, the great majority found it expedient to unite with the established Congregational churches.

The influence of the presbyterian element among the Puritans was somewhat stronger in Connecticut than in Massachusetts and extended over a longer period. A few of the churches were largely presbyterian in practice even though not in name. The Saybrook Platform, which was adopted in 1708, was a later attempt to merge presbyterian and congregational polity in a modified form of presbyteries called "consociations." They were composed of ministers and laymen from each church. In this cooperative body was vested authority in church discipline and in the ordination and installation of pastors. The powers thus conferred were quite similar to the usual powers exercised by a presbytery.

Though this presbyterianized form of congregationalism was not adopted by all Congregational churches in Connecticut and was subsequently modified, it created mutual interests and formed a distinct bond of communication with the developing Presbyterian churches in the Middle Colonies. It made much easier the transition from Congregational to Presbyterian churches in those areas where Presbyterianism was soon to be strengthened by the rapid migration of the Ulster-Scotch and by a considerable infiltration of Connecticut Congregationalists who were moving southward into New Jersey, New York, and Philadelphia.

This southward movement of New England Puritans began during the latter half of the seventeenth century and resulted in the organization of the earliest Presbyterian churches south of Mason and Dixon's line. It was destined to exert a marked influence upon the future development of Presbyterianism throughout the Middle Colonies as Presbyterians and Congregationalists worked and worshiped together in comparative harmony. Some of these New England émigrés came voluntarily in search of greater economic opportunity. Others were compelled to move because their distinctive presbyterian practices had made them an unwelcomed and disturbing minority.

Among the first of these presbyterian Puritan pastors to settle in the Middle Colonies was the Reverend John Young, who organized a church at Southold, Long Island, New York, on October 21, 1640. Here he continued to serve until death closed his pioneering pastorate in 1672. He was followed to Long Island by the Reverend Abraham Pierson, who brought with him from Lynn, Massachusetts, almost his entire congregation to settle at Southampton in 1641.[7] He subsequently preached for several years in Branford, Connecticut, leaving his congregation at Southampton in the pastoral charge of Joseph Fordham, another New England émigré, who had previously preached a year or two at Hempstead, Long Island. Later Pierson returned to establish what is now the First Presbyterian Church of Newark, New Jersey.

These two Long Island churches, Southold and Southampton, are sometimes referred to as the oldest Presbyterian churches in the Middle Colonies. Their claim can be disputed since it is difficult to determine whether they were organized originally as Presbyterian or as Congregational churches. Their presbyterian leanings are proved, however, by their subsequent inclusion in the Long Island Presbytery.[8] Similar claims for the honor of first priority have been presented on behalf of Mespat, near Newtown, Long Island, where a Presbyterian colony and church were established by the Reverend Francis Doughty, who was forced to leave Taunton, Massachusetts, because of his discordant presbyterian practices. Also, a priority claim can be argued on behalf of Hempstead, Long Island, to which the Reverend Richard Denton migrated with a portion of his Connecticut congregation.[9] Two of Denton's sons and other residents of Hempstead settled in nearby Jamaica, Long Island, where they formed what is also claimed to be the first church organized definitely as a Presbyterian Church.

The question of which of these churches has the most valid claim is not of vital importance. What is of distinct value to the historian is that Long Island was the scene of the birthplace of a strong and influential New England brand of Presbyterianism. This slow but steady stream of Puritan preachers continued to spread out with increased strength over Long Island and adjacent New York and New Jersey with the resulting development of other Presbyterian churches during the closing decades of the seventeenth century. The close of the century saw several other congregations being served by this influx of presbyterian Puritans both from England and New England. The number of these churches in New York and New Jersey has been estimated as between six and eleven. In New Jersey four congregations of Puritans had been established. Delaware could claim only two Presbyterian churches and Pennsylvania but one. Growth was slow. Presbyterians were only a scattered and persecuted minority, tolerated in some places but generally unwelcomed.

But with the turn of the century, the tide of Presbyterian fortunes also changed. The eighteenth century was destined to become the great century for American Presbyterianism. The Presbyterian Church was soon to develop into the largest and most dominant religious body throughout the Middle Colonies. Its growth from the organization of the first Presbytery in 1706 to its expansion into the General Assembly in 1789 is an outstanding achievement in the ecclesiastical history of the American colonies. Three factors may be regarded as the determining influences in that rapid growth and multiplied influence.

THE ARRIVAL OF A GREAT LEADER

The first of these three factors was the arrival of a creative leader in the person of the Reverend Francis Makemie. Following his ordination by the Presbytery of Laggan, Ireland, he responded to an urgent appeal for ministers from the Ulster Scotch settlers in Maryland. More than any other man he merits the title "The Father of American Presbyterianism." [10] His diverse gifts ideally fitted him for rugged service over a far-flung frontier. Lord Cornbury, the corrupt Governor of New York, bitterly hated Makemie and ridiculed his many-sided talents as "a Jack-of-all-trades, a preacher, a doctor of physic, a merchant, an attorney, a counselor-at-law and, which is worst of all, a disturber of governments." He was a young man of unbounded energy when he landed on the shores of Maryland in 1683. Here he soon established five Presbyterian churches. These churches, Rehoboth, Snow Hill, Manokin, Pitts Creek, and Wicomico, are among our oldest churches in continuous service.

Makemie was an inveterate traveler and an itinerant missionary whose extended parish reached from the Barbados to New York. Fortunately, he married the only daughter of a wealthy Virginia landowner and was a successful businessman. His business ventures provided the resources for his preaching and his missionary tours. Everywhere he sought out and encouraged the little groups of Presbyterians scattered south of Pennsylvania. His only complaint was that these widely diffused Presbyterians seemed never to collect themselves into towns. This he attributed to "some strange unaccountable humor."

Ulster-Scotch though he was, he appealed to his Puritan brethren in New England for additional ministers. They responded by sending various emissaries to preach and teach. Among them was Jedediah Andrews, a Harvard graduate, who after ordination in 1701 became pastor of the First Presbyterian Church of Philadelphia. It was the only organized Presbyterian Church in the entire colony of Pennsylvania. At that time this church could gather together only a struggling congregation. It was attempting to unite in harmonious worship a few Scotch, Welsh, Swedish, and New England families. The Episcopalian missionary, the Reverend John Talbot, wrote, with perhaps a touch of denominational prejudice: "The Presbyterians have come a great way to lay hands on one another. But, after all I think they had as good stay at home, for all the good they will do." [11] Andrews remained in Philadelphia throughout his entire ministry. Under his leadership the church steadily grew and required the services of an assistant pastor.

Makemie's search for additional resources of men and money to meet the needs of Presbyterians throughout the colonies brought him to London during the summer of 1704. His mission was successful. Funds to support two missionaries for two years were given to him.

With John Hampton, an Ulsterite, and George McNish, a Scotsman, as his two cooperating missionaries, Makemie returned to America. He was now ready to reap the ecclesiastical harvest of his previous years as an itinerant evangelist. He invited his Presbyterian brethren to meet with him in Philadelphia to organize the first independent Presbytery on American soil. It was an epoch-making achievement, a masterful stroke of policy which was to give the weak, scattered Presbyterian churches an organizational unity and impart to them a distinct advantage over other Protestant churches. It enabled them to license and ordain their own fellow ministers in a cooperative but independent effort to serve their extensive fields of labor. They could speak and act as a unit without interference from any European body.

The exact date of this first meeting of an intercolonial American Presbytery cannot be determined with certainty until the missing first page or pages of the manuscript minutes recording its organization have been found. The probable date is the spring of 1706. This conclusion is drawn because the second page of the original minute book [12] bears the date December 27, 1706, and because Makemie wrote a letter on March 28, 1707, describing the purposes of its organization. That historic event places the organization of the Presbyterian Church at least four decades earlier than that of any other intercolonial body among American churches.

The Congregational churches of New England, because of their polity, had developed no interdependent connection with one another. They were separate, independent congregations and formed local or colonial fellowship groups for mutual assistance only. They had no power apart from the colonial governments. The Episcopal Church looked to the Established Church of England for guidance and assignment of its ministers and waited until the close of the Revolutionary War before launching forth into a separate organization. Four decades after the Presbyterians had formed their expanding intercolonial bond of communication and control, the German Reformed Synod was organized in 1747. It was the second American church body to be formed, but it did not become fully independent until 1773. Then followed in rapid succession the formation of the First Lutheran Synod in 1748, the First Associate Presbytery in 1753, the Reformed Dutch Church in 1771, the Reformed or Covenanter Presbytery in 1774, and numerous others.

Beginning in 1706 and continuing throughout the entire colonial period, the regular gatherings of Presbyterian leaders in Presbytery and Synod became a strengthening bond of union between the colonies. As these Presbyterian ministers and elders from the colonies gathered in Philadelphia or New York, they discussed not only the religious interests of their people but also educational and political questions. United loyalties and unified plans were formulated which were to prepare the colonies for the struggle for free-

dom which began with the organization of the First Continental
Congress in 1774.[18]

Only seven ministers responded to Makemie's call to establish an
intercolonial Presbytery. Difficulties in travel limited the group to
those who were comparatively near. Most of the Puritan ministers
in New York and New Jersey held aloof until a more conveniently
located Presbytery could be organized later. Yet these seven men
represented the merging together of diverse national and cultural
backgrounds into a working unity which was to demonstrate in
miniature the broad scope of the American Presbyterian Church.

In imagination the calling of the roll can be heard and the different backgrounds visualized. Francis Makemie, who was chosen the
moderator, was Ulster-Scotch with strong ties of friendship with
London and New England. John Hampton, from Ulster, and
George McNish, a Scotsman, were missionaries supported by London Presbyterians. Three of the ministers were formerly from New
England but now were settled pastors. Jedediah Andrews was
pastor of the host church in Philadelphia, John Wilson was located
at New Castle, Delaware; Nathaniel Taylor was ministering to a
congregation at Patuxent, Maryland. The remaining charter member was Samuel Davis, who had come directly from Ulster and
had been serving as pastor in Lewes, Delaware, since 1692. The
congregations which these men served were likewise diverse in their
backgrounds and drew together Puritans from England and New
England, with Scotch-Irish, Dutch, Huguenot, and Welsh Presbyterians.

All were eager to work and worship as congregations united in
one Presbytery. Questions of doctrinal uniformity could wait until
an indefinite tomorrow. They did not question one another's orthodoxy. No constitution was drawn up. The Ulster form of Presbytery seemed mutually agreeable. The Presbyterian Church, from
its first organization as a Presbytery, was an American institution
and welcomed different backgrounds and viewpoints. Makemie
wrote:

Our plan is to meet yearly and oftener, if necessary, to consult the most proper measure for advancing religion and propagating Christianity in our various stations and to maintain such a correspondence as may conduce to the improvement of our ministerial abilities by prescribing texts to be preached on by two of our number at every meeting, which performance is subject to the censure of our brethren.[14]

Unfortunately, Makemie was not permitted to have any extended service in the Presbytery he helped organize in Philadelphia. He did live long enough, however, to lift the Presbytery from comparative obscurity to widespread prominence throughout the British colonies by waging a successful fight for religious liberty. Following the adjournment of the October meeting of Presbytery, in 1706, Makemie and John Hampton set forth on what might be called the first moderatorial tour. Their purpose was to enlist more ministers for service in the Middle Colonies and to enlarge the membership of the Presbytery. On their way to New England, Makemie was invited to preach to the Puritans in New York. Governor Cornbury refused to permit him to speak in the Dutch Church. He therefore preached in the private house of William Jackson, on Pearl Street. The same day Hampton preached at Newtown, Long Island. Two days later both men were arrested on a warrant from the governor on the charge that they were "strolling preachers" and had preached without his permission. With the courage characteristic of a martyr, Makemie informed the governor: "If your Lordship requires it, we will give security for our behaviour. But to give bond and security to preach no more in your excellency's government, if invited and desired by any people, we neither can nor dare do it." From January 22 to March 1, the two ministers languished in prison awaiting trial.

In the meantime news of the unjust confinement spread rapidly throughout the colonies. Interest heightened as the men were released on bail to stand trial in June. Makemie appealed to his brethren for help. The New England Puritans responded by sending a strong letter of protest to London. Three of the ablest lawyers in New York volunteered to defend him. They presented an elaborate and convincing defense.[15]

Makemie testified in his own defense. He produced a license to preach which had been issued in Barbados and which he maintained was valid throughout the queen's dominions. He answered point by point the arguments of Cornbury. He exposed the injustice of the charges against him and revealed a discriminating knowledge of English law. His brilliant defense resulted in a jury verdict of "not guilty." The spiteful governor, however, compelled him to pay the entire cost, not only of his own defense, but of the prosecution. These costs amounted to the large sum of more than eighty-three pounds. It was more than a minister's salary would be for an entire year. The complete story of the unjust trial was printed and widely distributed in Boston and reprinted in New York. The unfavorable publicity resulted in the recall of Governor Cornbury and an epoch-making victory for freedom of speech throughout the colonies. The trial lifted the Presbytery, of which Makemie was moderator, into widespread prominence and won for the heroic Presbyterians the favorable attention of many dissenters in the colonies.

This successful defense of his right to preach was Makemie's crowning act of service to Presbyterianism and the cause of religious liberty. The strain of prolonged imprisonment and the worry of the trial seemed to undermine fatally his expended strength. The following year he died, a comparatively young man of fifty years of age, and was buried on his farm in Virginia. He had laid a broad and strong foundation upon which the expansive superstructure of colonial Presbyterianism was soon to be built. A grateful church finds merited satisfaction in the poetical tribute written by Henry van Dyke in 1906 as part of the 200th anniversary of the organization of the first Presbytery in Philadelphia:

Francis Makemie, Presbyter to Christ in America, 1683–1708

> To thee plain hero of a rugged race,
> We bring a meed of praise too long delayed.

Oh, who can tell how much we owe to thee
Makemie and to labors such as thine
For all that makes America the shrine
Of faith untrammeled and of conscience free?
Stand here, gray stone, and consecrate the sod
Where sleeps this brave Scotch-Irish man of God! [16]

Though deprived of their trusted leader, the Presbytery developed steadily in the spirit of its original organization as the population increased. All of the members of the Presbytery had pledged themselves "to set on foot and encourage private Christian societies and to supply neighboring desolate places where a minister is wanting and opportunity of doing good offers." [17]

Thus they set the first of a determining series of precedents that were to form the policy of the developing American church. The Presbyterian Church from its very organization was to be and remain a missionary church. This action of the seven ministers at their second meeting as a Presbytery was the first of many missionary pronouncements that have been issued by the Presbyterian Church in America.

As a result of this missionary policy, new preaching points were established and new churches organized. Appeals for help were sent to Calvinists everywhere. Four additional ministers came from New England, six from Scotland, three from Wales, others from Dublin and Ulster. Most of the Puritan Presbyterian churches in Long Island and New Jersey also joined. The Presbytery was expanding by receiving these additional ministers with diverse backgrounds. It was a broad and tolerant body, alert to new opportunities, concerned more for the moral purity of its members than for their theological conformity and seeking to maintain high standards throughout the churches. Within ten years the Presbytery had increased its membership from seven to seventeen ministers with widely separated fields of labor.

These additional ministers were well educated men who had previously received their education in Europe or in the colleges of New England. Only one was educated by the Presbytery itself throughout that decade of growth. The single exception, the first fruit of Presbyterian theological education, was a young Welshman, David Evans. He was taken under care of Presbytery in 1710. For four years he continued in his Presbytery-directed course of study before the Presbytery would ordain and install him as pastor of the Welsh church in Philadelphia. High educational standards were being upheld. A precedent was thus set which was to have continuing effect upon the educational policy of a frontier church and which later was to result in the establishment of Presbyterian colleges and theological seminaries.

A Synod Is Organized

The Presbytery had now developed sufficient strength to take the second step in its expanding organization. It was ready to subdivide itself into four parts or presbyteries for regional supervision and then to come together annually for general reports and conferences and final decision on basic problems of theology and polity. The united body was known as the Synod of Philadelphia. The constituent presbyteries carried the names Philadelphia, New Castle, Long Island, and Snow Hill. Most of Pennsylvania and East and West Jersey were grouped together to form Philadelphia Presbytery. The churches on Long Island and throughout the province of New York were the responsibility of Long Island Presbytery. Snow Hill Presbytery was planned to cover the peninsula between Chesapeake and Delaware bays but was never formally constituted. This peninsula area was then transferred to the Presbytery of New Castle, which extended southward from the Great Valley in Chester County and included Delaware, Maryland, and Virginia.

The members of these three constituent or subordinate presbyteries came together for their first meeting as the Synod of Philadelphia on September 17, 1717. They represented a total Presbyterian strength of 19 ministers, 40 churches and 3,000 communicants.[18] After receiving various reports and communications, the first important item of business was the establishment of a "fund for pious uses." The Synod at its very inception was thereby setting another determining precedent in the expanding life of the church. Not only was the Presbyterian Church to be a missionary church by the action of the ministers at their initial meeting as a Presbytery in 1707, where the ministers pledged themselves "to supply neighboring desolate places when a minister is wanting and opportunity of doing good offers," but now the church was to be a benevolent institution with a program of brotherhood and human relief as need and opportunity became manifest. Its members were to share their financial resources for broader and more humanitarian causes than merely meeting the individual churches' financial needs. This fund was soon to be strengthened by a large contribution from Presbyterian brethren in Scotland. The fund thus established was a continuing policy of the growing American Presbyterian Church and the basis for all the missionary programs and benevolent enterprises of the denomination.

New resources were at once added to the Presbyterian Church by this formation of three conveniently distributed presbyteries. The added strength included most of the New York and New Jersey Puritan churches. Among the prominent ministers thus received were Jonathan Dickinson of Elizabethtown and John Pierson of Woodbridge, New Jersey. Both were Yale graduates of marked ability. Dickinson's leadership in Synod, with his tact and calm judgment, was a valuable asset in guiding the formative policies of the Synod during the period of controversy which was soon to follow. The Synod had been formed without any clear demarcation between the powers of Presbytery and Synod. Proper procedures had to be formed upon the anvil of heated debate. Differences of opinion arising out of contrasted phases of experience in other countries were inevitable. Controversy seems the unhappy price which a democratic form of government must pay before harmony can be purchased. The democratic Presbyterian

Church was no exception throughout its years of rapid growth.

The first of these major verbal struggles toward unity found a peaceful and permanent solution in the historic action of the Synod of Philadelphia in 1729.[19] The Synod by unanimous vote approved a compromise Adoption Act which gave permanent creedal unity to the developing Presbyterian Church. The occasion was a widespread doctrinal laxity throughout the British Isles and the resulting fear that Presbyterian ministers who came to America from these countries might be tinged with heresy. Some standard by which their theological views could be tested seemed necessary. The more conservative brethren thought that strict acceptance of the Westminster Confession and Catechisms was vital and should be required by presbyteries and synod. The more liberal group feared that doctrinal strife and possible schism would follow any requirement of strict subscription to the letter of any creed.

The discussion over a two-year period developed sharp differences of opinion. An acceptable compromise, however, was worked out largely through the wisdom, tact, and prestige of Jonathan Dickinson. The famous Adopting Act provided that "all ministers of this Synod shall declare their acceptance of the Confession of Faith, with the Larger and Shorter Catechisms of the Assembly of Divines at Westminster as being in all the essential and necessary articles good forms of sound words and systems of Christian Doctrine." [20] This compromise gave the Presbyterian Church a definite doctrinal basis and test for its ministers. It was sufficiently flexible, also, to allow reasonable differences of interpretation on the less essential articles of faith and did not attempt to define what were these "essential and necessary articles in doctrine, worship or government." The Synod and the constituent presbyteries were left free to use their own best judgment in receiving new applicants for membership who might have conscientious scruples about some articles which were considered not necessary nor essential.

The Presbyterian Church was now ready to go forward with its ministers and churches bound together in an adjustable bond of theological unity. Unfortunately, other perplexing problems of growth did not find as happy and unifying solutions and had to pass through the fires of schism before the melted elements of thought and experience would be merged and reshaped by the Holy Spirit and hardened into happy reunions.

As the years passed, the territorial bounds allotted to these three functioning presbyteries were frequently subdivided and additional presbyteries authorized. This flexible type of organization was part of the genius of the Presbyterian system. It was particularly well adapted to the needs of an ever expanding frontier. Whenever that frontier extended too widely for convenience in meeting or effectiveness in supervision, all that was necessary was a vote of the Synod cutting off a group of ministers and churches to be constituted a new presbytery with clearly defined territorial boundaries. Thus the Presbytery of Donegal was formed in 1732, the Presbytery of New Brunswick in 1738. In that same year the presbyteries of East Jersey and Long Island were merged and renamed the Presbytery of New York.

THE GREAT ULSTER-SCOTCH MIGRATION

The second major factor in the rapid growth of American Presbyterianism during the first half of the eighteenth century was the tide of Ulster-Scotch immigration which began to flow with increasing volume shortly after the organization of the Synod of Philadelphia in 1717. Basically they were native Scotch Presbyterians who had migrated from Scotland in the seventeenth century and settled in northern Ireland. Here they prospered until religious and economic persecution forced them to seek more advantageous conditions in the American wilderness. Immigration to America began with comparatively small numbers during the last two decades of the seventeenth century. It reached impressive volume throughout the second decade of the eighteenth century when from three to six thousand emigrants reached America annually. It rolled steadily onward to its peak from 1740 to the outbreak of the Revolutionary War. At least 12,000 sailed annually from Ulster. Perhaps as many as 30,000 came during the years 1771–1773.

The great majority of these new settlers were Presbyterian, at least in background and loyalty if not in character and conviction. New England seemed to be the choice of the first of the Ulster-Scotch when the tide of immigration first started to move. A large group numbering from six to eight hundred, including two ministers, arrived in Boston in 1718. But they were not welcomed by the more cultured New England Puritans, who shunted them off to the frontier as a protecting barrier from marauding Indians. Still they continued to come, and settled in sufficiently large numbers to establish the Presbyterian congregations which organized the Presbytery of Londonderry in 1729 and later the Boston, East, Grafton, and Salem presbyteries.

Pennsylvania, with its policy of religious toleration established by William Penn, soon became the popular home for these energetic pioneers. The broad, fertile valleys of Pennsylvania offered attractive agricultural opportunities. The new settlers swarmed over unoccupied land without concern for legal ownership as they moved westward in search of farms and homes. They defended their illegal squatting on unoccupied land by insisting that "it is against the laws of God and nature that so much land should be idle while so many Christians wanted it to labor on and to raise their bread." This disregard of the legal rights of absentee landowners frustrated any further attempts to establish the tenant system in colonial Pennsylvania. In 1729 James Logan, in a communication to Thomas Penn, wrote, "It looks as if Ireland is to send all its inhabitants hither for last week not less than six ships arrived and every day two or three arrive also." [21] The numbers steadily increased. In 1749 they totaled one-fourth of the entire population of the colony of Pennsylvania. Fifteen years later, according to the estimate of Benjamin Franklin, the proportion was one-third among the 350,000 inhabitants. In some years, as already noted, as many as 12,000 immigrants came to Pennsylvania from northern Ireland.

These newcomers from Ulster spread out in two separating streams of westward migration from the coastal ports. One followed the Delaware River into Bucks County and over the valley of the Susquehanna toward the foothills of the Alleghenies. As it gathered strength, it permeated the mountain valleys of western Pennsylvania until it reached the Ohio country which lay beyond. The other stream entered the Potomac Valley and proceeded in a southwesterly direction throughout the Great Valley of Virginia. From thence it flowed into the western areas of North and South Carolina and on to Georgia. These new migrants were searching primarily for desirable agricultural lands. They were an aggressive group of determined pioneers. Always liberty-loving, they proved somewhat lawless and distinctly individualistic and self-reliant. They were united in their distrust and hatred of English monarchy.

Pennsylvania, which before this infiltration of Presbyterian sympathizers from northern Ireland had only two weak Presbyterian churches, soon witnessed the multiplying of congregations among the scattered settlers on the westward-moving frontier.

Jedediah Andrews, the minister of the First Presbyterian Church in Philadelphia, in a letter written in October, 1730, reported:

Such a multitude of people coming in from Ireland of late years our congregations are multiplied in this province to the number of 15 or 16 which are all but two or three furnished with ministers. All are Scotch and Irish but three or four. Besides divers new congregations that are forming by these new comers, we all call ourselves Presbyterian, none pretending to be called Congregational in this province.[22]

In lesser numbers this Ulster-Scotch tide extended throughout all the colonies, especially the Middle Colonies.

The Presbyterian ministers saw in the arrival of these newcomers not only added strength, by the increased number of ministers and church members, but also a challenging missionary opportunity. Each member of presbytery felt that his responsibility extended beyond his own community and that he must heed the requests for preaching and the administration of the sacraments which came from neighboring groups where there was no minister. At almost every meeting of presbytery, an important item of business was the assignment of its ministers to preach on one or more Sabbaths at specified points in response to urgent calls. Failure to meet these assigned preaching engagements and missionary journeys was regarded as a breach of responsibility unless the reason for such failure was deemed satisfactory by the other brethren in presbytery. Ministerial students and licentiates also were used to supplement the inadequate supply of pastors. This missionary work of the licentiates was a forerunner of the home missionaries who in later years continued to play a vital part in the nation-wide extension of the Presbyterian Church.

The formation of new presbyteries was the natural result. Donegal Presbytery was thus organized in 1732 with responsibility for Lancaster County and beyond. It was long the Pennsylvania frontier Presbytery whose members labored diligently and strained their inadequate resources to meet the developing number of calls for service. To the missionary zeal of Donegal Presbytery, western Pennsylvania Presbyterians owe an eternal debt of gratitude.[23]

THE GREAT AWAKENING

The third major determining factor in the rapid growth of colonial Presbyterianism was a moral and religious revival known as the Great Awakening. It was an intercolonial and nonsectarian movement that manifested its regenerating influences in different denominations but with especial effectiveness among Presbyterians in the Middle Colonies. It was marred at times by excessive emotionalism and embittered controversy. Yet it stirred religious emotions with a dynamic power that lifted the moral standards of the colonies and released religious forces that changed the outlook and program of organized religion. Membership rolls of the churches were lengthened, community evils were restrained and humanitarian impulses stirred which found practical expression in the establishment of colleges and orphanages, schools for the Negroes, missions to the Indians and the Negroes and other agencies of human betterment. Revivalism was adopted as a valued asset in the church's program. Religion became a vital experience in all phases of life, not merely a formalized program of worship.

The Great Awakening was the divine answer to the needs of a careless and indifferent age that was being touched, but not transformed, by the comparatively few ministers whose resources in numbers and energy were inadequate to serve this rapid increase in population. The success of the revival movement was due to its timeliness and to the widespread moral and religious carelessness that called it into aggressive action. In the older New England communities and in the coastal cities, religion had lost much of its evangelistic zeal and had become self-centered in orthodoxy or in intellectualism. No less prominent a New England divine than Increase Mather bemoaned this loss of Puritan zeal and cried out passionately in 1721, "O degenerate New England, what art thou come to this day." [24] On the frontier, life was crude and callous, a succession of hardships, Indian wars, bereavements, and a monotonous struggle against nature which sought entertaining release in excessive use of liquor and lewd indulgences. Educational and religious activities were all too infrequent among the scattered settlers, who had no resources except their own habits and attitudes. Most of them had come from the lower economic groups in Europe where they had little more than a nominal contact with the church.

The New England phase of this needed intercolonial revival was centered chiefly among the Congregational churches under the leadership of Jonathan Edwards, a man of tremendous intellectual strength. As a precocious young graduate of Yale, he was called at the age of eighteen years to serve as pastor of a small Presbyterian congregation in New York. His brief New York pastorate proved unsuccessful after eight months. He returned to his native New England to serve for a few years as instructor in Yale.

In 1726 Edwards began his historic pastorate in Northampton, Massachusetts. After a few years of discouraging response, his evangelistic preaching finally bore fruit in a remarkable revival which began in 1734 and transformed the church and community. People flocked to him for counsel. "The place of resort," he wrote, "was now altered. It was no longer the tavern but the minister's house that was thronged far more than ever the tavern had been wont to be." [25] Reports of the revival spread throughout New England. Edwards was besieged with requests to preach in other communities. Almost every village in the Connecticut Valley was touched in some measure. Edwards called upon all colonial governments to appoint a day of prayer and fasting. "We in New England," he wrote, "are this day engaged in a more important war than that between England and Spain." The Great Awakening was now a quickening reality in New England.

Throughout the Middle Colonies the first evidences of the Great Awakening were the fruitage of the evangelistic preaching of Theodore J. Frelinghuysen. He was pastor of four small Dutch Reformed Churches in the Raritan Valley of New Jersey. The revival which soon swept over those congregations aroused the attention of other churches of all denominations throughout an ever widening circle. His emphasis upon individual regeneration and a personal experience of conversion profoundly changed the sermons of hosts of neighboring pastors.

This revival in the Dutch Reformed churches under Frelinghuysen in central New Jersey was the spark which ignited the Great Awakening among Presbyterian churches and spread rapidly throughout the Middle Colonies and especially Pennsylvania. It touched the heart of Jonathan Dickinson in Elizabethtown, New Jersey, and blessed his and other Puritan churches with notable results. But its real power came through the remarkable Tennent family. Associated with the Tennents were a group of capable and consecrated graduates of Log College, founded in 1728, where they had studied theology under the elder William Tennent's tutelage. The group included such outstanding Presbyterian leaders as John and Samuel Blair, John Rowland, Samuel Finley, and William Robinson.

Gilbert Tennent, the eldest of the four sons, was the most famous of the Tennent family and the greatest single factor in the Awakening Movement and in the resulting controversy and schism. In the autumn of 1727, he was called to serve the Presbyterian church at New Brunswick, New Jersey. He felt dissatisfied with his lack of spiritual success. By contrast, he noted the transformed lives and quickened religious zeal in Frelinghuysen's neighboring congregations. The two men became close friends and kindred spirits. A short time later Tennent was stricken with a severe illness. In prolonged prayer for recovery, he experienced an emotional change which sent him forth with flaming zeal for the similar regeneration of all men. He insisted that belief in the Bible and orthodox doctrines was not sufficient for salvation. A personal experience with God which resulted in high moral standards and religious fervor, he felt, was an essential manifestation of redemptive Christianity. "No one ever became a Christian," he thundered, "without first passing through the terror of realizing that he was not a Christian." [26]

Tennent accepted every possible opportunity to preach. Alone, and in the depth of winter, he set forth on an evangelistic tour that brought him to Boston. There he preached daily for about three months. He was convinced that he was called "in providence to attempt to arouse the Presbyterian Church from its profound sleep of carnal security and to bring about a Reformation in its body." Under the spell of his oratory and flaming denunciation of sin, strong men wept, groaned, and repented. Emotionalism carried many to conviction and consecration. The Great Awakening had begun in Presbyterian churches, especially in those churches whose pastors were from New England or were graduates of Log College.

The arrival in America of George Whitefield in 1739, on the

first of his numerous trips from England, added tremendous impetus to the revival movement. Whitefield was the greatest preacher of that period. Gilbert Tennent was second only to Whitefield. Together these two evangelists joined forces. They understood and admired each other as kindred souls. Sometimes they toured together. Sometimes they journeyed separately; but always they supplemented their efforts. Everywhere Whitefield drew tremendous crowds. No church was large enough to accommodate those who flocked to hear him. Whitefield then took to the fields, where his powerful voice and clarity of speech enabled him to be heard almost a mile away and every word understood at distances of four hundred feet.

His evangelistic tours carried him from New York and Philadelphia to Boston. Everywhere he emphasized the need of the new birth. It was the central theme of his preaching.

"Why, Mr. Whitefield," inquired a friend one day, "do you so often preach on 'Ye must be born again'?"

"Because," he replied solemnly and looking his questioner full in the face, "because you must be born again." [27]

Though Whitefield was an Anglican by ordination and a close associate of Wesley in England, he found himself most at home among his Calvinistic co-workers throughout the colonies. So forcefully did he preach Calvinistic convictions that some Ulster-Scotch Presbyterians invited him to join the Presbyterian Church. He rejected their invitation but replied: "I am of Catholic spirit and if I see any man who loves the Lord Jesus in sincerity, I am not very solicitous to what communion he belongs."

He was a powerful force in bringing the Great Awakening to the Presbyterian churches. Thousands throughout the Middle Colonies found their way into the membership of Presbyterian churches because of Whitefield's close association with Tennent and other Presbyterian preachers in this most effective and long-continued revival movement in the colonial era. Philadelphia, which became the center of the revival movement, was particularly quickened by Whitefield's preaching. Benjamin Franklin, who was an admirer of Whitefield and an attentive listener to his sermons, testified that "one could not walk through the town in an evening without hearing psalms sung in different families in every street."

The *Pennsylvania Gazette* reported:

The alteration in the face of religion here is altogether surprising. Never did the people show so great a willingness to attend sermons, nor the preachers greater zeal and diligence in performing the duties of their function. Religion is become the subject of most conversations. Instead of idle songs and ballads, the people are everywhere entertaining themselves with psalms, hymns and spiritual songs. All of which under God is owing to the successful labors of the Rev. Mr. Whitefield.[28]

One very visible result was the organization of a second Presbyterian Church in Philadelphia. Gilbert Tennent was called as its first pastor, and a large and impressive sanctuary was later erected. Philadelphia was soon to merit the distinction of being the strongest center of American Presbyterianism as the forces generated by the Great Awakening continued with steady effectiveness. Thus the Great Awakening became the third major determining factor in the rapid growth of the Presbyterian Church.

OLD SIDE AND NEW SIDE SCHISM, 1741–1758

But growth always presents inevitable problems arising from expansion and the need of assimilation. The growing Presbyterian Church was no exception. With its democratic form of church government, these problems could find an acceptable solution only through discussion and majority decision. For the growing Presbyterian Church, that process of solution was complicated by the contrasted backgrounds of the diverse elements which were being merged to form an American Presbyterian Church. It was further hindered by the divergent convictions cherished by strong and somewhat self-opinionated leaders.

The Great Awakening which was expanding and energizing the Presbyterian Church was also arousing regrettable bitterness and contrasted attitudes toward the procedures of revivalism. Strong and noble men were lined up on opposing sides. One group was composed of the friends and leaders of the revival movement. They regarded it as a glorious work of God's spirit and branded all those who disapproved of it as unconverted men and formalists. Those who opposed the revival based their objections upon the methods of the evangelists. They in turn accused the revivalists of placing too great stress in their preaching upon the terrors of the law and the horrors of the damned and of interpreting religion too exclusively in terms of emotional raptures and violent excitement.

Instead of being drawn together more closely by discussion, acrimonious debate deepened the chasm of thought separating the contrasted viewpoints. The divergent views proved temporarily insoluble by friendly conference and mutual trust. The unhappy result was the division of the Presbyterian Church into two separate and independent branches. These two divisions were called the New Side and the Old Side. The growing Presbyterian Church was now experiencing the first of a succession of schisms that have marked its developing progress toward unity and mutual understanding. The two divisions of the Synod continued in separate existence for seventeen years. In 1758 a more conciliatory spirit effected a reconciliation and reunion.

The explosive force which made impractical the continued organic unity of the Synod of Philadelphia was an irritating and denunciatory sermon preached by Gilbert Tennent at Nottingham on March 10, 1739. It bore the provocative title "The Danger of an Unconverted Ministry." By implication and direct statement, Tennent accused the ministers who opposed the revival movement as being themselves unregenerate. They were making the ministry, he charged, no more than another trade. They were dead at heart. They had no call of God to the ministry. He clothed his charges in cutting, scornful phrases that would either shock or shatter them out of their complacency. He describes these so-called unworthy ministers as

moral negroes, never so white in the mouth, yet who will hinder instead of help others in at the straight gate.

Look into congregations of unconverted ministers. Not a soul converted that can be heard of for many years together. These caterpillars labor to devour every green thing.

He likened them unto "a swarm of locusts, a crowd of Pharisees who give forth a very stinking odor in the nostrils both of God and good men." [29]

The sermon was printed by Benjamin Franklin. It circulated rapidly throughout the church. Tempers flared. Its effect was, as Tennent had planned, "like rousing a wasps' nest." Separation was inevitable when the Reverend Robert Cross at the Synod meeting in 1741 replied with answering invectives in which he accused Tennent and his followers of

preaching the terrors of the law in such a manner and dialect as has no precedent in the word of God but rather appears to be borrowed from a worse dialect and so industriously working on the passions and affections of weak minds as to cause them to cry out in a hideous manner and to fall down in convulsion-like fits and then boasting of these things as the work of God.[30]

This resolution of Cross and his associates carried the supporting signatures of twelve ministers. It concluded with the direct charge that "these brethren have no right to be acknowledged as members of this judicatory of Christ."

Amid the confusion of the embittered debate which followed, Gilbert and his supporters walked out. Later the entire New Brunswick Presbytery was read out of the Synod in an illegal action.

Subsequent efforts to heal the break failed. The separation was complete. New York and New Castle presbyteries withdrew later to join with New Brunswick Presbytery in the organization of the Synod of New York in 1745. The new Synod was composed of thirteen Tennent men and nine from New York. All were supporters of the revival. Under their leadership the fruits of the Great Awakening continued to strengthen and enlarge the Presbyterian Church.

But this provocative sermon of Tennent and the controversy over methods of revivalism were only the embittered surface causes of the schism. These could have been discounted easily as temporary un-Christian differences of opinion to be cured by the healing hands of time and penitent reflection. However, there were deeper causes arising out of the unsolved problems of growth. Until these problems were solved, unity was impossible whether the Synod was organized as one or two ecclesiastical bodies. At least three disruptive problems were most controversial.

The first was the problem of how to maintain an educated ministry. As long as the denomination was small, this was no pressing problem. The European universities and later the New England colleges could furnish a sufficient number of educated preachers. The problem began to be acute in 1735 as the tide of Ulster-Scotch migration was rolling westward. Up to that year the Presbyterian Church had received a total of seventy-eight ministers. Of these, twenty-three were graduates of the University of Glasgow, and nine were alumni of Edinburgh, Scotland. Harvard had supplied five graduates and Yale seventeen. The other four, of whom three were his own sons, had been trained by William Tennent. Additional ministers were in urgent demand because of "the great number of newly organized churches in this wilderness." [31]

William Tennent, who was both a profound scholar and a creative educator, made the first effort to solve the problem by organizing a school on his own farm near Neshaminy in Bucks County, Pennsylvania. His purpose was to educate for the ministry qualified young men who lacked the time and money to seek an education in the far-away New England colleges. It was only a log house, about twenty foot square. Tennent, with some assistance from his oldest son, was the entire faculty. His detractors dubbed it in ridicule "The Log College." The number of its students was never large, perhaps a total of twenty-one. The scope of the curriculum was necessarily limited. Yet it trained a remarkable group of men. They became notable preachers and outstanding educators and made a transforming contribution to religion and education. What William Tennent lacked in equipment he made up in zeal. He knew how to impart to others his own range of knowledge.

Doubtless the training these men received at the Log College, with its inadequate library and one-man faculty, was not as comprehensive as was the education of the preachers from the older universities and colleges. The graduates of these institutions looked with haughty disdain upon the Log College men who were seeking ordination and admission to the Synod. Resolutions were adopted by Synod which seemed to reflect on the education of Log College men and which subjected them to certain additional examinations by Synod. Gilbert Tennent defended his father's school amid embittered discussion. The elder Tennent retired in 1742 because of his advanced age. Evidently Log College with its meager resources could only be a controversial and not a satisfactory answer to the problem of how to train an increasing number of educated ministers.

Nor was the unifying answer to be found in Francis Alison's school, which was established at New London in Chester County by the Synod of Philadelphia in 1744 and supported by the congregation under the care of Synod. Nor could the succession of academies such as Pequea, Nottingham, and Foggs Manor be more than preparatory aids. The unifying answer came when the College of New Jersey at Elizabethtown, New Jersey, later removed to Newark, and thence to Princeton, was established by the New

School Synod of New York, in October, 1746. Its purpose was to carry forward the work of Log College, which no longer existed, and to train men for an evangelistic ministry. Moreover, its curriculum and standards were to be the equivalent of the New England colleges. To the support of this college, both New and Old schools could then contribute as the solution which satisfied both sides and helped to bring about the reunion in 1758. As the years passed, Princeton College became the only truly intercolonial college. The famous four founders of the Redstone Presbytery in 1781 were all graduates of Princeton College. They in turn established the earliest Presbyterian colleges in western Pennsylvania.

The second disturbing problem which could find a satisfactory solution only through the experimental years of the New and Old Side Schism was the perplexing question of the division of powers between the Synod and its Presbyteries. When the General Presbytery in 1716 voted to constitute an annual Synod, the three newly organized presbyteries were referred to as "subordinate meetings or Presbyteries." The limitations of the jurisdiction of the Synod and these three Presbyteries were not defined but had to be worked out as experience might prove expedient. Explosive differences of opinion did not appear until the Synod of Philadelphia refused to admit into its membership, without further examination, ministers who had been licensed or ordained by the Presbytery of New Brunswick. The problem was made irritatingly acute by the insistence of some of the members of that Presbytery upon what they felt was their right to preach in the bounds of adjoining Presbyteries without the permission of those Presbyteries.

The New Brunswick Presbytery had been erected in 1738 with five ministers, of whom three had been educated in Log College. Naturally, they favored ordaining other young men who had been similarly educated at that same college. Synod, however, charged that the educational facilities of that pioneer school were inadequate and so voted to admit into its membership without further examination only ordained ministers who held diplomas from the

New England or European colleges. The New Brunswick men believed this action was an undeserved reflection upon Log College and its graduates. They defied the Synod by licensing and later ordaining John Rowland and Samuel Finley, both Log College graduates.

The issue was now being clearly defined. Gilbert Tennent and those associated with him claimed that the real seat of authority in the presbyterian system was the Presbytery. The other and larger group, led by Francis Alison, argued that Synod was the authoritative body. Synod declared that the New Brunswick Presbytery was guilty of violating the laws of the church and pronounced Rowland's licensure illegal. The Log College men lost the decision in the church court. They had to await the experience of seventeen years of schism to find vindication in the compromises of reunion. The reunited church made the Presbytery the basic seat of authority on matters of ordination and procedure.

The third disruptive problem was the highly involved question of what constitutes the essential spiritual requirements for church membership and the ministry. This problem had appeared early in the contrasted views of the church which divided the Puritans into Congregationalists and Presbyterians. It came to the focus of controversy in the period of the Great Awakening as the Log College revivalists insisted upon some experience in regeneration. They believed that true ministers were called of God and should be motivated by an inner sense of divine compulsion to preach for the salvation of sinners. This consciousness of the moving of God's spirit in their souls, they contended, was as essential as education in the Arts, Sciences, and Theology. On the other hand, many of the older clergy had entered the ministry without experiencing any spiritual crisis in their lives. A regrettably large portion of the Old Side ministers were guilty of moral irregularities and were never severely disciplined by their too tolerant brethren in presbytery. These ministers seemed to be satisfied with high educational standards and formal regularity in belief and worship. There were similar differences of conviction regarding the need of regeneration and personal piety as tests for church membership.

These differences seemed too contrasted to be reconciled harmoniously in church councils. They had to await the test of the revival itself throughout the seventeen years of schism. The New Side leaders joined heartily in the revival in its emphasis on changed lives and experiences of conversion. Their membership multiplied fourfold. The Old Side, which looked askance at any emphasis on the new birth, stagnated. Its churches did not strive. It failed in its attempt to establish a college. The number of ministers on the roll of the Synod of Philadelphia was four less than before the separation. During that same period the Synod of New York increased its roll from twenty-two to seventy-three ministers.

These contrasted results made the answer clear and determined the future policy of the Presbyterian Church. Apparently even Calvinists need to be energized by religious emotions if their religion is to be a vital force. The Great Awakening altered the program and practices of the Presbyterian Church. The reunited church was lifted from a formalized emphasis on creed to a living and vital fellowship with Him "whom to know aright is life eternal." Every presbytery was soon ready to examine candidates for licensure and ordination in "experimental acquaintance with religion." Revivalism had demonstrated its power and was "owned as a definite work of God."

With these three divisive problems approaching satisfactory solutions, allied problems seemed of lessened importance after the years of schism. Tempers had cooled. Mistakes were acknowledged more readily as the healing hand of time allayed the wounded feelings of conscientious combatants. In 1758 the Old Side and the New Side synods worked out an acceptable Plan of Union. Both synods were ready for reunion. The very Gilbert Tennent, whose provocative sermon on "The Danger of an Unconverted Ministry" had split the church, became the leader in successful efforts toward reconciliation. His conciliatory pamphlet "The Peace of Jerusalem" was distributed widely. It helped draw the leaders together. The Plan of Union was adopted as the basis of reunion. The two synods were merged to form the Synod of New York and Philadelphia. As an appropriate act of Christian brotherhood, Gilbert Tennent was chosen to serve as the first moderator of the merged synods.

A strengthened and a more tolerant church was now ready to give united leadership to the colonies throughout the long and sacrificial struggle for independence which only the War of the Revolution could establish. Upon the members of the Presbyterian Church rested the main burden of leadership and sacrifice as the years of conflict brought the war to a triumphant close with the surrender of Cornwallis in 1781. The war greatly reduced the resources of the Presbyterian Church, but it remained the largest connectionally organized body of Christians in the new republic. With face and hope toward the future, the church redirected its missionary efforts for the spiritual salvation of the westward-moving frontier. In 1781 the Synod of New York and Philadelphia constituted the Presbytery of Redstone, the mother presbytery of upper Ohio Valley Presbyterianism, with the famous "Four Horsemen of Western Pennsylvania" as its original members and missionary evangelists and educators.

Further growth and expansion made necessary another reorganization for nation-wide service. No longer could the growing church be served adequately by the single Synod of New York and Philadelphia. Territorial jurisdiction was subdivided into four synods and sixteen presbyteries. All were united under the control of the General Assembly which held its first meeting in Philadelphia on the third Thursday of May, 1789. John Witherspoon, who had been a member of the Continental Congress, who was the only clergyman to sign the Declaration of Independence and who had fought for political and religious freedom, received the deserved honor of presiding as the first moderator of the General Assembly.

The Presbyterian Church was now completely organized, with its distinctive series of four ascending courts through the Session, Presbytery, Synod, and General Assembly. The foundation of a nation-wide organization was laid. A democratic self-governing church was ready to serve the newly born American nation which had adopted its own Constitution only two years earlier.

CHAPTER III

Beginnings in the South

ACCORDING to Professor Carl Bridenbaugh there was no South in 1776, and never had been. There were rather three different modes of existence: (1) the already old Chesapeake Society, erected on a tobacco base; (2) the youthful Carolina Society, burgeoning on profits from rice and indigo; and (3) the lusty Back Country, still in process of formation.[1]

Presbyterianism, during the Colonial period, developed little strength in the Chesapeake area or in the Carolina lowlands; its strength and promise for the future was in the Back Country— among the Ulster-Scots, most of whom had come down the Great Valley from Pennsylvania in the generation preceding the Revolution.

THE CHESAPEAKE SOCIETY

The earliest of the three Southern societies began with the settlement of Jamestown in 1607 and gradually spread along the lands served by the Chesapeake and its tributaries. When the Revolution began, it was the largest and most populous English society in America. A rural region, without stimulating centers, its metropolis was London, 3,000 miles across the sea.

The Anglican Church was established in Virginia from the outset. But all of the ministers brought to the colony under the Virginia Company, that is, before 1642, seem to have been Puritans, inclined, some of them at least, toward Presbyterianism.[2] The best known of these early ministers, Alexander Whitaker, whose father was professor of divinity in the University of Cambridge, wrote to a cousin in London, "I much more muse that so few of our English ministers that were so hot against the Surplis and subscription, come hither where neither are spoken of." [3] In 1624 direction of the colony was assumed by the Crown, and five years later the Assembly ordered "that all ministers residing and beeing, or who hereafter shall reside and bee within this colony, shall conforme themselves in all things according to the cannons of the church of England. . . ." [4] Vigorous enforcement of this law was begun by Governor Berkeley, a pronounced loyalist, in 1642—after the Puritan Parliament had impeached Charles I for high treason and imprisoned him in the Tower of London. In this year—1642 —three ministers from New England, called to the pastorate of as many Puritan parishes south of the James, were compelled to leave the colony. Many of the Puritans of Southside Virginia (three hundred in a single group), unwilling to conform to Anglicanism, finally migrated to Maryland, attracted by the more tolerant policy of the proprietor. Here some of them were later gathered into the early Presbyterian congregations gathered on the eastern shore of Maryland.

A number of ministers with Presbyterian ordination, Scotch as well as Puritan, held parishes in the Established Church of Virginia during the seventeenth century,[5] but no attempt was made to organize distinctly Presbyterian congregations until the century's end. In 1684 Francis Makemie ministered for some months to a number of Presbyterian families in Lynnhaven and the adjoining parish of Elizabeth River, near the present Norfolk. They had been previously cared for by the Reverend James Porter, a Presbyterian by ordination, but incumbent of the Anglican parish. Josias Mackie, who followed Makemie, took advantage of the Toleration Act,

and on August 15, 1692, was recorded as a dissenting minister,
pastor of the first Presbyterian congregation recognized as such by
the laws of the colony. Six years later Makemie registered two
preaching points near his home in Accomac County on the Eastern
Shore. But none of these or any other early Presbyterian group in
eastern Virginia survived more than a brief number of years. The
Presbyterians who remained in this portion of the colony were
finally absorbed into the dominant Anglican Establishment.

In Maryland, at the head of the Chesapeake Bay, the story was
slightly different. Lord Baltimore, the proprietor, encouraged Protestant settlers, and to Maryland they came, Puritans, Scots, Ulster-
Scots, Huguenots, and others. Francis Doughty, Matthew Hill,
and William Traill all labored here. The last-named came after
Laggan Presbytery in North Ireland had received a request from
Colonel William Stevens of Rehoboth, Maryland, for a "godly
minister." After widespread itineration in Maryland, Virginia, the
Carolinas, and Barbados, Francis Makemie settled down in Accomac County, Virginia, just across the Maryland line. Shortly
thereafter, about 1698, he organized churches in Snow Hill, Rehoboth, and other communities on the Eastern Shore of Maryland.
About 1703 Nathaniel Taylor was serving a strong church at Patuxent. Three years later, presumably under Makemie's leadership,
the first American Presbytery was formed with seven ministers,
four of whom labored in Maryland, one in Philadelphia, and two in
Delaware. For a few years Maryland Presbyterianism continued to
thrive. But after the Anglican Church was established (in 1691),
immigrants who were Presbyterians tended to avoid the colony.
Few ministers came to it, and gradually most of the Presbyterians
conformed to the Church of England.[6] When the Synod was organized in 1717, there were seventeen ministers and forty churches.
Four of the ministers served congregations in Maryland. There were
neither churches nor ministers in Virginia or further south, except
in the South Carolina lowlands.

THE CAROLINA SOCIETY

Charleston, settled in 1670, was the port through which Presbyterianism began to come into South Carolina. Here on the Ashley and Cooper rivers a notable planter society began to develop, based on the culture of rice and indigo. It spread ultimately over an area of approximately eleven thousand square miles, about one-fourth of the area of the Chesapeake country. At the end of the Colonial period it supported a population of more than 110,000.

Presbyterians were drawn thither from many sources—England, Wales, Scotland, and the north of Ireland, Holland, France, Switzerland, and Italy. A Huguenot church, composed of French Calvinists driven from France by religious persecution, was organized about 1687, just two years after the revocation of the Edict of Nantes. Other Huguenot churches, formed in the interior on the Presbyterian model, were absorbed ultimately into the Established (Anglican) Church of the colony. An Independent Church, including Puritans from Old and New England, Presbyterians from Scotland and Ireland, and Huguenots, was organized in Charleston about 1690. Later—about 1731—the congregation was divided over the issue of subscription to the Westminster Confession of Faith, and the Presbyterians formed their own organization. The Reverend Archibald Stobo, a Scotsman, was largely instrumental in the organization of six other Presbyterian churches in the neighborhood of Charleston in the early part of the eighteenth century. It was difficult for these Presbyterian churches to maintain their ground against the superior resources of the Established Church. Thus the English Society for the Propagation of the Gospel sent twelve Episcopal missionaries to the colony, and their support came chiefly from the public treasury. Presbyterians and other dissenters received no missionary aid and were taxed heavily to build Episcopal churches. Continued state patronage ensured the ascendancy of the Established Church both in numbers and in strength. Presbyterianism was kept alive, however, by Stobo, aided by a little handful of ministers sent out from Scotland and by a steady accession of immigrants from Scotland and Ireland. A presbytery was formed of the churches in and around Charleston in 1722 or shortly thereafter, but this presbytery was not connected with the main body of Presbyterianism farther north, and in the Revolutionary period it passed out of existence. A Presbyterian church organized in the town of Savannah, Georgia, in 1755, as a branch of the Church of Scotland, remains an independent Presbyterian church until the present time.

The first Presbyterians to come to North Carolina were Scotch Highlanders, who settled along the Cape Fear River. The date of the first settlement is not known, but Highlanders were there certainly as early as 1729, the year that North and South Carolina became separate provinces. They came, like their brethren from the north of Ireland, because of disabilities in their native land and because of unfavorable economic conditions.

The majority of the Highlanders came after the battle of Culloden in 1746. Some of the smaller clans in the Scottish Highlands raised their standards for the Pretender, Charles Edward Stuart, and fought against the House of Hanover. They were joined by young men from the larger clans. Defeated at Culloden, the Highlanders were hunted down like wild beasts and treated with great ferocity by their enemies. Large numbers were ultimately pardoned on condition that they take the solemn oath of allegiance and emigrate to the American plantations. In 1746–1747, with their families and friends, they arrived in North Carolina and settled a large expanse of country along the Cape Fear River, of which Cambelltown (now Fayetteville) was the center.[7] The emigration, once fairly begun by royal authority, was carried on by those who wished to improve their economic condition. Not until the Revolution did this migration from the Highlands cease.

Unfortunately, no minister accompanied the first Scotch immigrants, nor was any minister found to labor among them until James Campbell came to Cross Creek from Pennsylvania in 1757, and bought a plantation opposite Bluff Church. He organized three churches, Roger's Meeting House, Barbecue, and McKay's, all in Cumberland County, and preached to them regularly in Gaelic and English.

The fact that most of the Highlanders spoke only Gaelic (which continued to be used in some of the churches until after the Civil War) protected them from the nearby Baptist missionaries at Sandy Creek, and kept them faithful to Presbyterian Calvinism during the many years when they were without the ministrations of a regular pastor. Their custom of family worship also kept their faith alive. Children learned the Catechism from their elders and the church officers examined them frequently on it. Before each hearth where there was reverence for the forms of the Scotch church the whole family read the Bible aloud every day, and repeated the Shorter Catechism. So well informed on the doctrines and customs of the church was the congregation of Barbecue that the Rev. John McLeod, who came to North Carolina with a colony of Highlanders in 1770, said that "he would rather preach to the most polished and fashionable congregation in Edinburgh than to the little critical carls of Barbecue." [8]

Not until after the Revolution did the Scotch Presbyterians in North Carolina have adequate ministerial care.

The Back Country

The third Southern region settled prior to the Revolution was the so-called "Back Country," "Back Parts," or "Back Settlements." "The Back Parts," Bridenbaugh points out,

consisted of an irregularly shaped area running southwest from Mason and Dixon's line for more than 600 miles to just beyond the southern banks of the Savannah River and varying from 20 to 160 miles in width. Beginning west of the Monocacy River with Frederick County, Maryland, it included the Great Valley and that portion of the Virginia

Piedmont west of a line from Charlottesville due south to the North Carolina boundary, as well as the North and South Carolina Piedmont between the fall line and the Great Smokies. In extent this was a larger territory than the Chesapeake and Carolina countries combined.[9]

Before 1730 this country was virtually unoccupied. At the outbreak of the Revolution it had more than a quarter of a million inhabitants, most of whom had come into the Back Country by way of Pennsylvania along the Great Philadelphia Wagon Road. This road, following the meanderings of the old Indian trails, ran from Philadelphia west through Lancaster and York, crossed the Potomac into the Shenandoah Valley at William's Ferry, and proceeded southward to its original terminus at Wachovia (N.C.) on a branch of the Yadkin. After 1769 the road was extended to Pine Tree (Camden) in South Carolina, where the road from Charleston joined it as it bent westward, then south, forking beyond the Congaree for Ninety Six and Augusta (Georgia).[10]

Speculators obtained large tracts of land in the Shenandoah Valley of Virginia which in the 1720's and 1730's they offered for sale at a shilling an acre. Advertisements describing the beauty and fertility of the valley in glowing language and offering a home to prospective settlers on easy terms were given wide circulation among the recent immigrants in Pennsylvania and to the poverty-stricken folk in England, Ireland, and Germany.

THE COMING OF THE ULSTER-SCOTS

Ulster-Scot immigration into the Valley of Virginia, stimulated by this new land policy, began in 1732. In that year Joist Hite, a Hollander, migrated from Philadelphia with fifteen families in addition to his own, the most of them Ulster-Scots, and from that time the stream flowed full and strong. The only competitors of the northern Ireland Scots for the occupation of the valley were German folk, mostly Dunkard, who came in similar fashion by way of Pennsylvania. But the Ulsterites were more venturesome than the Germans, more venturesome indeed than any other people who had come hitherto to America. While the Germans congregated near the lower end of the valley, the former pushed on in larger numbers to its farther extremities, and on through into the Piedmont. By 1775 they had settled on the banks of the Holston and the Clinch and stood at the threshold of the Cumberland Gap. At the war's end they would pour rapidly into the new West —Kentucky and Tennessee.

Eight years after Joist Hite entered the Shenandoah Valley, scattered families from Pennsylvania followed the Indian traders' paths into the wide prairies of North Carolina between the Catawba and the Yadkin. After 1750 a steady stream flowed into the colony, drawn by the favorable reports of the pioneers and encouraged by the Colonial authorities, who hoped that they would protect the older communities from the Indians. They came driving their cattle, hogs, and horses before them, until the whole country from what is now Raleigh to Morganton was filled with them. Meanwhile other Ulster-Scotch pioneers had turned westward from the fertile plains of North Carolina into the wilderness beyond the mountains, where later along the banks of the Watauga, French Broad, and Clinch would be laid the foundations of the present state of Tennessee.

About the same time the stream began to flow into the South Carolina Piedmont and into Upland Georgia. In 1755 General Braddock was defeated, and the frontiers of Pennsylvania, Maryland, and Virginia were exposed to so much danger from the French at Fort Duquesne on the Ohio, and the Indians attached to them, that their inhabitants were strongly inclined to move southward. In the same year Governor Glen made a treaty with the Cherokee Indians by which much of what is now called the Upper Country was ceded to the King of Great Britain. Both events lured settlers to the western parts of South Carolina. In 1767–1768 other families came to Charleston direct from Ireland and moved on westward, aided by the Colonial government, which was eager to have settlers on the frontier. In the latter year a missionary from the Synod of New York and Philadelphia discovered thirty-eight Presbyterian settlements in South Carolina and five Presbyterian settlements in Georgia, possessing from twenty to five hundred families each.[11]

By the time of the Revolution there were Ulster-Scotch communities of considerable strength all along the Southern frontier from Maryland to Florida. There were one hundred communities, it is estimated, in Virginia, Maryland, and Tennessee; fifty in North Carolina; and seventy in South Carolina and Georgia.[12] The Ulster-Scotch settlers constituted "a shield of sinewy men thrust in between the peoples of the seaboard and the red warriors of the wilderness."

IN WESTERN VIRGINIA

But the Ulster-Scots would have been lost to the Presbyterian Church if it had not been for a vigorous missionary activity on the part of the presbyteries of the North and East. To follow these hardy pioneers into the Back Country of Virginia, the Carolinas, and Georgia the early system of missionary itineration was greatly extended. Pastors were ordered by presbyteries and synod to leave their congregations and to take extended tours among the Ulster-Scotch settlements. Young men who wished to enter the ministry were not ordained until they had made a visit to the frontier.

The initial move was taken ordinarily by the settlers themselves. They moved into the wilderness without ministers, but they had their Bibles, their catechisms, and their Confession of Faith. No sooner were settlements effected than their appeals were sent up to presbyteries, perhaps hundreds of miles away, for the ministry of the Gospel. A good part of the presbyteries' time was given to the consideration of these appeals. The communities were widely scattered; the roads, often nothing more than Indian trails, were difficult; the distances seemed enormous; and the number of ministers available was insufficient for the task.

Presbyterians had been handicapped in eastern Virginia by the hostility of the Colonial government to dissenters. In 1733 the Church of Scotland was requested to use its good offices with the government in England

so as to lay a restraint upon some gentlemen in said neighboring province, as may discourage them from hampering such itinerant ministers by illegal prosecutions; and if it may be, to procure some assistance from his majesty for our encouragement by way of regium donum.[13]

In 1738, "upon the supplication of John Caldwell, in behalf of himself and many families of our persuasion, who are about to settle in the back parts of Virginia," the Synod of Philadelphia drafted a letter "To the honourable William Gooch, Esquire, Lieutenant Governor of the Province of Virginia." Said the petitioners:

We take leave to address you in behalf of a considerable number of our brethren who are meditating a settlement in the remote parts of your government, and are of the same persuasion with the Church of Scotland. We thought it our duty to acquaint your honour with their design, and to ask your favor in allowing them the liberty of their consciences, and of worshipping God in a way agreeable to the principles of their education. . . .[14]

The Governor replied as follows:

As I have always been inclined to favour the people who have lately removed from other provinces to settle on the western side of our great mountains [where, it is to be remembered, they protected the older settlements on the seaboard from the Indians] so you may be assured that no interruption shall be given to any minister of your profession who shall come among them, so as they conform themselves to the rules prescribed by the act of toleration in England, by taking the oaths enjoined thereby, and registering the places of their meeting, and behave themselves peaceably towards the government.[15]

From this time on more earnest efforts were made to supply the frontier settlements. In 1737 Samuel Gelston had been sent into the Valley by Donegal Presbytery; he was followed three years later by

James Anderson from the Synod of Philadelphia, and the following year by John Thomson and John Craig, also from the Presbytery of Donegal.

In 1740 John Craig returned to Augusta County to become pastor of Augusta (Old Stone) and Tinkling Spring churches, the first settled pastor in western Virginia. He spent the rest of his days serving the Presbyterians of the valley. Samuel Black settled shortly afterward in Albemarle County, and Alexander Miller came to share the work in Augusta County. In 1744 John Thomson, who had itinerated earlier through the frontier settlements, made his home in the upper valley and carried on an extensive missionary work throughout the whole region.

For some time these four, Craig, Black, Miller, and Thomson, were the only pastors in the valley; the majority of the settlers continued to depend on the occasional visits of itinerants for their religious ministrations.

In 1741 the Presbyterian Church suffered its first division, owing to differences over the Great Revival, which was then spreading through the colonies. Presbyterians were almost equally divided between the Old Side Synod of Philadelphia, which opposed the methods of the revivalists, and the New Side Synod of New York, which included the chief representatives of the great revival in the Middle Colonies, and who were also the first to bring it into the South.

The schism, which lasted for seventeen years, was seriously felt by the churches in the valley. The great majority of them were firmly attached to the Old Side. Lack of ministers did not allow the presbyteries on which they had previously depended to care adequately for their needs. And before the schism was healed the visits of their missionaries had almost ceased.

The New Side, more aggressive and growing more rapidly, did not wait for invitations to send men anywhere in the colonies. Virginia, in particular, engaged a large share of their attention, and many of their ablest ministers, John and Samuel Blair, John Roan,

Samuel Finley, Gilbert and William Tennent, visited the congregations on both sides of the Blue Ridge. John Blair, for example, in 1746 organized churches at North Mountain, New Providence, Timber Ridge, and Fork of the James—all in Augusta County (now Rockbridge). From these original congregations grew the large and flourishing bodies which shortly after the Revolution were gathered into the Presbytery of Lexington.

So Presbyterianism grew in the Valley of Virginia and the Back Country of the Piedmont. No other church sent its missionaries to compete with them until, shortly before the Revolutionary War, Baptists and Methodists appeared on the scene, representing the second and third waves of the first great American Revival.

The Hanover Revival

Meanwhile there were interesting developments in eastern Virginia. The Established Church—long the exclusive church—had failed to satisfy the religious needs of the masses of the people. About 1740 there grew up a spontaneous revival in the country around Hanover (the present site of Richmond). Several individuals, the chief of whom was a certain Samuel Morris, became interested in reading religious books, including Luther's Commentary on Galatians and the Sermons of Whitefield, and began to hold meetings in one another's homes. Gradually attendance increased; private homes could no longer hold the crowds. A building was erected and called Morris' Reading House. The movement spread to other communities. Attendance on the parish churches began to decline, and the authorities became alarmed. Called before the Governor's Council at Williamsburg "to declare their creed and name," Morris and his friends claimed after some hesitation that they were Lutherans, remembering that Luther was a great reformer and being grateful for the help they had received from his books. Thereafter, for a time, they were allowed to carry on their simple religious services unmolested.

A later account states that on the road to Williamsburg they chanced upon a copy of the Westminster Confession of Faith. Finding it a splendid statement of their tenets they presented it to the Council as their own confession. The governor, who was a Scotsman, informed them that they were Presbyterians and, therefore, able to come under the Toleration Act. This later version of the story is almost certainly apocryphal. The probability is that they had never even heard the name of Presbyterian until the visit of William Robinson in 1743.[16]

The Reverend William Robinson—"one-eyed Robinson" he was called—was the son of a rich Quaker, who became a zealous Presbyterian and an ardent apostle of the Great Awakening. Smallpox had robbed him of an eye and left his skin badly scarred, but "a rather rough exterior clothed a warm heart and a passion to serve men." Ordained by New Brunswick Presbytery in 1741, he was sent the next year to visit the Presbyterian settlements in western Virginia and North Carolina. He was arrested near Winchester for preaching without a license, but so impressed the sheriff that he was soon released and allowed to continue unmolested. News of his successful preaching in the valley and on the eastern side of the Blue Ridge, in what was then Lunenberg and Amelia counties, came to Hanover, where Morris's awakening was in full progress. Robinson was requested to pay them a visit. He turned his horse eastward and arrived in Hanover in July, 1743. It was a momentous visit. Hitherto missionary activities of the Presbyterian Church had been confined to Presbyterian communities. But in Hanover Presbyterianism entered upon a larger work; it was the first church to bring the revival and so to break the hold of the Establishment in eastern Virginia.

Robinson remained in the neighborhood only four days. But Morris refers to those four days as the

glorious days of the Son of Man. Such of us as had been hungering for the word before were lost in agreeable surprise and astonishment and some could not refrain from publicly declaring their transports. . . .

Many that came through curiosity were pricked to their heart; and but few of the numerous assemblies on those four days appeared unaffected. They returned alarmed with apprehensions of their dangerous condition, convinced of their former entire ignorance of religion, and anxiously inquiring what they should do to be saved.[17]

So many were attracted by Robinson's powerful evangelistic preaching that the Reading House could not contain them, and services were conducted out in the open.

Robinson's visit marked the beginning of Presbyterianism in eastern Virginia. Finding themselves in accord with their evangelist's views, the Hanover dissenters adopted the name Presbyterian and attached themselves to the Presbytery of New Castle at the first opportunity. Other evangelists, John Blair, John Roan, Gilbert and William Tennent, Samuel Blair, and Samuel Finley, fanned the flames of the revival, and the movement continued to spread. Irresponsible and abusive utterances directed against the Established Church by some of the revivalists, none of whom had secured a license, or even attempted to do so, led to new opposition on the part of the Colonial government.[18] Morris, as their leader, was fined again and again for non-attendance at the parish church and for "keeping up unlawful meetings." The governor issued a proclamation "strictly requiring all Magistrates to suppress and prohibit, as far as they lawfully could, all itinerant preachers." [19]

This was the situation when Samuel Davies came to Virginia. Davies was born in Pennsylvania in 1723 and ordained by the Presbytery of New Castle in 1746. His health was very delicate, and he was thought to be in the early stages of consumption. Davies himself was sure he would not live long, but he entered upon his work with all the vigor that his feeble body would allow, preaching as a missionary evangelist in Pennsylvania, New Jersey, and Maryland. In the spring of 1747 he was sent on his first visit to Hanover, directed to supply the congregations in that region for six weeks. He at once secured from the Colonial Court a license to preach at four meeting houses in and about Hanover. The following year, at the urgent request of the people, he returned to Hanover as a settled pastor, bringing a friend, John Rodgers, to assist him in extending the Gospel to other points. The Council at Williamsburg refused to grant Rodgers a license, and Davies was forced to return to Hanover alone. That fall he secured permission to preach at three additional points, one each in Louisa, Goochland, and Caroline counties. No two of his seven preaching points were closer together than twelve or fifteen miles; and some of his parishioners had to travel thirty or forty miles to reach the nearest meeting house. For eleven years this great man, the most eloquent preacher of his day, preached throughout this territory, hampered by the opposition of the attorney-general, Peyton Randolph, and by the refusal of the General Court to license additional preaching points.

As the work progressed, Davies brought in other helpers to carry on the work which he had developed. In 1752 John Todd was installed as pastor of Providence Church in Louisa County. Three years later Robert Henry became pastor of Cub Creek in Charlotte County and Briery in Prince Edward County. In December, 1755, the Presbytery of Hanover—representing the New Side, or evangelistic wing of the church—was organized, the first Southern presbytery except for the independent and languishing presbytery in the South Carolina Lowlands. There were only six ministers in the presbytery—four in the Davies country and two in the valley—but Presbyterianism in the South had begun its organized existence, and from this one presbytery the Southern Presbyterian Church was, in large part, to take its rise. The new presbytery was active in its missionary endeavors. It included the greater portion of Virginia and of the Carolinas as well. North Carolina was its particular missionary territory, and regular supplies were sent to the congregations in that colony.

Nor were the Negroes neglected. Samuel Davies, in particular, gave a large part of his time to the slaves who lived in the homes of his flock. About three hundred attended his preaching regularly, and a hundred or more were baptized. Friends in England sent him Bibles and copies of Watts's hymns for distribution among the Negroes. Many of the Africans learned to read that they might receive these coveted books. Some of the slaves, Davies wrote, "have the misfortune to have irreligious masters, and hardly any of them are so happy as to be furnished with these assistances for their improvement." [20] The English "Society for the Promotion of Religious Knowledge among the Poor" became very much interested in the efforts of Davies to teach the Negroes, which they called the "first attempt of this nature that has ever been made with any considerable success." Collections were made to supply him with Watts and other religious books. Davies replied:

Your letter, with the large donation of books that attended it, gave me the most agreeable surprise that ever I met with in my whole life. . . . The books were all very acceptable, but none more so than the Psalms and Hymns which enable them to gratify their peculiar taste for psalmody. . . . In this seraphic exercise some of them spend almost the whole night. . . . There are thousands of Negroes in this colony who still continue in the grossest ignorance, and most stupid carelessness about religion, and as rank pagans as when they left the wilds of Africa.[21]

Davies was assisted in his labors among the Negroes, and his work was continued after his departure by his young co-laborers, Todd, Wright, and Henry. The fruit of their work continued for many years.

In 1759 Davies left Virginia to assume the presidency of Princeton College. Evangelistic zeal declined in Hanover after his departure. Missionary interest centered once more on the Ulster-Scots. The Presbyterian Church, which was the first church in eastern Virginia to appeal to the people neglected by the Establishment, and which, by means of its favored position should have become the leading church in the colony, was passed rapidly by the Baptists and the Methodists, who represented later but more vigorous waves of the Great Awakening. Baptist missionaries, in particular, came in great numbers, and by the beginning of the Revolution had claimed the colony as their own.

In the Western Carolinas

The first known Presbyterian minister to visit the Carolina Back Country was William Robinson, sent out as an itinerant in 1742 to visit the Presbyterian settlements in Virginia and North Carolina. Other missionaries followed him, some of them sent by the Old Side Synod of Philadelphia, but most of them by the New Side Synod of New York. The first of these missionaries to leave us an account of his journey was Hugh McAden, a graduate of Nassau Hall (later Princeton College), licensed by New Castle Presbytery in 1755, and sent out immediately on a missionary tour of the Carolinas. He went farther south than any previous missionary and was probably the first minister to be heard in some of the regions traversed. According to his account there were at least seven houses of worship constructed in North Carolina and many worshiping assemblies, but few organized churches, if any, and no settled minister. He preached generally at private houses or in the open air. It grieved the young preacher to find that some who had been brought up under the influence of the Gospel in other parts had become dissolute and were indulging infidel notions, "since their abode in this region where the Gospel was not regularly preached, and in fact scarcely heard." In one community he found that

many adhere to the Baptists that were before wavering, and several that professed themselves to be Presbyterian; so that very few at present join heartily for our ministers, and will in a little time, if God prevent not, be too weak either to call or supplicate for a faithful minister.[22]

All in all, McAden preached in about fifty settlements in North Carolina. Many of the places he visited have flourishing Presbyterian churches at the present time; some have passed into other hands.

John Thomson, who had pioneered as a missionary in the Valley of Virginia, visited the Presbyterian settlements in Iredell County in 1751, the first minister of any denomination to preach in that region. He settled near Statesville and ministered, until his death two years later, to new settlements within a radius of twenty miles.

In 1758 Alexander Craighead found his way into North Carolina from the western frontiers of Virginia. After Braddock's defeat, large numbers of the valley inhabitants fled southward because of their fear of the Indians, and Craighead followed his flock. The same year he became pastor of the Rocky River Church, and three years later pastor of the Sugar Creek Church. He remained the only settled pastor in the whole district between the Yadkin and the Catawba until his death in 1766.

McAden returned to Carolina in 1759 and became the settled pastor of the congregations in Duplin and New Hanover.

In 1764 McWhorter and Spencer, missionaries sent out by the reunited Synod of New York and Philadelphia, organized a number of congregations in the western part of the state near Sugar Creek, and the next few years pastors were called to Steel Creek, Providence, Hopewell, Centre, Rocky River, and Poplar Tent, all except Centre being in Mecklenburg County, which remains one of the most populous centers of Presbyterianism within the bounds of the Southern Church.

In 1770 seven ministers laboring in North Carolina were set off into the Presbytery of Orange, the second presbytery to be organized in the South, its territory coextensive with the Carolinas. It was strengthened from time to time by the accession of new members, many of them originally from the North, but coming to North Carolina at an early age as missionaries. By the time of the Revolution there were about thirty organized churches in the upper part of the state, and a number of preaching points in addition.

The Ulster-Scotch settlements in the South Carolina Piedmont were supplied by occasional itinerants from the North, as were the settlements in North Carolina and Virginia. Robert Miller, ordained by the independent Presbytery of Charleston in 1756, served the Waxhaws and the Fishing Creek congregations for a little more than twelve months when he was deposed for irregularities. William Richardson, who set out to be a missionary to the Cherokees but found little opportunity to be of service there, accepted a call to the Waxhaws church in 1759. Richardson traveled far and wide through these regions near the headwaters of the Catawba and Broad rivers in the upper part of South Carolina, and many of the churches in this region owe their origin to his wide vision and indefatigable labors. The long rides through the forests, the fording of the deep streams, the constant exposure to the elements, at length broke down his strength. He died, a martyr to the cause, in 1772.

When the Revolutionary War began there were only three settled ministers in the whole South Carolina Back Country.

The Revolutionary War checked Georgia's development, broke up the Presbyterian settlements, and ended the supply of Presbyterian missionaries until 1784, when the Presbytery of South Carolina was formed and missionary labors in Georgia were resumed. During the war there was no Presbyterian minister in Georgia so far as known, save the pastor of the Independent Church in Savannah.

Before the Revolution only two Southern presbyteries (besides the independent presbytery in South Carolina) were erected—Hanover in Virginia and Orange in the Carolinas. At the close of the war a number of additional presbyteries were formed: South Carolina in 1784; Abingdon in 1785, with five ministers and twelve congregations at least partially organized, all in Kentucky. In the same year Hanover Presbytery was divided, Lexington taking the territory west of the Blue Ridge, Hanover retaining the territory to the east.

When the General Assembly was organized in 1788, two Southern synods were erected—Virginia and the Carolinas. The Synod of Virginia had thirty ministers in four Presbyteries: Hanover, Lexington, Transylvania, and Redstone—the last being the grow-

ing missionary edge of western Pennsylvania. The Synod of the
Carolinas, with three presbyteries—Orange, South Carolina, and
Abingdon—covered a territory which forty years earlier lacked a
single Presbyterian minister. Now there were twenty-seven ministers—ten in North Carolina, eleven in South Carolina, and six
in Tennessee; there were more than a hundred preaching points,
and the field was growing rapidly to the south and west.

Comparative Failure

In spite of its great gains the Presbyterian Church in the South
had not lived up to its opportunities or met the needs even of its
own people. The cries of the Presbyterian communities in the
South had come up to Presbytery and Synod and they had sent all
the supplies they could spare, but the number of missionaries was
altogether inadequate for the need. Congregations could not be
built or even held together by occasional visits from itinerants.
Ordinarily the traveling missionaries visited only congregations
which had sent in a request for their services. Little or no effort
was made to gather new congregations. And so ultimately the
great majority of the Ulster-Scots were lost to Presbyterianism, if
not to the Church of Christ.

Presbyterian missionaries were not able to retain their own people. They made little or no effort to reach the non-Presbyterian
folk, in spite of the fact that the Established Church in the Southern colonies had failed to meet the needs of the great mass of the
people. The one exception to this rule was in Virginia, the strongest of the Southern, and the most populous of all the American,
colonies. The spontaneous revival that grew up in Hanover came,
we saw, under the control of the Presbyterians, and Presbyterians
thrived for a while under the vigorous leadership of Samuel Davies.
But when Davies departed the revival languished, and the missionary zeal disappeared. The Baptists, who brought the second
wave of the Great Awakening into the South, swept everything be-

fore them, even in the Davies country. Before the end of the Colonial period they had taken that numerical lead in the South which they have never since surrendered. Their growth was due not to immigration but to evangelism.

Presbyterians were handicapped so far as numbers were concerned by the high educational standards which they required of their ministers. The College of New Jersey on which they so largely depended could not produce enough ministers to serve established congregations, to say nothing of reaching out for the unchurched. Baptists had no educational restrictions. Their ministers outnumbered the Presbyterians ten, perhaps twenty, to one, and in addition they spoke to the people in language they could understand. As W. M. Gewehr, historian of the Great Awakening in Virginia, has pointed out: "Presbyterianism, 'with its intellectual demands of an elaborate creed' and its high standards of education for its ministry, was at best restricted in its appeal. It was never able to reach and to stir the common folk as the Baptists did." [23]

COMPENSATIONS

In spite of the failure of the Presbyterian Church to reach the masses of Southern people, it made significant contributions not only to the religious, but also to the social and political life of the new nation that was coming into being. I shall mention only four:

First, its contribution to an ordered society. As Bridenbaugh states, "Organized Protestantism was the most influential institution in the Back Country." (The same could not be said of the Chesapeake or Carolina societies.) As he recognizes, the dominant church in this area during the Colonial period was the Presbyterian. Its churches became nuclei, not only of the religious life, but of social, educational, civic, and military activities as well. It was a force making for social stability—in some regions before the Colonial authorities were able to establish law and order.

Second, its contribution to religious liberty. Samuel Davies won a fuller right of religious toleration in Virginia not only for Presbyterians but also for all dissenters from the Established Church. After the battle for religious toleration came the long and decisive struggle for religious freedom, for complete separation of church and state, a struggle whose successful issue marks an epoch in the history of religious liberty. Credit for this significant victory is generally given to the well known Virginia statesmen Patrick Henry, James Madison, and Thomas Jefferson. But much of the credit should go to the dissenters. Baptists were the first and the most consistent champions of absolute separation of church and state, but equal, if not greater, influence was wielded by the telling deliverances of the Presbyterians.

Third, its contribution to political freedom. Presbyterian dissenters who occupied the frontiers beyond the mountains were forced to bear the burden of the French and Indian War. Braddock's defeat at Pittsburgh in 1755 spread terror throughout Virginia. It was proposed to abandon all territory beyond the mountains to the enemy. In this panic of souls it was Samuel Davies who counseled calm and courage and who cheered the volunteers who went to the front from eastern Virginia. Meanwhile the inhabitants of the valley were exposed to the raids of ruthless savages, and the helpless inhabitants in utter consternation were counseling safety in flight. John Craig wrote in his diary:

I opposed "that scheme as a scandal to our nation, falling below our brave ancestors, making ourselves a reproach among Virginians, a dishonor to our friends at home, an evidence of cowardice, want of faith, and a noble Christian dependence on God, as able to save and deliver from the heathen; it would be a lasting blot forever on our posterity."

He advised the building of forts in convenient places for refuge. His appeal and example had its effect.

"They required me to go before them in the work, which I did cheerfully," he wrote, "though it cost me one third of my estates. The people very readily followed, and my congregation in less than two months was well fortified." [24]

And they maintained their homes most bravely through all the fiery trials of those times.

In 1764 Governor Dobbs of North Carolina wrote to the Society for the Propagation of the Gospel in London requesting that a missionary or a schoolmaster be sent for the benefit of the inhabitants of Mecklenburg County, "who," he said, "are mostly now Presbyterians or other foreign sectaries, which may be of great use in those back western frontier settlements." The Reverend Andrew Morton, the minister whom they dispatched, describes his experiences in a letter which he wrote to the Secretary of the Society from Northampton, North Carolina, on August 25, 1766:

Reverend Doctor, I wrote to you in June last informing you of my Journey to my new mission in Mecklenburg County— From Newbern I pursued my Journey to Cape Fear where I received such Intelligence as discouraged me from proceeding any further— There I was well informed that the Inhabitants of Mecklenburg are entire dissenters of the most rigid kind— That they had a solemn league and covenant teacher settled among them— That they were in general greatly adverse to the Church of England—and that they looked upon a law lately enacted in this province for the better establishment of the Church as oppressive as the Stamp Act and were determined to prevent its taking place there, by opposing the settlement of any minister of the Church of England that might be sent amongst them— In short it was very evident that in Mecklenburg County I could be of little use to the honorable Society and I thought it would be but prudent to decline embroiling myself with an infatuated people to no purpose and trusting that the venerable Society, upon a just representation of the matter would not be dissatisfied with my conduct.[25]

The teacher to whom Mr. Morton refers was the Reverend Alexander Craighead who, holding to the Solemn League and Covenant of his Scottish forebears, had taken an advanced position in regard to civil and religious liberties some years earlier in Pennsylvania and had had his brushes with the authorities also in Virginia. In North Carolina, where he was further removed from the Colonial authorities, he apparently refused to recognize the rights of the British government to grant land titles and inculcated principles of independence which bore fruit in "The Sugar Creek War" of 1765, in the Regulators' resistance of 1768–1771, and in the Mecklenburg Convention of 1775.[26]

Ulster-Scotch Presbyterians in the Valley at Abingdon were among the first to raise their voice for independence. The Presbytery of Hanover in 1776 presented a memorial to the legislature of Virginia which said: "Your memorialists are governed by the same sentiments which have inspired the United States of America, and are determined that nothing in our power or influence shall be wanting to give success to their common cause." Some of the Scotch in South Carolina and the Highlanders in North Carolina who had vowed their allegiance to the crown before they were allowed to sail for America remained loyal to the mother country. But there were few Tories among the Ulster-Scots.

Presbyterian pastors supported the war undeterred by any theory regarding the spirituality of the church. In Virginia, for example, William Graham encouraged the members of his congregation to enlist, and himself served as their captain; John Brown and Archibald Scott, neighboring pastors, entered warmly into the American cause, and exhorted the people to fight for their freedom; Dr. James Waddell was one of the first and most earnest vindicators of liberty from the pulpit; David Rice warmly declared that only fools, cowards, and knaves would decline to hazard their lives in defense of freedom and independence; Moses Hoge interrupted his preparations for the ministry to serve in the army of the Revolution; and John Blair Smith was an active patriot and captain of a company of students of Hampden-Sydney College, of which he was the president. Military officials suggested that he could serve his country best by making speeches, which may cast some reflection on his ability as a military leader. But he was counted as one of the best recruiting officers in the colony. Ministers in North and South Carolina had a similar record.

Fourth, its contribution to education. John Craig, the first settled pastor among the Presbyterians in the Back Country, combined teaching with his other ministerial duties, and so did many, if not most, of the pastors who followed him.

Augusta Academy, later known as Liberty Hall, and since the Civil War as Washington and Lee University, was established by Virginia Presbyterians west of the Blue Ridge as early as 1749. Hampden-Sydney, the second oldest college in the South, opened its doors, in the face of Anglican opposition, as a non-sectarian institution on the first day of January, 1776, and received its charter as a college from the first General Assembly of Virginia after the cessation of hostilities (1783).

In North Carolina there were numerous classical schools opened after 1755 by ministers who had received their training in the College of New Jersey. Best known of these was David Caldwell's celebrated "Log College" in Guilford County, in which many of the most eminent men in the South—lawyers and statesmen, as well as clergymen—were educated. In 1771 Presbyterians of Mecklenburg County sought to expand the classical school, which the Reverend Joseph Alexander had opened at Sugar Creek, into a college. The Act of the Legislature toward this end was disallowed by the King-in-Council (apparently because the school was in the hands of Presbyterian Whigs), but Queen's Museum, as it came to be called, and then Liberty Hall continued to instruct boys, of whom there were eighty in 1776, "in the languages and other literary attainments." In 1780 the school was moved to Salisbury and soon thereafter fell by the wayside. Presbyterians in North Carolina were not yet strong enough to support their own institution of higher learning, but took a leading part shortly thereafter in the establishment of the University of North Carolina.

The importance of these various contributions to education by the Presbyterians in the Back Country is more appreciated when it is realized that there was no system of public education south of Mason and Dixon's line in the Colonial period or long thereafter; that there were few schools of any sort in the older and wealthier Chesapeake and Carolina societies; that the prevailing theory of education brought to these regions from England was that education was for the upper class only, and of no concern to the people; that the Anglican Church, which prior to the Revolution was the established church in all Southern colonies, and which had sponsored William and Mary College, the one institution of higher learning in the South before 1776, was declining in strength; and that neither of the other evangelical denominations which had come into the South on the wings of the Great Awakening accepted as yet any educational responsibility.

Presbyterianism had not succeeded in reaching the masses in the South, but at the beginning of our national era it occupied the strategic place along the Western frontier, and its influence among thoughtful and intelligent men was unexcelled.

CHAPTER IV

The United Presbyterian Church

SCOTTISH ORIGINS

Having considered the early history of the Presbyterian family in Scotland and America, with special reference to the churches north and south, we turn our attention now to a sister denomination, which, while coming out of Scottish and northern Ireland backgrounds, has always had an independent life here in America. In this chapter we deal with the United Presbyterian Church.

A sort of ecclesiastical equilibrium in Scotland was reached with the glorious Revolution of 1689. With the coming of William and Mary to the throne of Great Britain a kind of *modus vivendi* was established which has continued, more or less, to the present time. That is, Episcopalism was decisively recognized as the religion of England and Presbyterianism as the religion of Scotland. No longer would England try to force Anglican prelacy into Scotland, nor Scotland try to introduce Scotch presbytery into England. It is worthy of note, however, that the covenanting Scotch were not satisfied with this settlement. It was all right as far as it went, but it did not go far enough to suit them. It did not recognize the Solemn League and Covenant of 1643, which they regarded as still binding; and it did not completely eradicate every trace of Episcopalism from the government of the Church of Scotland. This is not only worthy of note for the understanding of the covenanting position, but for the later thinking of Erskine and the Seceders. For the vast majority of Presbyterians, tired of struggle and suffering, it was an eminently agreeable solution.

Ebenezer Erskine was the acknowledged leader of the Secession of 1733. He was one of the several children of Henry Erskine, who himself was a Presbyterian minister who had suffered greatly under the Anglicizing policies of Charles II and James II. Ebenezer, after graduation from Edinburgh, took charge of a church at the lovely little village of Portmoak. It is interesting to note that Erskine, the leader of the Secession, like Thomas Chalmers, the leader of Free Church movement a century later, was converted after being several years in the ministry. Erskine then became noted for his great evangelical preaching. Indications are that his pastoral work was every bit as distinguished.[1] His general standing with his people was such that they gave him this tribute:

. . . we own the sweetness of his temper, and the mildness of his manners, except in the matters of his God, for whom appearing and against sin, he is all in a holy flame, being very jealous for the Lord God of hosts; and, through the bounty of heaven, he is *above all our eulogies.*[2]

It is true that the Secession Church came into existence in connection with the patronage issue. As already indicated,[3] it was Ebenezer Erskine's vigorous protests, in his moderatorial sermon against the settlement of pastors by unauthorized persons, which brought on his rebuke and the beginnings of strife. This was the reemergence of something akin to the great medieval struggle concerning lay investiture. Its importance in the origination of the Secession is difficult to overestimate.

It has, however, frequently been overestimated. It is a very common mistake to suppose that because the Secession took place in connection with the patronage issue, it took place because of it. History clearly reveals that that was the occasion rather than the cause. The real cause lay elsewhere. It was not church polity primarily, but practical theology, and Christian lethargy, then called "moderatism."

Before the Secession actually took place, the Marrow Controversy had occurred. In brief, here is the story. There was felt to be a growing moral lethargy in the Church of Scotland. Ministers, as Erskine noted in his preaching, were merely moralizing with a minimum of Christian living. Now, the great Presbyterian principle is that the grace of God teaches us to deny ungodliness, worldly lusts, and so on. But it seemed that many were coming to think that merely exhorting to deny ungodliness, and so on, would make the dead to rise morally. The rise of the Moderate party to a place of determinate influence in the Church of Scotland was proof that this charge of the Evangelicals was not unfounded. Then, looking back in the history of the church to the Revolution Settlement of 1689, we find the probable source of this defection in the low quality of many ministers of that time:

Bishop Burnet, who cannot be suspected of any groundless prejudice against them, says: "They were the worst preachers I ever heard; they were ignorant to a reproach, and many of them were clearly vicious. They were a disgrace to their orders, and were indeed the dregs and the refuse of the northern parts. Those of them that rose above contempt and scandal were men of such violent tempers, that they were as much hated as the others were despised." [4]

Into these ecclesiastical doldrums came a breath of evangelical Christian fresh air. It was a book entitled *The Marrow of Modern Divinity*. Having been written by an Englishman with the initials E. F. in the preceding century, it was now republished in Scotland to awaken her evangelical zeal. It was a keen, warm presentation of modified Calvinistic doctrines in an interesting dialogue form.

Now a strange thing happened. The "Marrowmen" were charged with heresy in their attempt to revive orthodoxy—and the fact is, they were guilty as charged. [5] They republished this book and inculcated it because it was a strong advocacy of neglected phases of Calvinistic doctrine. It really was just that. It did teach the universal offer of Atonement which the opponents twisted to mean that all come to salvation. The Marrowmen did not believe this misrepresentation. They felt that this was a fabricated charge by men who had a distaste for the basic Calvinism of the book. But, on the other hand, it was in general a very healthy statement of evangelical Calvinistic orthodoxy, and probably the Marrowmen were right in suspecting that men who singled out some minor faults were really after its major virtues.

So, a decree went out from the General Assembly in which they

> strictly prohibited and discharged all the ministers of the church to use by writing, preaching, catechising or otherwise teaching, either publicly or privately, the positions condemned, or what may be equivalent to them or of like tendency, under pain of the censures of the church conformed to the merit of their offence.[6]

Heads began to fall. That of Thomas Boston, for one, who says that

> his physicians having assured him that the air of Ettrick was extremely injurious to his health, he had ground to hope the Church would have removed him to a parish more favourable to his bodily constitution, "till I fell under their displeasure," adds that worthy man, "in the affair of the Marrow, which I reckon to have staked me down in Ettrick." [7]

The tension was very great. The Secession would very probably have taken place at this time on the basis of theology and not ten years later on the basis of polity had it not been for the restraining influence of the secular government. It did take place ten years later, but it was this rise of a zealous form of Christianity which produced it and perpetuated it.

INNER DEVELOPMENT

What has been the most characteristic feature of the inner life of United Presbyterianism? We believe it has been the Church's ardent attachment to the Reformed theology. A militant, sometimes too militant, attachment to Calvinism was, and to a degree still is, her genius.

Indication of the theological character of the Secession is the fact that after the Secession had taken place, it could have been healed but for a theological problem more basic than the patronage issue itself. When the Seceders were invited to return, after the Established Church had done much to rectify the previous conditions, the reasons they gave for refusing were:

It was not violent intrusions, it was not the act of 1732, neither was it any other particular step of defection considered abstractly and by themselves, upon which the Secession was started; but a complex course of defection, both in doctrine, government and discipline, carried on with a high hand by the present judicatories of this church, justifying themselves in their procedure, and refusing to be restrained.[8]

In other words, the trouble was not merely that heritors were presenting pastors, but that the General Assembly was dealing leniently with Professor Simson, who had been proved by the court guilty of Arianism, and also with Professor Campbell, while actually suspending from the ministry men such as Erskine for speaking out for recognized Presbyterian principles of great importance.

Whilst such severity was employed against the friends of evangelical truth, it was deservedly noticed as in singular contrast that those who were charged with the most grievous errors, as has been already stated, were treated with utmost lenity.[9]

A strong Calvinistic emphasis has characterized the Secession churches from the beginning. This persisted in the next century and in this country. In 1813 the Associate Presbyterian Church made a strong deliverance.[10]

Likewise in the union of 1858 which formed the United Presbyterian Church of North America as we have it today, the same Reformed principles were zealously affirmed in the adoption of the Westminster Symbols and the Eighteen Articles of Testimony. At the time of union there never was any question about Calvinism as the basis. That was taken for granted. The points which were discussed were minute details within the system, but no question about the system itself.

There have been considerable and serious claims that the adoption of the *Confessional Statement* in 1925 marked the abandonment of high Calvinism in favor of a considerably modified testimony. In this claim there is truth.[11]

In addition to this general theological tradition now thus modified, the United Presbyterian Church and its ancestries have been characterized by various particular emphases. The former may have accounted for the original Secession; it has been the latter which has kept the denomination apart from other Reformed bodies. Indeed, they almost prevented the union in 1858.

Dr. Wayne Christy [12] has noted some eight of these points which entered largely into the union negotiations of a century ago: first, closed communion; second, public testimony; third, covenanting; fourth, the magistracy; fifth, Psalmody; sixth, the purchase by Christ of common benefits; seventh, slaveholding; and, eighth, secret societies. Of these issues we will comment briefly on only a few.

First, the closed-communion principle came near to dividing the United Presbyterian Church shortly after its formation. Recently a seminarian asked the writer if United Presbyterian law permitted him to have a Methodist minister administer the Lord's Supper for him. We replied that there was today no law against it. But we also said that if a student had asked Dr. Pressly that same question in the same seminary a hundred years ago, the answer would have been an emphatic negative with horror thrown in at the very raising of the question. That is a general reflection on the fact that the historic position of the United Presbyterian Church has been closed communion. For example, here is a declaration of the Associate Reformed Church:

Resolved, That this Synod disapproves of the principle and practice of open communion, or that scheme of communion which would obligate or allow the ministers or members of the Associate Reformed Church to unite in sacramental communion with other Churches, and the ministers and members of other Churches to unite in communion with ours, on the ground merely of a general or partial agreement of opinion respecting the doctrines set forth in our Confession of Faith; and the Synod hereby enjoins all the ministers to conform to the constitutional doctrine of the Associate Reformed Church.[13]

This principle reaches back into the beginnings of the church where we find some sorry illustrations of it, such as John Erskine of the Anti-Burgher division (concerned with the legitimacy of taking a certain oath of office) refusing to allow his father to pray with him on his deathbed because he belonged to the Burgher group, and funny illustrations such as the relationship of Alison Scott to her husband, the Reverend James Scott. This daughter of Ebenezer Erskine sided with her father in the Burgher controversy and against her husband. Consequently, although this man and wife had a happy married life, it did not include church fellowship. For Alison Erskine Scott would not attend her husband's church. Rather, he was obliged to put her on her horse to ride ten miles to the nearest Burgher church every Sunday morning. This same principle broke up cordial relationships between the Secession and the great George Whitefield. Defection from the position was one of the causes of the many divisions of the Associate Reformed Church about 1820. Differences concerning it delayed the union of 1858. The argument between John T. Pressly and W. C. McCune and other proponents and opponents of closed communion almost destroyed this union a decade later.

Exclusive Psalmody was the most conspicuous practice of the United Presbyterian Church until 1925. In insisting on the use of the Psalter only in public worship, the Secession churches were true to John Calvin, who favored "singing the words God has put in our mouths." The Associate Reformed Synod declared, characteristically, in 1799:

. . . the will of God, that the sacred songs contained in the Book of Psalms be sung in his worship, both public and private, to the end of the world; and the rich variety and perfect purity of their matter, the blessing of God upon them in every age, and the edification of the

Church thence arising, set the propriety of singing them in a convincing light; nor shall composures merely human, be sung in any of the Associate Reformed Churches.

The exclusion of all else was most specific; thus, hymns are defined:

Under that expression are included all those religious poems, however pious and sound in themselves, of which, though the subject be Scriptural, yet the structure and management are the work of human genius, and which aim at anything more than adapting the Psalms given in the Bible by the inspiration of God, to the Christian worship, by a version as close as the laws of versification will admit.

There was at one time a family quarrel concerning the legitimacy of versification of portions of Scripture other than Psalms. A General Assembly at New Castle, Pennsylvania, observed that such had been used from the beginning, and pointed to Ralph Erskine's "Paraphrases." When the time for change came in connection with the adopting of the *Confessional Statement* in 1925, Article 28, simply entitled "Of Praise," and allowing the use of meritorious hymns in worship, occasioned more debate than all of the other forty-three articles of the *Statement* combined, and was very narrowly carried in a revised form.

Considering the fact that the slavery issue loomed large in the division of the Presbyterian and other churches of the North and South, it is interesting to note the stand of the United Presbyterian Church on it. The Secession churches can claim a long-time and consistent opposition to this institution. As far back as 1788 the mother churches in Scotland were opposing it. Isolated protests were occurring in this country at the turn of the nineteenth century. By 1811 the Associate Synod defined slavery as an evil and directed its members to free slaves. By 1815 we have congregations moving up from the South in order to protest the condoning of slavery in the South. By 1831 the Associate Synod had taken the drastic action of excommunicating her slaveholders. When, however, in 1840 these actions were pressed in the South, the reader of an official ecclesiastical communication, the Reverend Mr. Kendall, was seized and driven out of the state of South Carolina. And the Presbytery made its declaration of independence of the Synod.[14] At the time of the union of the Associate and Associate Reformed churches to form the United Presbyterian Church, three years before the outbreak of the Civil War, one of the eighteen Articles of Testimony read:

We declare, That slave-holding, that is the holding of unoffending human beings in involuntary bondage and considering and treating them as property, is a violation of the law of God and contrary both to the letter and spirit of Christianity.[15]

In addition to these distinctives there are a number of others into a discussion of which we cannot enter here. Public covenanting, or vowing together to defend a particular principle or cause, has been a characteristic of all the Secession churches and not only the Reformed Presbyterian which is popularly known as the Covenanter Church. This practice dates back to 1558 and was still common in 1858. It has become an obsolete practice in the United Presbyterian Church. Opposition to secret societies and refusal to accept any as members of the church who were members of such societies is another practice now abandoned.

OUTER DEVELOPMENT

One may sketch the outer history of the United Presbyterian Church in the United States in terms of three dates: 1782, 1820f. and 1858. To 1782 we have the first or informal period of union. Beginning in 1820, we have the period of divisions. With the formation of the United Presbyterian Church of North America in 1858, we have the realization of the most significant union in the history of the United Presbyterian Church. For the last century there has been neither division nor union. So we can see that

during the first hundred years of the United Presbyterian Church
and its ancestries in this country there was much union and division,
while for the last hundred years there has been no more of either
—though a great deal of discussion of union.

The union of 1782 was the climax of a tendency of the Secession
churches in this country. The Ulster-Scotch immigrants to America
who formed what Theodore Roosevelt called a "shield of sinewy
men thrust in between the people of the seaboard and the red
warriors of the wilderness" [16] had a good proportion of Covenanters
and, later, Seceders among them. In the early decades of the
eighteenth century this exodus from the Old Country began. Both
of the groups found immigration inviting because of the unfavorable situation in Scotland and, later, because of Anglican pressures,
in North Ireland. So, many isolated, pastorless groups were sprin-
kled throughout New York, Pennsylvania, South Carolina, and
elsewhere. The first ordained minister to come to them, in 1751,
was the Reformed Presbyterian John Cuthbertson, followed a year
later by the Anti-Burgher Alexander Gellatly. Though the Covenanters arrived first with a minister, the Associate Presbytery was
formed much earlier; indeed, the next year, in 1753. Very soon the
possibilities of union were discussed between the two groups. It is
worth noting also that the Burgher-Anti-Burgher issue which divided the Associate Church in Scotland and produced such sad
antagonisms within the Erskine family never really developed in
this country. Historians usually account for this fact by observing
that there were no oaths in this country similar to the Burgess oath
in Scotland and no comparable problems in the relation of church
and state. We do not question the fact but we doubt it as an explanation. These Scotsmen were people of very strong principle,
and how a person stood on it, whether it related to his present
situation or not, was often considered important. The reason the
Burgher controversy did not continue in this country has a simpler
explanation, we think. It was simply the fact that there were scarcely

any organized Burgher groups in the United States. And even among Scotsmen it takes two to make a quarrel. As Scouller notes in his *History of the Presbytery of Argyle:*

> Only three distinctly Burgher congregations were ever gathered in this country: those of Salem, Shippen Street, Philadelphia, and Cambridge; the others were organized under Antiburgher auspices, although the most of them contained a Burgher element in their membership.[17]

At any rate, with the union between Burgher and Anti-Burgher taking place almost incidentally, the Associate Church was able to think as a unit about the union with the Reformed Presbyterians. So, after much thinking, praying, and informal talking about it, a conference was held at Donegal, Pennsylvania, in 1777. Five years later the union, with all the Covenanter congregations and pastors and many Associate groups merging to form the Associate Reformed Synod, brings this union era to a climax.

From the year 1782, the year of the union forming the Associate Reformed Synod, divisions occurred. In the first place, though the organized Reformed Presbyterian groups joined the union, the small unorganized groups did not. The opposition of the Associate Church was much more formidable and effective. Some ministers and congregations refused the union and were almost immediately approved in their stand by the Scottish Synod, which sent them a steady stream of new ministers beginning with the well known John Anderson in the very next year.[18] What this continuing Associate Church felt about the union which formed the Associate Reformed Church in 1782, even a quarter-century later, is bluntly stated:

> The plan, on which the advocates for this union proposed to effect it, was gradually discovered; and was found to be a laying aside, or expressing in ambiguous terms, every thing about which the parties mentioned could not agree.[19]

Nevertheless, the Associate Reformed Church grew only to divide as it did, and even because it did. Soon it formed a Synod of

Pennsylvania, later the Synods of Carolina, New York, and the West. Carolina withdrew in 1820 because of its feeling of isolation from the Pennsylvania area which it felt was being too domineering. This factor also caused the Synod of the West to secede. New York and even part of Pennsylvania synods rejected the unconstitutional action of the Associate Reformed Synod in deciding that, in spite of the vote of the presbyteries and without an adequate proportion of the Synod itself, it had favored union with the Presbyterian Church in the United States of America. So this period began with a split and ended with splinters. And some of the divisions were produced because some were too eager for union.

By 1820–1822 it appeared that divisions had run their course and the Secession churches were determined to heal the breaches between Judah and Ephraim. This period was as remarkable for its unions as the preceding was for its divisions. And by 1858 the union movement reached its peak in the formation of the United Presbyterian Church. In contrast to the union of 1782 which caused so many divisions, the union of 1858 was the result of long deliberation and serious debates on every point of difference, even where the difference was nothing but a point of emphasis on an unessential detail. We noted earlier that the continuing Associate Church refused the Associated Reformed union in 1782 because it felt that it was based on an ignoring of all real differences. No one could have said this about the union of 1858. The discussions revealed differences; many of them. There was no ignoring of them —if anything there was an overemphasizing of them. But everyone saw them. And the vast majority, clearly seeing them, felt that they were differences concerning which forbearance was a possibility. No vital point of Calvinistic orthodoxy was questioned or union would not even have reached the discussion stage. Intricate details were the only points of difference, and this was seen and made union possible and desirable to almost all. There were no pigs in the poke. Everything essential was agreed upon in advance. Only adiaphorous administrative details were left to the future.

Hence there was not only satisfaction at the time, but no dis-illusionment afterward.

The event of union took place in Pittsburgh, Pennsylvania, May 28, 1858. The Associate Reformed delegates, having voted favor-ably, joined the like-minded Associate delegates at the corner where the Brimstone Methodist Church now is. Arm in arm they marched up Wood Street to the Old City Hall where the union meeting took place. A bronze marker shows the site of this meeting. Dr. John T. Pressly, first full pastor of the First Associate Reformed Church, Allegheny, first long-time professor in Allegheny Seminary, first editor of the *United Presbyterian*, became the first Moderator of the United Presbyterian Church of North America.

During the century following 1858 there have been no less than seventeen different unsuccessful union efforts. Dr. Christy in his *The United Presbyterian Church and Church Union* remarks:

In the 88 years (to 1946) since 1858 there have been only 24 years in which there were no union activities. During the first 50 of those years, 1858–1908, the United Presbyterians were favorably inclined toward union. Ten times during that interval, church union involving the United Presbyterian Church was voted on and only once was the nega-tive vote cast by the United Presbyterians. During that period union was discussed with the General Synod of the Reformed Presbyterian Church four different times, 1865–1871, 1887–1888, 1890–1891, and 1904–1905. A very long period of union discussion was engaged in with the Associate Reformed Synod of the South from 1874 until 1908. There were negative votes in the highest court of this small Southern body in the years 1882, 1887, 1894, 1905 and 1908. During the years 1888 and 1899 union discussion was carried on with the Holland Chris-tian Reformed Church. Twice during the interval this Reformed Church voted against consummating a union. The only occasion on which the United Presbyterians drew back from union was in the case of an early invitation from the Presbyterian, U.S.A., when an offer from the large church was rejected in 1872.

Since 1908 there have been three discussions of union with the Presbyterian Church U.S.A. and two with the Presbyterian Church U.S.; all of these, when they came to the vote, received a negative majority from the United Presbyterian General Assembly. On the other hand, the United Presbyterian Church's efforts to unite with the Reformed Church in America and later with the Associate Reformed Presbyterian Church were voted against by these churches. At this time a union of the Presbyterian Church, U.S.A., the Presbyterian Church, U.S., and the United Presbyterian Church is being considered.

While the denomination may have stood still as far as ecclesiastical mergers are concerned, she has forged ahead in most other areas. The following statistics tell the story:

Date	Ministers	Congre- gations	Members	Contri- butions	Per Capita Giving
1858	419	660	54,789	$ 242,014	
1890	774	904	103,921	1,134,223	
1908	1,098	1,082	127,700	2,400,023	19.
1924	937	924	165,186	5,847,370	35.39
1940	893	853	187,470	4,137,122	22.07
1953	914	829	222,201	12,251,549	55.14

These are figures for the American Church. But it is to be remembered that one-fourth of the total membership of the denomination is in Asia and Africa. The second largest synod in the entire denomination is in the Punjab, in Pakistan.

The United Presbyterian performance in the field of foreign missions is good, but not unparalleled. The work of the Women's General Missionary Society, however, is exceptional even in the wonderful annals of mission endeavor. As early as 1872 the female members of the church were asked, by the General Assembly, to take a special interest in the female heathen of the mission fields. By 1887 the Women's General Missionary Society was fully organized. Today these women support one hundred full-time foreign missionaries, not to mention the short-term foreign missionaries and the home missionaries. Annually they receive a special offering, the thank-offering for foreign missions. The first year it amounted to less than six thousand dollars; in 1950 it was more than a quarter of a million. Last year the total of that one day's offering was $273,990.72. Today, some feel that the ladies of the church have succeeded too well—that is, so well that the men are willing to put virtually the whole responsibility on them. Steps have been taken to prevent that disaster: one of them being the changing of the name of the magazine *The Women's Missionary Magazine* to that of *Missionary Horizons*, with more accent on the mission work as a whole.

In the realm of theological education, the United Presbyterian Church has a history possibly unparalleled in this country. This church and its ancestries have had more seminaries in relation to the size of its constituency than any other group of which we know. It is rather interesting to contrast the fact that with its growth as a denomination, it has continued to reduce the number of seminaries until now, with one-quarter million members in this country it has only one seminary: Pittsburgh-Xenia. Among the professors we have had some notable ones such as John Mason, James Harper, Melvin Grove Kyle, J. G. Moorehead, and others. Probably the most influential in the seminary's life were the three Johns: John Anderson, the first professor at old Service Seminary, the first or second oldest theological school in the United States; John Pressly, who for one-half of last century was the dominant influence in seminary affairs; and John McNaugher, whose fifty-five years of distinguished service in this institution justified his being referred to as one of the greater educators in the country.

In the collegiate field the church has also displayed its dedication to the cause of learning. Consider the colleges in this country alone: Muskingum, first started in 1837; Westminster, 1852; Monmouth, 1853; Knoxville, 1875; Tarkio, 1883; and Sterling in 1887. All of these schools have maintained creditable academic standing and some of them the highest standing for small liberal arts schools.

Many and varied are the other activities of the United Presbyterian Church. Some one has declared that

the first Sabbath School in the United States is credited to David Bethuen, a member of the Associated Reformed Church in New York; that in our ancestry is the first theological seminary west of the Allegheny Mountains; that at least fifteen years before Francis E. Clark founded the Christian Endeavor Society, a flourishing young people's society was organized in the United Presbyterian Church at Bellefontaine, Ohio.[20]

This leads us, in conclusion, to an over-all summation of the trend of this church as indicated in its history. There are many specific comments which would be in order here. But we submit only the most general evaluation. That which stands out in the big perspective of two centuries is this: The United Presbyterian Church has, under God, gradually corrected the schismatic tendency which was inherent in the movement from the beginning and which came close to becoming canonized in the last century. Dr. John McNaugher and his associates then and since have greatly increased the feeling for catholicity and for a more irenic disposition toward those without this particular Presbyterian family.

CHAPTER V

The Reformed Presbyterian Church
in America

ON June 22, 1680, Richard Cameron, with some twenty followers, rode into the town of Sanquhar in the southwest of Scotland and posted on the market cross a document disowning Charles Stuart "as having any right, title, or interest to, or in the said crown of Scotland and government," and officially declaring war on him and all who should support him. Beginnings are difficult to locate exactly; but from that day the paths diverged sharply. The majority of Scottish Presbyterians chose one path; the ancestors of what was to be the Reformed Presbyterian Church followed their convictions down the other.

The Sanquhar Declaration made three charges against the king: perjury, usurpation, and tyranny—all based on his breach of covenant with God and with man. In order to gain Scotland Charles I had signed the covenants, National and Solemn League. The practice of covenanting with a specifically religious purpose, by analogy with Biblical models, began in Scotland about 1555, when a group of Protestants associated with John Knox banded themselves together to support him and "the trew preaching of the Evangell of Jesus Christ." The first document in which the term "covenant" is used is the National Covenant which was in process of formation from 1581 to 1638, in which latter year it became the Scottish answer to the introduction of a prayer book into Scotland by Charles I. Dr. Philip Schaff described this covenant as follows:

It was drawn up in English and Latin by the Rev. John Craig, a noble, well-educated, and devoted man, a colleague of Knox and author of two Catechisms. It is a solemn indorsement of the Confession of Faith of 1560, with the strongest possible protest against "all kinds of papistry in general and particular heads," especially against the "usurped tyranny of the Roman Antichrist upon the Scriptures of God, upon the Kirk, the civil magistrate, and consciences of men; all his tyrannous laws made upon indifferent things, against our Christian liberty; . . . his five bastard sacraments, with all his rites, ceremonies, and false doctrine added to the ministration of the true sacraments without the Word of God; his cruel judgment against infants departing without the sacrament; his absolute necessity of baptism; his blasphemous opinion of transubstantiation; his devilish mass; his blasphemous priesthood; his profane sacrifice for sins of the dead and the quick; . . . his worldly monarchy and wicked hierarchy; his three solemn vows; his erroneous and bloody decrees made at Trent, with all the subscribers and approvers of that cruel and bloody band conjured against the Kirk of God." No other Protestant Confession is so fiercely anti-popish.

The renewal of the Covenant in 1638, which is more particularly called the National Covenant, marks the Second Reformation. It includes the old Covenant of 1581, the Acts of Parliament condemning popery, and a protest against the government of the Kirk by bishops, and all those measures of King Charles I. which "do sensibly tend to the re-establishment of the Popish religion and tyranny, and to the subversion and ruin of the true Reformed religion, and of our liberties, laws, and estates." The additions were prepared by Alexander Henderson and Johnston of Warriston, to meet a great crisis.[1]

The Solemn League and Covenant which included the substance of the National Covenant together with condemnations of Anglican "prelacy" was signed in 1643, an agreement between the Scotch Covenanters and the Parliament party in England looking toward "the reformation of religion" in England, Ireland, and Scotland "according to the Word of God and the example of the best reformed churches," specifically denouncing prelacy, the government of the church by bishops.

As soon as Charles I came to power he had the parchments of

the covenants publicly burned; and he violated their substance by his establishment of prelacy and by his persecution of all who would not conform. The Sanquhar Declaration was therefore a declaration of loyalty to the covenants. Those who adhered to it thereby separated themselves from any ecclesiastical organization in connection with the government. To support each other they organized local societies; to achieve a unified testimony they sent delegates to quarterly General Meetings.

The "society people" continued to maintain a separate existence after the Revolution Settlement (1689), for they felt that it was false to the covenants. Presbyterianism was established, not by divine right, but by the will of the king, who continued, through the presence of his commissioner at meetings of the General Assembly, to exercise control over the church. Though Cameron was dead on the field of battle and the only living ministers joined the established church, the remnant continued their identity and unity through their society meetings. In 1706 they were joined by the Reverend John Macmillan and in 1743 by the Reverend Thomas Nairn; and on August 1, 1743, Macmillan and Nairn constituted the Reformed Presbytery.

Perhaps at this point a word about names is in order. They have been called many things, these people. Cameronians, after Richard Cameron, Macmillanites, after John Macmillan. Mountain men, because during the days of persecution many of them fled for safety to the hills; "society people" because of their special form of organization. The name under which they published their *Informatory Vindication* was "a poor, wasted, misrepresented remnant, of the Suffering, Anti-popish, Anti-prelatic, Anti-erastian, Anti-sectarian, true Presbyterian Church of Christ in Scotland." [2] Today the church glories in the name Covenanter, because it has maintained a separate existence out of loyalty to the principles of the covenants. Its legal name is "Reformed Presbyterian," derived from the original Reformed Presbytery. Why they chose that name for their organization is not altogether clear—not of course because they were Presbyterians who had reformed. It has been seriously suggested that the name was chosen because they had been able to "form again" a presbytery, as they felt, loyal to the covenants and the Word of God, hence the "re-formed presbytery." This is an intriguing suggestion, but I doubt its truth. Already in the same year, 1743, Alexander Craighead was speaking of "the true Reformed Presbyterian religion," [3] with obvious reference to the attainments of the Scottish reformation. This was the official explanation published in 1806:

It is at least their honest intention faithfully to adhere to the whole of our reformation attainments, . . . On this account . . . they may . . . be called the *Reformed,* or *Reformation-Presbytery.*[4]

MIGRATION TO AMERICA—ALEXANDER CRAIGHEAD

The route by which the society people and their beliefs reached America is a difficult one to trace. The records of the Privy Council of Scotland indicate that many of those who would not take the oath to the king were banished to the colonies. Old Tennent Church in Monmouth County, New Jersey, in which was held an early recorded presbytery meeting of the Presbyterian Church in America, was founded by a group of these emigrants. Their absorption in the Presbyterian Church seems typical of those whose careers are traceable.

That they came we know. That some of them maintained their independence we learn from the career of Alexander Craighead. A kind of stormy petrel of Presbyterianism, he associated himself briefly with the Covenanters, provided a rallying point for them, and began the series of events which eventually led to the organization of an American Reformed Presbytery.

Craighead began his ministry as a Presbyterian, in the period of the Great Awakening, when American Presbyterianism was being torn apart over its reaction to the revivalism of men like Gilbert Tennent. Craighead was in the curious position of being vigorously on both sides at once. An outspoken preacher of "experimental religion" (the religion of experience), he was on the side of the revivalists, a friend of Whitefield. At the same time he believed in careful statements of doctrine and church government, and was therefore a "subscriptionist." Demanding such written assent to the historic documents of the church had become the mark of the anti-revivalist party.

Originally, the first issue seemed more important. His revivalist activities came to the judicial notice of Donegal Presbytery after his "intrusion" upon Francis Alison, the Presbyterian pastor at New London, in Lancaster County, Pennsylvania. That is to say, he had preached within the geographical bounds of the territory assigned to the New London congregation without Alison's invitation. Manifestly, Craighead would consider it no crime to preach "true, practical religion" [5] in a congregation unaccustomed, as he thought, to hearing it. Alison resented it and complained to the Presbytery. The matter was brought to trial at Middle Octorara, Craighead's congregation. The Presbytery gathered, to find Craighead preaching to a considerable crowd from Matthew 15:14, "They be blind, leaders of the blind," and making specific application to members of the Presbytery.

After his sermon, Craighead invited the people into the churchyard, where two of his sympathizers read a paper in his defense, "containing," says the Presbytery, "a long and numerous train of most Slanderous reproaches." [6] The next day the paper was read again in Presbytery meeting, while the company outside was exhorted, the result eventually being that the Presbytery had to retire to a neighboring house to conduct its business in peace. Craighead insisted that he had tried to quell the tumult; Presbytery claimed that he postponed action "till ye people got into Such an uproar that they could not hear him; w^h . . . he uttered a few words in a low voice, so that it could be of little use to calm a tumultuous multitude." [7] Of the whole proceeding, Presbytery's clerk recorded the handwritten minute: "In sum, we cannot but look on Mr. Craighead's whole conduct in ye above instances, to be extremely irregular and disorderly. So that we have not known a parallel instance since we have been capable to mark anything in the world." [8]

The upshot of the whole matter was Craighead's suspension by Presbytery. When the case came before the Synod, it precipitated a debate on the whole revivalist controversy and the withdrawal of the Tennent group from the Synod of Philadelphia to form the Conjunct Presbyteries of New Brunswick and Londonderry.

Craighead, in his new association with those commonly called the New Side, found that ground for disagreement still existed. The new group, born of a revival spirit, tended to underemphasize theology and church government. For Craighead, the talisman against defection from the truth was subscription to the covenants. He therefore proposed to the new organization that they renew the National and Solemn League and Covenant. He stood alone in his conviction. The presbyteries replied to his demand by saying "that they supposed they were not called unto any other measure or methods for the carrying on a true Reformation, and promoting of real Godliness, than they already plainly aim at and endeavor after. . . ." [9]

COMING OF THE CAMERONIANS

Craighead, if he could gain no clerical support, did find those who were interested in the proposal. These were the Cameronians, the society people, who had themselves in Scotland in 1712 renewed the covenants. How many there were, or where, or in what state of organization we have little information. The ones whom Craighead contacted lived in scattered settlements on both sides of the Susquehanna River in southern Pennsylvania. It is presumable that they had established some sort of organization patterned after their Scottish experience. In response to Craighead's call, they gathered at Middle Octorara, in Lancaster County, Pennsylvania, and on November 10 and 11, 1743, one hundred years after the Solemn League and Covenant, they renewed the covenants.

The most interesting part of the proceeding is the declaration and testimony there issued. It is extensive, detailed, and in language little restrained. After testifying against Charles I, Cromwell, and Charles II, and for the acts and declarations of their Scottish forebears, they reach the issues which particularly concerned them. They continued their dissent from the British government, their reasons for withholding allegiance from George I and II consisting in

their being sworn Prelaticks, the Head of Malignants, and Protectors of Sectarian Hereticks, and Electory Princes of Brunswick, in chusing of new Emperors, which is their giving their power to the Beast; and for their confederacy with Popish princes, directly contrary to the second Commandment; and for want of their Scriptural and national Qualifications . . . ; and for their being established head of the Church by the Laws of England.[10]

They also would not adhere to the Revolution Settlement

which established an Erastian power in the Kings Hands (as they term him) to appoint Time and Place, when and where General Assemblies should be holden, and obliged Presbyteries to settle such qualified Preachers (as they call them) to vacant Congregations, as should be presented by the pretended King or Laick Patrons.[11]

They strenuously maintained the right of the church and of each congregation to govern itself under Christ.

The renewal of the covenants provided a rallying point for the Covenanters. We have from the next year (1744) records of a General Meeting of the American societies. Craighead, as the only minister, could not constitute a presbytery; he therefore wrote for aid to the new Reformed Presbytery in Scotland. They concerned themselves with the matter, but were, of course, in no position to render immediate aid. Craighead, discouraged, appealed to the Associate Presbytery, likewise without immediate result. Eventually he returned to the Presbyterian Church, preaching first on Cow-pasture Creek in Virginia and later founding the Presbyterian churches in Mecklenburg County, North Carolina.[12]

JOHN CUTHBERTSON

Seven years later, the repeated pleas of the American Covenanters to the Scottish Presbytery were answered by the arrival of the Reverend John Cuthbertson. Many have seen the small leather-bound volume in which he recorded the day-to-day experiences of his remarkable career.[13] For nearly a quarter of a century, from his arrival at New Castle, Delaware, August 5, 1751, until he was joined by Matthew Lind and Alexander Dobbin in 1773, he was the only Covenanter minister in America. His first Sabbath in America he lectured on a passage from Luke's gospel which begins, "Take no thought for your life," and which ends, "But rather seek ye the Kingdom of God." These words are symbolic of his career.

Over such roads as there were in eighteenth century Pennsylvania, or without them, he rode, visiting the scattered settlements of Covenanters, until he had covered more than sixty-nine thousand miles. Lost on the Blue Mountain on a dark October night (until the Lord brought him to Isaac Bushwa's), lying in the snow all night near York, tossing sleeplessly in Conrad Weiser's tavern while the card game kept him awake, recording in his diary after an itching night the *Bugs*—but always riding. One of the most familiar words in the diary is the word *tired*, but still he rode, back and forth across the Susquehanna, many times to visit the Covenanters along the Hudson, once to follow his parishioners who had moved west over the mountains, once to Massachusetts, where he thought he might find adherents to the Covenanter cause.

And all this besides that which came upon him daily, the care of all the churches. During one of his first weeks in America he preached eleven times (and Cuthbertson never used old sermons), baptized several children, "conversed with several weak, well-meaning" persons, held a long theological conversation with someone now unknown, had a three-hour session meeting, examined three elders, did the jobs of rebuking and admonishing which were required. Week after week he spent himself giving spiritual sustenance to his scattered flock.

In this diary—there was another one, lost when the home of its owners burned—he says little of his spiritual experiences. One catches only an occasional glimpse of his inner life. Once, having read one of Ralph Erskine's sermons, he writes: ". . . a real conviction of one's original guilt; actual transgressions of childhood; riper years, especially in the great office of the ministry; pride, carnality, indifference, want of true zeal for Christ's cause and the welfare of Immortal souls . . ." and concludes, "O father of mercies, be merciful to me." [14] Though there are few such references in the diary, there stands everywhere through it a phrase, often abbreviated, a terse testimony to his recognition of the source of his spiritual life and of his deep desire to glorify God: "Give all praise to my gracious God." Those words are an epitaph worthy of his career.

FIRST REFORMED PRESBYTERY

In 1773 Cuthbertson was joined by Lind and Dobbin from the Reformed Presbytery of Ireland. This accession not only meant a division of Cuthbertson's labors and the fuller supply of gospel ordinances to his people. It also meant that a proper ecclesiastical organization could be formed. And so, at Paxtang, near Harrisburg, Pennsylvania, on March 10, 1774, the Reformed Presbytery of America was constituted.

It was a short-lived organization. Two years later, the colonies declared their independence of Great Britain and vindicated that declaration by force of arms. This separation from the mother country and from her sins and defections against which the Covenanters had so long testified suggested that perhaps there was no longer reason for separate existence. The Covenanters and the Seceders—the Associate Presbytery—entered into negotiation, and after long conferences and some compromise of differences, the Associate Reformed Presbyterian Church was constituted in 1782.

There remained some Covenanter laymen who did not enter the new church. They again petitioned Scotland for ministerial aid. In the years 1789 and 1790 the Reverend James Reid visited the American Covenanters. He left no record of his experiences, but he apparently visited all areas where he knew of Covenanter societies. Next came the Reverend James McKinney, encouraged to emigrate from Ireland by an indictment on the charge of treason. This was the period of the United Irishmen, the government was unduly sensitive, and the dimly understood principles of Covenanters made them susceptible to such charges. McKinney lived ten years after his escape to America, traveled widely, and laid the foundations for the re-forming of the American Reformed Presbytery. In the constitution of the court (in May, 1798, in Philadelphia) he was joined by the Reverend William Gibson, likewise escaping from the political difficulties created by the United Irishmen. The year 1798 thus marks another beginning in the organized history of the Reformed Presbyterian Church in the United States.

FOREIGN MISSIONS

In dealing with the century and a half of history since that time, I should like to suggest first two areas in which Covenanters have been typical Presbyterians.

Foreign mission activity was proposed to the Synod in 1818. At that time resources for such a program were lacking. Congregations were small, few were wealthy, most were somewhat parochial in their outlook. So it was not until 1841 that the Synod appointed a committee to consider a foreign mission program. In 1846 the Reverend John B. Johnston was sent to make a survey of the island of Haiti. His favorable report led to the appointment of the Reverend

John W. Morton as missionary and the beginning of mission work. Morton secured property, translated some of the psalms into French verse, and was working on the Shorter Catechism, when his views on the propriety of keeping the first day of the week as the Christian Sabbath changed. His pamphlet on the subject, sent to all ministers of the church, effectively put an end to the mission in Haiti.

The experience dampened the enthusiasm of the church for foreign mission work and led rather naturally to the question of the providential meaning of what had happened. The rapid migration of Covenanters to the West, increased by the potato famine in Ireland, laid heavy burdens of home mission work on the church —perhaps Covenanters were not meant to carry on foreign missions.

Within a decade, however, there was a renewed interest in the cause of missions. Syria was chosen as a field of operations, and the first missionaries were sent out in 1856. The outstanding Covenanter missionary to the Near East was undoubtedly David Metheny, who began his career in 1864 and died in 1897 in Mersine, Turkey, where he had founded and long carried on mission work. Physician, minister, philanthropist, American consul, he combined a wide missionary vision with an extraordinary personality, to achieve wide influence in that corner of the Mediterranean coast. From the city of Latakia, which continues to be the center of mission work, a widespread program was carried on. The changed attitude of the Turkish government after the First World War led to the abandonment of all stations within modern Turkey. In the meantime, the missionaries had extended their activities to the island of Cyprus, where the church has made a great contribution, especially to the educational life of the island.

In 1895 the foreign mission program was expanded to South China, in the province of Kwangtung along the West River, in 1930 to Manchuria, and in 1950, as American missionaries were no longer welcome in China, to Japan.

In the United States, besides the program of church expansion, there have been missionary activities among the Jews, the Chinese immigrants, the Indians, the Negroes, and in the Kentucky hills.

EDUCATIONAL INSTITUTIONS

The Covenanter Church shared the value placed on education by Presbyterians. Many of her ministers made contributions to the educational life of their communities through private academies. This was often dictated by necessity, for many congregations could not furnish support for a minister. The most distinguished career of a Covenanter minister in education was that of Samuel B. Wylie, pastor of the Philadelphia congregation, who became professor of Greek and Latin in the University of Pennsylvania, was for a while vice-provost, and played some part in the early nineteenth century renaissance of the institution.[15] John Black, pastor of the Pittsburgh congregation, was professor of ancient languages and classical literature in the Western University of Pennsylvania from its foundation.[16]

At every level of the educational process the church demonstrated its concern. The first educational enterprise was, understandably, a seminary. The very differences of the church from other denominations were a stimulus in this direction, for its distinctive position in regard to politics involves many questions of theology and political philosophy. The seminary was founded in 1810 and was for many years peripatetic, existing wherever the chosen professor lived. It faced financial vicissitudes, for this also was before congregations developed a tradition of support for church-wide institutions. It meant to give thorough training, though, judging by the extent, both in time and subject matter, of the early examinations. In 1856 it was established in the Pittsburgh area, where it continues.

As early as 1841 the church manifested a concern for a "collegiate institution" in which, as New York Presbytery said, the youth of the church might prosecute their studies "free from the dangerous influences to which they are so often exposed in the higher seminaries and colleges now." [17] The introduction of the subject to church courts was frequently associated with the name of James R. Willson, who was greatly concerned over the study of pagan literature, disguised as classics, in the colleges of the day. He and his son, who edited one of the church magazines, carried on an extensive campaign for the use of Christian authors as text-books in Latin and Greek and for the study of Hebrew with the Old Testament as a text.

At the end of the decade, two such institutions were established. One, called Westminster College, without any connection with the present institution of that name, was founded in Wilkinsburg, Pennsylvania, under the care of Pittsburgh Presbytery. Eventually it was taken over by its principal and became Newell Institute, a private academy of some note in Pittsburgh. A second, called Geneva Hall, was founded in the village of Northwood, Ohio, in 1848. It had many trials, financial and otherwise, and was hard hit by the Civil War. But it survived, and moved in 1880 to its present campus in Beaver Falls, Pennsylvania.

There was concern likewise for Christian education at the elementary level. A report was adopted by the Synod in 1845, recommending the establishment of parish schools in which "scriptural instruction shall be given collaterally with the secular branches of education." [18] The experience of Illinois Presbytery was probably typical: they reported that they found obstacles, owing to "the scattered situation of our people, . . . the prejudice . . . against such an institution, . . . and the too general indifference of our people to the importance of religious schools." [19]

THE MAINTENANCE OF IDENTITY

One of the most interesting inquiries in connection with the history of the church is the attempt to discover how the church, small as it has been, maintained its identity. This is the second topic I should like to discuss. The distinctive beliefs of any group operate in two ways—to discourage the unconvinced and to increase the group feeling of the convinced. Both these tendencies have been at work in the Covenanter Church. Besides this almost automatic action, what conscious steps has the church taken to sustain its own existence?

First of all, besides its interest in formal educational institutions, the church has made consistent efforts, with varying degrees of success, at adult education. Its earliest church-wide fund was for the printing of Christian literature.[20] Its first extensive project was the preparation of a testimony, which should be a "means of instruction to their connections and to others." [21] From the beginning, ministers preached on the distinctive beliefs of the church, and not infrequently they published their sermons. The bibliography of such items is extensive. It would include Gilbert Mc-Master's *Apology for the Psalms*, J. R. Willson's *Prince Messiah*, J. M. Willson's *Civil Government*, James Milligan's *Account of the Secession Controversy in Vermont*, David McAllister's *Christian Civil Government*, J. M. Coleman's *Social Ethics*, D. H. Elliott's *Trail of the Totalitarian*, and many other polemical works on the issues of the day. Alexander McLeod and W. L. Roberts published catechisms for instruction in doctrine.

After James R. Willson had broken ground with the *Evangelical Witness* in 1882, the first periodical edited especially for Covenanters, the church was seldom without a magazine. The first official publication was the *American Christian Expositor*, edited by Alexander McLeod, which began in 1831 and died prematurely of battle wounds in 1833. The *Reformed Presbyterian*, begun in 1838, and the *Covenanter*, the first number of which appeared in 1845, merged their identity and titles in 1863. More recently have appeared the *Christian Nation* and its successor the *Covenanter Witness*, which continues. Other periodicals, of shorter life or more limited purpose, have also contributed in their various ways to the group consciousness of the church.

Another factor in the unity of the church was its exercise of discipline. This is an overly familiar aspect of church life, for it appeals to the curiosity of all of us and has provided a happy hunting ground for the critics of church morality. Undeniably the dry pages of routine business do come vividly to life when the scandalous and the tragic appear in session minutes. From the point of view of social institutions, the most important thing to notice is the extent to which the authority of the session was sought, the extent to which the session exercised its authority, and the very wide degree of submission to that authority. In the pages of one session book a man is rebuked for assignation of his property to others than his creditors, a household for an unpleasant difficulty unnamed, a son for ordering his mother out of the house (he eventually paid her board bill elsewhere), another for having been four years in America without joining a church, another for a New Year's Day altercation (when asked whether he was intoxicated he said that "he was led to indulge with greater freedom in talking than in ordinary circumstances"), a husband and wife for "criminal and scandalous strife and contention." [22] The point is not that such situations existed but that the sessional action in each one of them was accepted. This not only demonstrates, but was itself one cause of, the cohesion of a congregation. The focal point of the exercise of discipline was, of course, the communion service. Covenanters, with their high concept of the church and of church membership, have always recognized the responsibility of the church to guard the administration of the sacraments. They continue to set the same standards for partaking of communion that they do for church membership.

THE SOCIETY MEETING

One of the most interesting aspects of the organizational history of the church is the "society" meeting. It would be difficult to overestimate its importance as a centripetal force in the church.

It was carried to America from the Covenanter experience in Scotland where during persecuting times some relatively informal means of meeting for worship had to be devised. The first Covenanters in America, likewise without ministers, used the society meeting. When Alexander Craighead proposed the renewing of the covenants, he found societies scattered along the Susquehanna River. After the dissolution of the church in 1782, the first known organization was a General Meeting, held on the Conococheague Creek in 1791, which ordered "that two societies for prayer and Christian conference be erected to meet at such convenient times and places as each society shall from time to time agree upon." [23] As Covenanters followed the frontier West, they carried society meetings with them. In the history of nearly every early congregation is the account of meetings for "society" in some central home—or barn. Often a minister had a widely scattered charge and would meet from Sabbath to Sabbath with one after another of the societies of a congregation. Obviously the institution, developed for a very different purpose in Scotland, was of the greatest utility in meeting the particular problems of the frontier.

The society meeting had a much wider use than its simple use on the frontier. It was a part of the regular organization of the congregation, meeting during the week, if there were regular preaching on Sabbath, for Christian fellowship, study, and prayer. It was an important part of the educational program of the congregation. To it the children brought their newly learned catechism questions to say. Each adult was expected to contribute to the subject under discussion. The phrase "I pass the question" was an embarrassed admission that one had nothing to say. Society meetings also had governmental functions. The session of the First Church in Philadelphia ruled that no new members were to be received unless recommended by a society,[24] and occasionally a member not so introduced was asked to attend society meeting and to seek such a recommendation. Each society was asked to report on the Christian conduct of its members before each communion. Frequently intimation of the decisions of session about cases of discipline or the work of the congregation was made through each society.

PRACTICE OF COVENANTING

Another means of maintaining the identity of the church was through the old Scottish device from which the church takes its name. Alexander Craighead, when he led the Covenanters in renewing the covenants in 1743, added a "declaration, protestation, and testimony" bringing the century-old documents up to date. Covenanters have always believed not only in adherence to the doctrines of the Scottish covenants but also in the application of those doctrines to the contemporary situation. In practice it has been difficult to achieve the agreement necessary for covenanting; but the attempt has been almost continuous. At the meeting of the Reformed Presbytery in 1802 the action was taken "that a draught of a covenant, containing the spirit of the National and Solemn League, shall be prepared by each committee and laid before the Presbytery at their next meeting." [25] There are regular references to the matter until in 1843 a draft of a covenant was adopted by the Synod and sent down in overture, only to be rejected. The chief fault complained of, surprisingly enough, was its indefiniteness. In the 1850's another form was prepared and adopted; and the Synod met especially for the purpose of covenanting in 1859; still there was no feeling of hearty unanimity, and they did not proceed. Finally, after seventy years of effort, the members of the church joined in covenant with one another and with God in 1871, reaffirming their belief in the principles of the Reformed faith and promising to pray and labor for the extension of God's kingdom. In 1930 it was proposed that the covenant be again renewed; and after nearly twenty-five years of consideration a form was adopted in 1953 for use by the Synod next year. This Covenant of 1953 reads, in part, as follows:

We believe in and accept the standards of the Reformed Presbyterian Church of North America as being in agreement and founded upon the Scriptures. In particular we believe in the Reformed faith, emphasizing the sovereignty of Christ, the Presbyterian form of church government, and the New Testament pattern of worship, with its exclusive use of the Psalms, sung *a capella*.

We covenant with God that we will seek to conform our lives to the teaching and example of our Lord Jesus Christ; that we will endeavor to forsake all that is sinful and that would compromise our witness for Him; that we will separate ourselves from all associations, especially secret societies, which would hinder the development of Christian character; and that we will encourage by our example, temperance, love, and godliness.

We do solemnly purpose to seek first the Kingdom of God and His righteousness in all the relationships of life. We therefore oppose all the systems, religious and secular, that undermine faith in the Scriptures, in the deity of Jesus Christ, and His redemptive work. We will continue to advocate the separation of church and state and strive to bring each to the proper acknowledgment of Christ's sovereignty. We therefore will not avail ourselves of those rights and privileges of citizenship that may tend to neutralize our testimony to the rights and claims of Christ over the nations.

SOVEREIGNTY OF CHRIST IN THE CONSTITUTION

This brings us naturally to the third and most important topic of the paper: What is distinctive about the Reformed Presbyterian Church? How does it differ from those general "aspects of American Presbyterianism" which we have gathered to consider?

The basic belief of Covenanters, which has kept them a separate denomination, is the lordship of Jesus Christ in the life of the individual, the church, and the nation, and the specific applications of that belief which it makes. The church believes that the individual's complete commitment to Christ prevents him from giving his sworn allegiance to a religious institution not specifically Christian. Its members therefore do not belong to oath-bound secret societies. It believes that its own allegiance to Christ as head of the church involves submission to His rule in the matter of worship. It therefore continues what it believes to be the New Testament pattern, the Presbyterian tradition of the psalms sung without instrumental accompaniment.

The most distinctive application of the belief in the sovereignty of Christ is the practice of dissent from political institutions which do not recognize that sovereignty.

The civil government of the nations is subjected to the Lordship of Messiah: the Prince of the Kings of the Earth. . . . Nations are bound, in the constitutions of their governments, to recognize formally the authority of the Mediator as their King.[26]

In the Testimony, adopted in 1806, the church applies this general principle to its circumstances. After commending the constitution for its many good qualities, the Testimony continues:

such a constitution must, however, be founded upon the principles of morality . . . before it can be recognized by the conscientious Christian as an ordinance of God. . . . There are moral evils essential to the constitution of the United States, which render it necessary to refuse allegiance to the whole system. In this remarkable instrument there is contained no acknowledgment of the being or authority of God—there is no acknowledgment of the Christian religion, or professed submission to the kingdom of Messiah.[27]

Covenanters are not anti-government men. The Testimony begins its chapter on civil government with these words:

Civil government is an ordinance of God. Man by creation is a political being, to whom government is natural and necessary.[28]

They have always considered politics a proper sphere of concern. The first committee appointed by the Reformed Presbytery was that of "signs of the times," which, under the heading Causes of Fasting and Thanksgiving, annually discussed the current political situation. Alexander McLeod, pastor in New York City, in a stirring series of sermons on the War of 1812, devoted a whole sermon to justifying the attention to current events, with this stated theme:

"Ministers have the right of discussing from the pulpit those political questions which affect Christian morals." [29] James R. Willson, a noted Covenanter preacher in Albany, was burned in effigy for the pointed political references in one of his sermons and dismissed, after long discussion in the New York State Legislature, from his post as one of its chaplains. He kept a voluminous diary full of such remarks as

General Harrison . . . is undoubtedly cowardly, lazy, and ignorant. The nomination by the Whigs is as base a truckling to the South—as infamous a sacrifice to the Moloch of slavery as Van Buren's inaugural speech.

Or, speaking of diplomatic difficulties with Great Britain in 1840:

The arm of the helmsman in the national vessel too feeble for the rising storm. Such weather as is ahead requires a Captain & other officers "who are able men, such as fear God, men of truth—hating covetousness." O quam deficiunt.[30]

Covenanters have never felt politics beyond the proper scope of their interest or discussion. They do believe that it is the duty of governments to recognize the authority of Jesus Christ, and therefore "separate from the government at the point where the government separates from Christ." [31] Christians, the Testimony continues, are "under moral obligation to relinquish all such privileges of citizenship as may tend to neutralize their testimony to the regal rights and claims of Christ." [32] The two major breaks in the church's organizational history have come over that issue, in 1833 and 1891. In the years before 1833, there had been a growing difference of opinion over the application of this principle, so much so that a leading minister of the church, S. B. Wylie, had openly taken the oath to the Constitution, had been naturalized, and had voted. The matter reached the church courts when a committee appointed to draft a pastoral address to the congregations in the church included the doctrine that political dissent be left to the individual conscience. After sharp debate, the address was ordered printed without the offending paragraphs. The committee published the original draft. The ensuing trial led to the separation of the church in 1833 into two independent bodies, each calling itself the Reformed Presbyterian Church. The group which no longer emphasized political dissent is called the General Synod, or New School, and continues to exist with about thirteen hundred members.

Two generations later the question of political dissent came up again, in very much the same form. On July 22, 1890, a meeting was called in the East End Church in Pittsburgh, which reached the conclusion that persons desiring admission to church membership should be admitted without any statement with regard to political dissent. This position led likewise to judicial trial and the suspension from the ministry of the church of those known to have signed the statement.

FOR THE ABOLITION OF SLAVERY

The church has not been content with the somewhat negative position of dissent from a Constitution it believes is unchristian. It has essayed also the more positive task of trying to change the Constitution. There were two moral evils which Covenanters felt especially needed change: the Constitution's condoning of slavery and its failure to recognize Jesus Christ as the source of its authority. Much of the activity of the church has centered around the attempt to remedy these two evils.

The slavery question reached its conclusion in the Civil War and the Emancipation Proclamation. Therefore it is perhaps more logical to consider it first.[33]

Slavery was the subject of judicial action by the Reformed Presbytery in 1800, two years after its constitution. The action came about on this wise: licentiate Alexander McLeod received a call from the Walkill congregation in Orange County, New York, one of whose members was a slaveholder. Mr. McLeod had strong convictions on the subject of slavery and declined before presbytery to accept the call. Presbytery then established the rule "that no slaveholder should be retained in their communion." A committee was sent to convey this information to the Covenanter settlement in South Carolina. The report is that three thousand guineas in slaves were sacrificed on "the altar of principle." Of the four members of the church known to have violated the rule, three came to tragic ends. "Thus was the brand of Cain put on the sin of slavery."

From that time Covenanters stood in the forefront of the abolition movement. Alexander McLeod published in 1802 a sermon entitled "Negro Slavery Unjustifiable," and that became the battle cry of the church. Its ministers were outstanding abolitionist speakers. James Milligan, lecturing in New Hampshire, was threatened with a coat of tar and feathers. He offered to help pay for the tar if his audience would hear him out. They listened, and he left in peace. More than once he and others came home with the smell of rotten eggs on their clothing. Covenanters were the friends and supporters of abolitionists. James M. Willson opened the Cherry Street Covenanter Church in Philadelphia to the famous British abolitionist George Thompson, and stood with him on the platform after threats had been made to burn the building to the ground. N. R. Johnston, J. R. W. Sloane, James Milligan, and others were affiliated with William Lloyd Garrison in his lecturing.

While their ministers influenced public opinion from the platform, the rank and file of Covenanters served the cause of abolition through the underground railway. The report of Illinois Presbytery to the Synod in 1849 reads:

The circumstances that some reckless characters are watching their opportunity to catch poor fugitives, to make gain by the price of blood, and others are willing to hide the outcasts, makes a kind of civil war among us all the time. The Covenanters have led the latter class.[34]

Wilbur H. Siebert, in his study of the underground railway, pays tribute to the work of Covenanters in southern Illinois, where the prevailing sentiment was pro-slavery, as well as in areas where there was more sympathy for the fugitive slave. Wherever there were settlements of Covenanters there were stations on the railway. One Covenanter student at Indiana University said he would pay no more attention to the Fugitive Slave Law than "if it had emanated immediately from Satan." There is a tradition in the First Church of the Covenanters in Philadelphia that children inattentive to the sermon might if they glanced around see black faces peering over the gallery railing. Covenanters, each in his own situation, contributed far more than their share to the battle against slavery.

After the legal battle had been won in the Emancipation Proclamation, Covenanters devoted themselves to the care of the freedmen. In Washington, D.C., in South Carolina, Florida, Mississippi, and Arkansas they carried on work. They made definite efforts to find worthy Negro students for Geneva College. In 1874 mission work was established in Selma, Alabama, which continues. For many years the church supported Knox Academy, which made a distinguished contribution to Negro education in that part of the South.

Very early in the history of the church, attention was paid to the possibility that the Constitution might be amended to recognize the authority and law of Jesus Christ. In 1823 it was proposed that the cooperation of other churches be sought in achieving that end.[35] This action seems not to have been implemented, and shortly the church was involved in the controversies leading up to the division of 1833. Agitation began again in the 1840's. John Quincy Adams presented to Congress two petitions from Covenanters in 1843 and 1844, asking for amendment of the Constitution.[36] This time the movement seems to have been swallowed up in increasing abolitionist activity.

Moved to a consideration of national sins by the terrible calamity of the Civil War, the church again turned its attention to the amendment of the Constitution. A committee was appointed by the Synod in 1863 to visit President Lincoln to confer with him on the duty of the nation "to submit to Jesus Christ, the King of Kings and Lord of Lords." Lincoln is reported to have said:

"I know these Covenanters well. They have made two demands of this nation—submission to God, and freedom for the slave. One of their demands has been granted during my first administration; and perhaps, during my second they will obtain the other." [37]

In 1864 the National Reform Association was formed. Called at first the National Association for the Amendment of the Constitution, it had a Christian amendment as its original purpose. Though generously supported by Covenanters, its moving spirit and first president was a United Presbyterian, and it enlisted the cooperation of many noted leaders. One historian has cogently remarked that the ending of the Civil War left many men of reforming temperament without activity. Working for a Christian Amendment was one new channel many of them found. Such a bill was introduced into Congress repeatedly during the rest of the century.

After the National Reform Association had turned its special attention to other areas of reform, the church continued its own agitation through the "Witness Committee." Various ministers of the church served as lecturers, speaking on the subject especially in colleges. In 1942 the church again began a particularly active campaign to amend the Constitution as follows: "This nation devoutly recognizes the authority and law of Jesus Christ, Savior and Ruler of nations, through whom are bestowed the blessings of Almighty God." The Christian Amendment Movement was organized in cooperation with ministers of other churches, and continues its efforts through many avenues of publicity.

Besides these two special areas, the church has cooperated in a wide variety of reform movements in an effort to achieve a Christian America. Covenanters have recognized the need of applying Christian principles in the economic and social life of the nation.

For many years a committee on social justice reported to the Synod. The church has supported actively efforts to protect the Sabbath and to prohibit gambling. Its ministers early began support of the temperance cause. After a series of increasingly definite deliverances on the subject, the Synod in 1841 prohibited the engaging in "traffic in ardent spirits." [38] In 1883 the further step was taken of forbidding the use of intoxicating beverages by any member of the church.[39] The church continues to practice and to advocate total abstinence. In many ways, therefore, Covenanters have sought to achieve a social order recognizing the authority of Christ and obeying his law.

As long as I can remember I have watched Covenanters walking down the aisle of the church to the white-covered communion table singing from the Forty-fifth Psalm:

> Thy royal throne, O God, forever shall endure.
> The sceptre of thy kingdom is a sceptre right and pure.
>
> To triumph ride in state, for meekness, truth, and right,
> And thy right hand shall teach to thee the deeds of dreadful might.

Their partaking of the bread and wine of the sacrament is their oath to God that they will labor for the triumph of that kingdom. The service closes with the Seventy-second Psalm:

> On hilltops sown a little grain like Lebanon with fruit shall bend,
> New life the city shall attain; she shall like grass grow and extend.

It is the hope of the Covenanter Church that the small grain it has been able to sow may grow and bring forth fruit, so that the prayer of the psalm may come true:

> And blessed be his glorious name,
> Long as the ages shall endure.
> O'er all the earth extend his fame.
> Amen, Amen, for ever more.

CHAPTER VI

The Founding of Educational Institutions

CALVINISTS in the educational history of the United States, up to about the year 1835, are credited with being directly and indirectly responsible for the founding of more academies, colleges, and universities here in America than can be attributed to any other of the groups arising out of the Protestant Reformation. Be reminded that they were to be found among the Congregationalists, the Anglicans, the Dutch and German Reformed, and the early Baptists as well as the Presbyterians. While it is conceded that there are other factors which may furnish the urge to found institutions of learning, it is the consensus that so far as early American educational history is concerned, Calvinism had a very determining influence.

When the guiding principles, the predominant motives, and the stated reasons that were uppermost in our early college founders are examined, very much of the phraseology used by Calvin and his associates as they founded the Academy and the University of Geneva appears. At Geneva these institutions were held to be necessary "to secure political administration, to sustain the church unharmed and to maintain humanity among men." Calvin, in his famous *Institutes*, stated that "God has furnished the soul of man with a mind capable of discerning good from evil and just from unjust; and of discerning, therefore, by the light of reason what ought to be pursued or avoided. . . . To this He has annexed the will" (I. xv. 8). In interpreting the Word of God, Calvin made a very determined use of the intellect. His system of theology called for the exercise of a highly educated mind. He integrated the application of the basic doctrines of his system with the Christianization of the political and social order. Nothing short of a highly educated citizenry could carry out the Christian layman's vocation and the Christian minister's calling. Consequently, when the Calvinists of Europe and the British Isles came to America, they, being steeped with such principles and emphases, lost little time before they began, as the necessary material help arising out of Calvinistic Christian stewardship was provided, to found academies, colleges, and universities.

During the Colonial period nine colleges were established, all but one of them—what is now the University of Pennsylvania— founded by the Colonial churches wherein Calvinism was dominant. Harvard, Yale, and Dartmouth were established by the Congregationalists; William and Mary and Columbia by the Anglicans; Princeton by the Presbyterians; the College of Rhode Island, now Brown University, by the Baptists; Queens, now Rutgers, by the Dutch Reformed. All but three of these Colonial colleges were founded as the direct or indirect result of the new life and strength given to the Colonial churches by the great eighteenth century revivals. At least five of them were in a peculiar sense revival colleges. This was particularly true of Dartmouth and Princeton.

Of great interest is the story of Princeton's founding. In 1728, on the Neshaminy, northeast of present-day Philadelphia, William Tennent established what came to be called the Log College which schooled approximately forty men, many of whom were to be outstanding leaders in the planting and extension of Presbyterianism.[1] All of them were sympathetic with the Great Awakening dating from 1725–1745. Certain of them, notably Gilbert Tennent, son of William, were among the outstanding leaders of this Awakening. But Presbyterians in certain parts, notably in and south of Philadelphia, objected to any of the Log College men being ordained for the Presbyterian ministry. The Presbytery of New Brunswick, which did so, was outlawed. As told elsewhere, this opposition to Log College men on one hand, and the zeal on behalf of these same men and for the Awakening on the other, ultimately led to the division into the Old Side and New Side groups in 1741, this division not to be erased until 1758.

It was Jonathan Dickinson, formerly a Congregationalist, later a Presbyterian on the New Side, who joined with others in the founding of the College of New Jersey in 1746, this college being housed in his manse in Newark, New Jersey.

On this college's first board of trustees were none of the former teachers or students of the Log College. Hence it is an error to hold that the new college was an organic continuation of William Tennent's Log College. The first trustees of the institution, now known as Princeton University, included nine clergymen and four laymen, one of the latter being the Honorable John Hamilton, president of His Majesty's Council for the Province of New Jersey. The other three laymen were graduates of Yale and residents of the colony of New York. Of the clergy members, several, including Jonathan Dickinson, were graduates of Yale, and all nine, except for David Cowell, were in the New Side Presbyterian Church, which zealously favored emancipation from doctrinaire formalism, hyper-orthodoxy, and unwillingness to accept as clergy the newly converted leaders, which emancipation characterized the great religious awakening of the early eighteenth century.

On the board of trustees under the second charter there were twenty-three members. Of these, six were Yale, three were Harvard, and three were Log College graduates. Two, Kinsey and Shippen, were Quakers; one was an Episcopalian; one, Governor Jonathan

Belcher, chairman of the board and a graduate of Harvard (1699), was, in his early days, a Puritan Congregationalist and later a Presbyterian (member at Elizabethtown), a man very much in sympathy with the revival under George Whitefield and Jonathan Edwards. All the remaining nineteen were Presbyterians, each with a liberal education and outlook. Three of these trustees came from New York and three from Pennsylvania, the remainder from New Jersey. Within this group were representatives of both the Puritan English and the Scotch-Irish Calvinists.

Something of the zeal and determination which actuated the evangelicals of the Log College group and those closely associated with them, causing them to join, under the second charter, in the founding of Princeton, so that there might be educated under evangelical leadership young clergymen who would not be punished for their evangelicalism favoring revival standards and methods, may be seen in the fairly well established fact that it was the expulsion of David Brainerd from Yale which was a contributing factor in forcing the evangelicals to join in the founding of Princeton. To make plain just what we mean, we quote at length from President John Maclean's *History of the College of New Jersey.* He wrote:

It has been said that the College owes its origin to the expulsion of David Brainerd, the celebrated missionary, from Yale College, and to the refusal of the President and Trustees to admit him to the first degree in the Arts at the same time with members of his class. The following extract is taken from Dr. D. D. Field's *Genealogy of the Brainerd Family*, page 265:

"It is clear enough that the Reverend Jonathan Edwards was not satisfied with the refusal of a degree to David Brainerd by the Faculty and Trustees of Yale College, after all his readiness to confess his faults, and to confess them openly and fully. Others in New England sympathized with him, and others at a distance. Among the former were the Rev. Moses Dickinson, pastor of the church in Norwalk, Connecticut; among the latter, the Rev. Jonathan Dickinson, pastor of the church in Newark, who pleaded for Brainerd before the authorities of Yale College in behalf of the Society for Propagation of Christian Knowledge in Foreign Parts, which had appointed him their missionary.

"And now I will state a fact that may not be known to the very many that will read this book. I once heard the Hon. John Dickinson, Chief Judge of the Middlesex County Court, Connecticut, and son of the Rev. Mr. Dickinson, of Norwalk, say that the establishment of Princeton College was owing to the sympathy felt for David Brainerd, because the authorities of Yale College would not give him his degree, and that the plan of the College was drawn in his father's house."

Charles W. Shields, one-time professor at Princeton, writing on the subject "The Origin of Princeton University," and evaluating the service of Governor Jonathan Belcher, chairman of the board of trustees under the second charter, pointed out that he secularized (in the best sense), liberalized, and nationalized the college, features which have characterized Princeton University throughout its more than two centuries of life. It was the first truly inter-Colonial, interdenominational educational institution for higher learning, and as such wrought a great service in giving the colonies under the Continental Congress an added sense of unity as its alumni assumed positions of leadership.

Vital religion declined during the Revolutionary generation, partly under the impact of the so-called liberal ideas coming out of revolutionary France and English Deism and partly as a consequence of the disturbed political and social conditions of the time. Free thought and infidelity, if one is to believe the contemporary accounts, permeated the colleges, and, generally speaking, the religious forces of the new nation were on the defensive. Consequently it was during these years that the first colleges under secular control were established in North Carolina, in Georgia, in Tennessee, and in Vermont. Efforts were also made during these years to secure state control of several of the older colleges and for a time Dartmouth, Pennsylvania, and Columbia were actually taken over by the states in which they were located and they became temporarily state institutions, while Harvard, Yale, and William and Mary had state representatives in their controlling bodies.

Other Factors Leading to the Founding
of Church Colleges

Four factors were mainly responsible for checking the trend toward the secularization of higher education in the new nation at the turn of the century and for the beginning of the great college founding era. These four factors were, first, the writing of the great principle of the separation of church and state into the fundamental law of the land; the second was the Dartmouth College decision of the Supreme Court in the year 1819 which guaranteed to privately owned and denominationally controlled colleges the right to carry on independently of state control; the third factor was the impact made upon the religious forces of the nation by the Second Great Awakening, which began in 1786 and continued for nearly a generation; and fourth, the challenge to the religious and moral leadership of the nation made by the vast movement of population into the trans-Allegheny west, which by 1860 had added twenty-one new states to the original thirteen.

Principle of Separation of Church and State

In nine of the thirteen colonies there were established churches. In the five Southern colonies, together with the three counties surrounding New York City, the Church of England was the established church. In the three New England colonies, Massachusetts, Connecticut, and New Hampshire, Congregationalism was established by law. Only in the three Quaker colonies, New Jersey, Pennsylvania, and Delaware, and the Baptist colony of Rhode Island were there no church establishments. It is a significant fact that by the opening of the War for Independence the Presbyterians had become the dominant religious body in the Middle Colonies, the colonies in which there were no established churches. In fact the Presbyterians were more numerous in these colonies than all other religious bodies combined, and as a consequence it was there that the Presbyterians opened their first schools. It was there that the Log College movement had its beginning and there that the College of New Jersey opened its doors in 1746.

Following independence the Anglican establishments, more or less, automatically disappeared under the impact of the Revolutionary ideas, except in Virginia, where after ten years of agitation, disestablishment was accomplished by the passage of Jefferson's Act for the Establishment of Religious Freedom in Virginia in 1786. In New England disestablishment of Congregationalism came more than a generation later. As a consequence the post-revolutionary colleges founded in New England were all Congregational institutions—Williams College opened in 1783, Bowdoin College in 1784, Middlebury College in 1800, and Amherst in 1825. On the other hand the disestablishment of the Anglican Church in the Southern states led immediately to the founding of two Presbyterian colleges in Virginia—Hampden-Sydney in 1776 and Washington, with certain academy antecedents, now Washington and Lee, in 1749. Thus the writing of the principle of separation of church and state into the fundamental law of the land ended the exclusive right of the former established church colleges and cleared the way for the opening of colleges of the former dissenting bodies. In Connecticut, for instance, where Yale College had a monopoly on higher education since its establishment in 1701, when Congregationalism was disestablished in 1818, the Episcopalians opened Trinity College at Hartford in 1823 and the Methodists established Wesleyan University at Middletown in 1831. The creedal similarity between the Congregationalists and the Presbyterians, and the rapprochement between them created by the Plan of Union of 1801, were responsible for the failure of the Presbyterians to establish any New England colleges.

DARTMOUTH COLLEGE CASE

A second legal factor which further paved the way for the founding of church colleges throughout the nation was that formulated by the Supreme Court of the United States in the famous Dartmouth College case. This is one of the most far-reaching of the many important decisions of John Marshall. As has been noted above, Dartmouth College for a time was taken over by the state of New Hampshire and placed under the control of the state authorities. This high-handed action was resisted by the Congregational trustees of the college who brought suit in the courts to regain control. The case finally reaching the Supreme Court of the United States, the Court ordered the return of the college to its founders, the Congregationalists of New Hampshire. The decision was based on the principle that the original charter of the college, granted by the English crown, was a contract which could not be revoked without the consent of both parties to it. Previous to this decision there was no guarantee that private colleges might not be subject to state interference; thus this decision was an event of major importance in American educational history. It secured to the trustees of privately established and endowed colleges the right to conduct such institutions, choose presidents and faculties, and determine the curriculum without fear of political interference. Thus the way was now fully opened, legally, for the multiplication of church colleges, not only in the older sections of the nation, but even more significant, in the newer states in process of formation as population pushed westward.

SECOND GREAT AWAKENING

A third factor which furnished a major incentive for college founding by the churches was the Second Great Awakening, which came after more than a generation of moral and religious decline. This great religious reawakening had two distinct phases. The first, or eastern, phase centered largely in the Congregational and Presbyterian colleges along the eastern seaboard, and in its beginning was largely a student movement. Its earliest manifestations occurred in the two little Virginia Presbyterian colleges, Hampden-Sydney and Washington, where some thirty or more students professed conversion, most of whom entered the Presbyterian ministry.[2] Thus was created a band of young men "consecrated to the Church," not a few of whom later furnished a college-trained leadership for Presbyterianism west of the mountains, particularly in Kentucky and Tennessee.

What took place at Yale College under the leadership of President Timothy Dwight from 1797 to 1817 represents another phase of the second awakening. When Dwight came to the presidency of Yale College, to use Lyman Beecher's phrase, the college "was a hot-bed of infidelity"; when he died twenty years later there were but few students who were not deeply "pious," and the college had become one of the most active centers in the new nation for the training of young men for every kind of Christian service. We are told that he abandoned the traditional metaphysical type of preaching, with its emphasis upon dogma, which was often so tedious as to be useless, and centered his appeal "to the heart and conscience," and he always succeeded in "moving his hearers intellectually and emotionally." [3]

The College of New Jersey was another revival center. Two Princeton graduates, Samuel Blair Smith and Samuel Doak, who were members of the first faculties of what were to become Hampden-Sydney and Washington colleges, were both flaming revivalists. Thomas Craighead, Hezekiah Balch, Samuel Carrick, Philip Lindsley, David Rice, and John McMillan were all college founders west of the Alleghenies, and the products of the College of New Jersey.

Not only were these young men school founders in the trans-Allegheny West, they were also revivalists, and the beginning of the second, or western, phase of the Second Awakening was largely due to their activity in the early west. James McGready, who was the most important single figure in the opening phase of the western revival and the father of the camp meeting, attended Joseph Smith's Academy in western Pennsylvania and studied theology under John McMillan. John Lyle, one of the Presbyterian preachers in attendance at the Cane Ridge camp meeting in Bourbon County, Kentucky, in August, 1801, perhaps the largest meeting of the kind ever held in the West, and who later became a leading opponent of overemotionalized revivalism, was educated for the ministry at Princeton. Thus the eastern phase of the Second Awakening furnished the principal leadership in the Presbyterian phase of the western revival.[4]

Here is an appropriate place to call attention to the historic relationship between revivalism and the founding of schools and colleges in the United States. As already noted, five of the nine colleges established during the Colonial period were the direct or indirect product of the Colonial Awakenings. And the same set of influences which produced these eighteenth century colleges were responsible for the great college-founding era in the region between the Alleghenies and the Mississippi. Just as the older colleges had become the centers of a deep and fervid religious life, so the newer colleges on the advancing frontier became revival centers.[5]

THE CHALLENGE OF THE FRONTIER

Nothing in the history of the United States exerted such a challenge to the religious forces of the nation as did the vast movement of population into the great unoccupied areas over the Alleghenies during the first forty years of the last century. By 1830 the trans-Allegheny states had an aggregate population of 3,600,000, equaling the total population of the new nation at the time of Independence. Unlike their forefathers who had settled along the Atlantic seaboard, this western migration was not motivated by religion but almost solely by economic advantage. The great mass of the early settlers, who were steadily moving westward, were too poor to acquire more than eighty acres, the minimum amount of land that could be purchased, while not a few were entirely without financial resources and became mere squatters, known as preemptors, who moved ahead of the surveys. There were doubtless not a few educated and well qualified young men and women among those rushing westward, but these were far outnumbered by the "rude-minded and ignorant masses," by "luckless and impoverished families," fleeing westward from economic disaster. It is true that the frontier produced many admirable qualities which are both commendable in themselves and important from the standpoint of the development of the American character. Self-reliance, courage, the spirit of freedom and adventure, stanch and rugged individualism, and the democratic spirit were all nourished in the West. But all of these fine qualities would have gone for naught had not the seeds of moral, spiritual, and cultural life been planted in the far-flung rising communities of the West. The danger inherent in migration in lowering standards, both moral and cultural, was forcibly pointed out by Horace Bushnell in an address before the American Home Missionary Society in 1847 entitled "Barbarism the First Danger."

On every American frontier, life was crude, and ignorance and lawlessness were everywhere in evidence. The great majority of the people were indifferent to the prevailing conditions and accepted them as a matter of course. But fortunately for the future of the nation, the religious forces rose to meet the challenge and "gathered strength as they laid plans to meet the spiritual destitution of the new frontier," and by the end of the first generation of the last century the forces of irreligion were checked on all fronts and organized religion gained a dominance over American life that went largely unchallenged until the opening of the Civil War. De Tocqueville, that keen observer of American life, after a visit to the United States in 1831, stated:

There is no country in the whole world in which the Christian religion retains a greater influence over the souls of men than in America.

By regulating domestic life it regulates the state. Religion is the foremost of the institutions of the country.

The churches which made the largest contributions to the spiritual and cultural reformation of the trans-Allegheny frontier were the Presbyterians and the Congregationalists working together under the Plan of Union of 1801, together with the Baptists and the Methodists. Each of these bodies made its own distinctive contribution to the spiritual conquest of the early West and each developed its own methods and its own type of ministry. It was the combined efforts of the farmer-preacher Baptist ministry, of the Methodist circuit rider, together with the schoolmaster ministry of the frontier Presbyterians which wrought the transformation.

By the year 1850 the membership of each of the four most successful frontier religious bodies, was, in round numbers, as follows: the Methodists led with 1,324,000; the Baptists came next with 815,000; the Presbyterians were third with 525,000; while the Congregationalists, who had stood first in membership at the end of the Colonial period, now came fourth with 192,000. In other words those religious bodies that found the most effective way of following population west became the largest if not the most significant frontier religious bodies. The Methodists and Baptists had far outdistanced the Presbyterians and Congregationalists in gaining numbers. Neither the Baptists nor the Methodists had a trained ministry, and both made large use of lay leadership. The Methodist circuit riders in their preaching laid stress upon religion as an experience; its primary purpose was not to instruct but to sound the alarm, to call men to repentance. Basically the early Methodist circuit rider had but one sermon, which came largely out of his own experience, and it dealt with life rather than with ideas.

The frontier Baptist farmer-preacher stressed the simplicity of the gospel, which he insisted was so clearly set forth in Scripture that it did not require an education either to understand it, to apply it, or proclaim it. The Baptist farmer-preacher came along with the pioneers, for like the others he too was looking for land as well as for souls. He was not sent out by any overhead authority, but was self-propelled, for like the early Quakers, the gospel was as a hammer and anvil in him, driving him forth to proclaim it. He was also self-supporting and not until the formation of the Baptist Board of Home Missions in 1832 was there an overhead agency to superintend Baptist work in the West.

In sharp contrast to the ministry and methods of the Baptists and the Methodists was the emphasis upon an educated ministry among the Presbyterians. Theodore Roosevelt, in his *Winning of the West*, has stated that the Presbyterian Irish were America's first frontiersmen and that the Presbyterian Church in America in its early years was essentially a frontier church. The Methodists considered the gaining of knowledge a good thing, but the saving of souls a better one; the Presbyterians proceeded on the assumption that gaining knowledge was essential for the saving of souls. The Presbyterian emphasis upon an educated ministry was brought from North Ireland and Scotland, and it was a requirement of Presbyterian law that all candidates for the ministry must have a diploma of a Bachelor or Master of Arts from some college or university, or at least testimonials of having gone through a regular course of learning. And these standards were maintained to an astonishing degree on the American frontier by the establishment of schools and colleges on the edge of settlement.

The Presbyterians were responsible, as we have already noted, for sending to the frontier the first body of college-trained men, and in the very nature of the case, the vast need all about them, as well as the necessity of increasing their meager means of livelihood, naturally led the college-trained Presbyterian minister to open a school. The historic importance of William Tennent's Log College at Neshaminy, Pennsylvania, was not alone due to the fact that it was precursor of Princeton University, but also because it was the seed which eventually produced a large crop of other Log

Colleges over the mountains. Thus Samuel Blair, a graduate of Tennent's Log College, established a similar institution at Fagg's Manor in Chester County, Pennsylvania. From the Fagg's Manor school came Samuel Davies, later to become the fourth president of Princeton, as well as John Rodgers, James Finley, and Robert Smith, all of whom became educational and religious leaders of distinction. Another Log College was that at Nottingham on the Maryland border, the most famous of whose graduates was Dr. Benjamin Rush, the best known physician of his time as well as an influential Presbyterian layman who had a part in founding Dickinson College. Pequea in Lancaster County, Pennsylvania, was another of the famous Log Colleges, where John McMillan went to complete his theological studies under Robert Smith, after his graduation from Princeton. The Log Colleges above were the originals which furnished the pattern for a whole series of such schools on successive frontiers.

The Presbyterian educational influence on the Pennsylvania frontier has but recently been admirably portrayed by Dwight R. Guthrie in his *John McMillan: The Apostle of Presbyterianism in the West, 1752–1833.*[6] Washington and Jefferson colleges will serve to illustrate how full-fledged colleges grew out of Log Colleges established by the earliest Presbyterian preachers in southwestern Pennsylvania. John McMillan and Thaddeus Dodd were the first settled Presbyterian ministers on the Pennsylvania frontier, and both established schools at about the same time. Dodd's school was opened at Washington in 1787; McMillan's was opened in Canonsburg in 1791, only fourteen miles away. The Washington school was chartered as Washington College in 1806; the Canonsburg school was chartered as Jefferson College in 1802. Fifty years of college warfare waged in good Presbyterian fashion finally ended with the merging of the two institutions as Washington and Jefferson College in 1865. The present University of Pittsburgh also had Presbyterian origins. Chartered as Pittsburgh Academy in 1787, its incorporators were five Presbyterian ministers, four of them graduates of Princeton and the fifth educated in Scotland; associated with them were fourteen laymen. In 1819 the Pittsburgh Academy was reincorporated as the University of Pittsburgh, its charter providing that there were to be no religious tests applied either to faculty or to students.[7]

The educational history of Kentucky and Tennessee likewise opens with schools founded by Presbyterian preachers. Hezekiah Balch, Samuel Carrick, Philip Lindsley, and Thomas Craighead, early Presbyterian preacher pioneers in Tennessee, all had a hand in establishing schools. In 1794 Carrick's school was chartered as Blount College with Carrick as first president; the same year Balch became the first president of Greenville College. Philip Lindsley accepted the presidency of Cumberland College in Nashville in 1824 and exercised a major influence in making Nashville one of the chief early cultural and educational centers in the South. The educational history of Kentucky begins with a school opened in the home of Father David Rice near Danville. In 1793 Transylvania Seminary was chartered and was granted twenty thousand acres of land by Virginia with David Rice as the first president of the board of trustees. The struggle of the Kentucky Presbyterians to keep control of Transylvania, later to become Transylvania University, has been skillfully told by M. H. Sonne in his *Liberal Kentucky, 1780–1828*.[8] When the Presbyterians finally lost control of Transylvania, they established Centre College at Danville in 1819.

North of the Ohio where the Presbyterian and Congregational streams of influence came together, a number of colleges were established by the two bodies jointly. These jointly established institutions might well be termed "Presbygational" colleges. Ten such institutions were established before 1860—among them Illinois College, Beloit, Knox, Rockford, Ripon and Grinnell. Of these colleges only one, Illinois College, is now associated with the Presbyterians.

The Covenanters and the present United Presbyterians, who began their organized activity in America at about the turn of the century, were also active college founders. Before 1860, five colleges under their auspices had been opened—Muskingum at Concord, Ohio, in 1837; Erskine in South Carolina in 1839, and Geneva in Pennsylvania in 1848; Westminster in Pennsylvania in 1852; and Monmouth in Illinois in 1857. The Cumberland Presbyterians, who separated from the parent body in 1810 as a result of a controversy over revival methods, founded three colleges before 1860, Cumberland, Waynesburg, and Bethel.

In 1831 Dr. John P. Durbin, the editor of the Methodist weekly periodical the *Christian Advocate*, which had the largest circulation of any weekly paper in America at the time, stated that "of all the colleges in the United States they [the Presbyterians] have possession of a large majority." The facts that have been presented above will show that this statement is approximately correct. By that time the Presbyterians had opened seventeen permanent colleges, the Congregationalists seven, the Episcopalians five, the Baptists four, while the Methodists had succeeded in establishing only two, though three earlier attempts had all proved failures. The years between 1800 and 1860 were the most active period in college founding in the history of the nation. By the latter date the Presbyterians listed forty-nine permanent colleges; the Methodists thirty-four; the Baptists twenty-five; the Congregationalists twenty-one; the Catholics fourteen; and the Episcopalians eleven. Nine other religious bodies had founded twenty-six colleges, making a grand total of 180 denominational colleges in the United States by the opening of the Civil War.[9]

The wide distribution of the Ulster-Scotch immigration in the eighteenth century was basically responsible for making the Presbyterian Church a national rather than a sectional body. At the opening of the War for Independence there were at least five hundred distinct Ulster-Scotch communities in the colonies, located largely in the back country from the province of Maine on the north to Georgia on the south. A recent estimate has placed the number of Ulster-Scots who came to America in the eighteenth century at 385,000, the largest immigration group of the entire Co-

EDUCATIONAL FOUNDERS

ohn McMillan

William Graham

Philip Lindsley

saac Ketler

John Holt Rice

Robert Dollar

L. H. Severance

Charles C. Beatty

Cyrus H. McCormick

PREACHERS

Jonathan Edwards

Lyman Beecher

Moses Drury Hoge

William S. Plumer

PREACHERS

Henry Sloane Coffin

Henry van D

Albert Barnes

Hugh T. Kerr

George A. Butt

lonial period. This wide distribution of the Presbyterian Irish meant that the Presbyterian college movement was national in scope. By the Civil War, forty-three Presbyterian colleges had been founded in fifteen states east of the Mississippi, and five colleges in five states west of the Mississippi.[10] Pennsylvania led with a total of ten Presbyterian colleges, two of which eventually became Methodist institutions; Tennessee, New York, and Illinois had five each; Wisconsin had four, while Indiana, Ohio, Kentucky, and Virginia had two each. Eleven states—New Jersey, Michigan, North Carolina, South Carolina, Georgia, and Mississippi, east of the Mississippi, and Missouri, Iowa, Texas, Oregon, and California, west of the Father of Waters, had one each.

MOTIVES IN COLLEGE FOUNDING

The principal motive in the founding of Presbyterian colleges before the Civil War was to provide an educated ministry for the church. Colleges were considered a necessity to the church, since to the colleges the church looked for their future ministers and guides. The later college founders would have agreed with Cotton Mather, who, in speaking of the founding of Harvard College, stated that "our fathers saw that without a College to train an able and learned ministry, the church in New England must have been less than a business of one age, and soon have come to nothing." These early pioneer colleges, however, were not intended solely for the training of ministers, but that was their great design. At that time the church furnished not only religious leadership, but the minister was also looked upon as the principal cultural leader in society, and took a prominent part in the social, political, and intellectual interests of his day. The following statements of the purpose of early Presbyterian college founders bear out the above generalizations: "The ultimate purpose of the founders of Washington and Jefferson colleges was to fit some of them [sons of pioneers] to become ministers and missionaries." "At first the great and ultimate object of the founder [of Hanover College] was the education of young men for the gospel ministry." Wabash College "was founded in response to the painful destitution of educated leaders . . . the great and leading object [for the founding of Davidson College] shall be the education of young men for the gospel ministry."

A glance at the proportion of ministers among the graduates of Presbyterian colleges during their earlier years will further indicate the purpose of their founders. Of the first sixty-five graduates of Wabash College, forty-five, or more than two-thirds, devoted themselves to the ministry. Of the first ninety-two students who graduated from Hanover College, forty-seven entered the ministry. At Hampden-Sydney College in Virginia, up to as late as 1916, 50 per cent of all graduates entered the gospel ministry. As late as 1928, almost 40 per cent of the graduates of Monmouth College became ministers. A study of the graduates of a group of American colleges made in 1855 showed that of forty thousand graduates, one of every four had entered the ministry.[11]

A factor of importance in the founding of colleges west of the Alleghenies was the growing conviction that the older colleges in the East could not meet the demand for ministers in the rising new communities on the advancing frontier. In an address before the Society for the Promotion of Christian and Theological Education in the West in 1848 are these words:

Western colleges are hereafter to be the chief sources of a Western ministry. The ministers sent from the East to the West are not one twenty-fifth of the number which are immediately needed. . . . We at the West shall never be completely supplied from Eastern Churches. Western colleges as sources of supply are wholly indispensable.[12]

By-Products

Not only did the Presbyterians set the pattern for establishing denominational colleges, particularly in Trans-Appalachia, but the part they played in the founding of the first state colleges and

universities in the newer states, west of the Alleghenies, is significant. The part taken by Kentucky Presbyterians in the founding of
Transylvania University in Lexington, Kentucky, the first institution in the West which had state support, has already been noted.
Blount College, founded by Samuel Carrick in East Tennessee,[13]
was chartered as East Tennessee College in 1807 and became a
state college; it later developed into the University of Tennessee.[14]
From its opening in 1818, Miami University at Oxford, Ohio, was
carried on almost exclusively under Presbyterian influence, and for
sixty years its presidents, without exception, were Presbyterian
ministers. In its early years, Ohio University at Athens, Ohio, was
carried on under Presbyterian and Congregational leadership. In
1830 Mississippi College was opened as a state institution, but in
1840 it was taken over by the Presbyterians.[15]

The early years of what is now Indiana University furnish an
especially relevant illustration of the part played by Presbyterians
in the founding of a state institution. Indiana State Seminary was
chartered in 1820 under a federal land grant. In 1828 it was raised
to collegiate rank and became Indiana College under two boards,
a board of trustees and a board of visitors, both of which were self-
perpetuating and both dominated by Presbyterians. This situation
led to protests from the other religious bodies and was an important
factor in the establishment of both the first Baptist and Methodist
colleges in the state—Franklin College and Indiana-Asbury University, now Depauw.

In 1832, in a petition to the State Legislature of Indiana, the
Indiana Methodist Conference called attention to the fact that
literature belonged to no one denomination and insisted that no
one group "should be allowed to possess the keys that unlock her
treasures." They noted that there were 24,000 Methodists in Indiana and only 4,000 Presbyterians, yet the Methodists had no influence at the State College and doubtless there was a live sus-
picion also that the Methodist boys attending the state college—
if any—were in danger of being Calvinized. The presentation of

such memorials aroused a storm of protest among those in control of the college who accused the Methodists of trying to capture the college for their own purposes. In the course of the debate in the state legislature one of the Presbyterian members, Samuel Bigger, later to be elected governor of the state, remarked that "there was not a Methodist in America with sufficient learning to fill a professor's chair if it were offered him." It was stated that this remark was the cause of Bigger's defeat when he ran for reelection in 1844, and that Methodist revenge accomplished it.[16]

Thus one of the important by-products of Presbyterian dominance in the great college movement of the first half of the last century, was the competition it aroused among the other religious bodies, which led them to follow the Presbyterian example.

THE BEGINNING OF THEOLOGICAL SCHOOLS

The rise of special training schools for ministers, as distinct from liberal arts colleges, was a post-revolutionary phenomenon and was due to four principal factors. The first was the shutting off of the Old World supply owing to the winning of independence. This caused such foreign-language churches as the Dutch Reformed to open their first Seminary at New Brunswick, New Jersey, in 1784. A second cause was the drying up of the supply from the older colleges such as Yale and Princeton, which for the first time began to turn out more lawyers than preachers.[17] A third factor was the increased demand for ministers because of the great revivals which swept the country at the beginning of the nineteenth century, which led to the establishment of numerous new churches, particularly in the new West. A fourth cause was the inadequacy of private theological instruction. There was scarcely a Presbyterian minister in the early West who at one time or another did not have in his household a young man training for the ministry.[18] Of the first twenty-eight members of the Erie Presbytery, twenty-two of them had received their theological instruction under John Mc-

Millan, and during his long ministry some one hundred young men had come under his instruction. It was partly due to the lack of adequately prepared ministers in the West that Presbyterianism suffered two serious Western schisms. Such was the background which led to the demand for seminaries in the West.

But before we tell the story of how the General Assembly assumed the sponsorship and helped in the further organization of formal institutions devoted wholly to the training of ministers in the regions west of the Allegheny Mountains, we pause to state that in the year 1812 the Theological Seminary at Princeton, New Jersey, was founded by General Assembly action. This institution was wholly a new school without any closely related antecedents. It was located next to the campus of Princeton College but was not a part of the college. From its beginning, and throughout all its history since, this seminary has helped in the training of a great company of Christian leaders who have served not merely within Presbyterianism, but in other denominations in all parts of the world. In the year 1818 Auburn Theological Seminary was founded at Auburn, New York. In recent years it has been combined in close association with the Union Theological Seminary hard by Columbia University in New York City.

The action of the General Assembly in 1825 sets forth the purpose of the Presbyterian Church in sponsoring a seminary for the West:

The General Assembly taking into consideration the numerous and rapidly increasing population of that part of the United States . . . situated in the great valley of the Mississippi, and believing that the interests of the Presbyterian Church require it, and that the Redeemer's kingdom will thereby be promoted, do resolve that it is expedient to establish a Theological Seminary in the West, under the supervision of the General Assembly.[19]

Thus it was decided that the General Assembly should "establish" the Seminary in the West. An appointed committee, after considering the inducements offered by numerous communities, finally chose the town of Allegheny as the site. This was a logical choice. A study of the records of the Synods of Ohio and Pittsburgh indicates that the continuation, under Dr. John McMillan, of the theological department of Jefferson College was the guiding desire. Allegheny, at the "Gateway of the West," was made to be the successor of Canonsburg, where John McMillan taught.[20] There was general dissatisfaction expressed by the Synods of Kentucky, Indiana, and Ohio with this choice of site. They refused to co-operate with the new Seminary at Allegheny. Their principal objection was that its location was too far east to serve adequately the great and expanding new sections of the country. This opposition was led by the able and indefatigable Joshua L. Wilson of the First Church, Cincinnati, which opposition eventually gave rise to other Presbyterian Seminaries in the West. Out of this movement eventually came Lane Theological Seminary at Walnut Hills, Cincinnati, and McCormick Theological Seminary in Chicago. These two have now joined their resources in the present McCormick Theological Seminary in Chicago.[21]

Of these several western Presbyterian Seminaries, Lane Seminary at Cincinnati had a very colorful early history. It was named after two wealthy Baptist merchants, the Lane brothers of Boston who were convinced, as a result of their observations on a trip to New Orleans, that a school for the training of ministers was sorely needed in the West and had resolved to found such an institution. Failing to secure Baptist cooperation, they presented their offer to the Presbyterians, who at once accepted. Lyman Beecher was called from the pastorate of a church in Boston to the presidency of the New Lane Seminary. Arthur Tappan, the wealthy New York merchant and philanthropist, agreed to found a professorship in the seminary provided Lyman Beecher should be the incumbent. As the records tell us, Lyman Beecher came to Lane Seminary and there he remained until the end of his active life. There Henry Ward Beecher received his theological training and it was there that Harriet Beecher (Stowe) got her inspiration and much of her information for the writing of *Uncle Tom's Cabin*. There Lyman Beecher prepared his *Plea for the West,* which was a dramatic appeal for education in the West. He contended that to secure the civil and religious liberty of the West, education was the only hope. It could not be done with prayers and supplications, nor by tracts, Bibles, or missions alone, but by establishing "permanent, powerful and moral institutions" in the West; for he insisted that the great body of Western teachers must be educated in the West. The Western minister must be eloquent and talented as well as pious, for nowhere on earth is "talent, and learning, and argument and eloquence" more "highly appreciated, and regarded." Education, both intellectual and religious, "is the point on which turns our destiny," and the "period of our probation is short." And I think it can be said without fear of overstatement that the Presbyterians stood first among those who answered that educational challenge.[22]

CHAPTER VII

Service in Founding
and Preserving the Nation

THE spirit of democracy has been cradled in religion—and with confidence we can say that the spirit of American democracy has been nourished at all times by the spiritual zeal of devout members of the Church of Christ. Although it is a cherished principle of our country that there shall be no union between church and state, the facts of history prove decisively that Christian creed and ideology have contributed very much to the founding of this "land of the free and the home of the brave." Righteousness not only exalts a nation; it can literally give it birth. Within the narrow confines of this chapter, we shall seek to examine the evidence in this field —namely, that the founding of America was in large part a direct consequence and outgrowth of the doctrine and practical principles of Calvinism prevalent in most of early American church life. In setting forth this thesis we shall be as objective as possible, divorcing ourselves from denominational pride. Calvinism was the theology of the Congregationalists, the Anglicans, the Baptists, the Reformed, the Presbyterians, and others. Presbyterian polity, as opposed to the English prelacy, was the preferred scheme of government of most of the Puritans, of the Reformed, and of the Presbyterians. This type of polity, in Colonial days, was in especially bitter opposition to the British government.

When James I of England made the emphatic declaration, "No bishop, no king," he announced a fundamental concept cherished by monarchy and hierarchy, but one decidedly at variance with the representative ideas of free men. Long had the Scotch and Ulster-Scotch settlers of America stood in violent opposition to any such "divine right" idea of government; and it seemed inevitable that this clash in ideological thinking would result in the clash of arms. The American Revolution came as the inevitable consequence of men of conviction, acting not from impulse but from principle, who, despite the cost, were willing to follow their principles through to their legitimate and honorable conclusions. History is molded and made by men with crystallized ideas. The embodiment of Christian ideas is seen in the rupture of the Medieval Church to give us the Protestant Reformation, and likewise in the revolt of the British colonies in the New World to give us the American Republic. Anglo-Saxon democracy may be considered the product of a severe theological system with an accompanying democratic polity rising from the New Testament, and flourishing in Switzerland, Scotland, and Holland. This fact was recognized by the German historian Leopold von Ranke, when he said, "John Calvin was the virtual founder of America." [1] There is an undeniable connection between Calvinistic doctrine and constitutional government. Bancroft further supports this position by saying, "He who will not respect the memory of John Calvin knows nothing of American liberty"; and again, "Insofar as religion had any place in the War of the Revolution, that place must belong to Presbyterianism."

CALVINISM'S INFLUENCE

Now back of every great movement lie its proponents. Who were the people that fostered rebellion and revolution in the New World? Who spoke openly against the tyrannies and indignities they experienced? Who stepped forward with ready hearts, willing to die in resistance to the injustices meted out to them in the wilderness of this remote continent? They were mostly as follows: Huguenots from France; men of the Reformed faith, presbyterians of the Continent, who had come from the Palatinate, Switzerland, and the Low Countries; Lutherans who had fled the agonies of the Thirty Years' War; German Baptists who had endured persecution; and Presbyterians and Seceders (ultra-Presbyterians) from Scotland and Ulster; also the Puritan Congregationalists from England. Practically all of these were Calvinists, or neo-Calvinists, and a large number of them were Ulster-Scotch Presbyterians. C. A. Hanna points out clearly their commensurate numbers prior to the Revolution, by saying:

> No other one people, of uniform race, customs, religion and political principles, made such extensive settlements in so many of the thirteen American colonies as did the Scotch and the Ulster-Scots. . . . They alone, of the various races in America, were present in sufficient numbers in all of the colonies to make their influence count.[2]

On the eve of the hostilities with the British, there were approximately seventy communities of these democratically minded people in New England; thirty to forty in New York; fifty to sixty in New Jersey; more than one hundred and thirty in Pennsylvania; more than one hundred in Virginia, Maryland and East Tennessee; about fifty in North Carolina; and about seventy in South Carolina and Georgia—all in all an estimated five hundred of these communities scattered throughout the thirteen original colonies. Of the three million Americans at the time of the War, some nine hundred thousand were Scotch and Ulster-Scotch; with other Calvinist groups, such as German, Dutch, and Puritan English numbering approximately one million more. Wherever the sons of Scotia and Ulster settled, their somewhat clannish ways of life gave a homogeneity and a solidarity to a community. Theirs was a uniformity in worship, in church polity, in morality and discipline, in integrity and spiritual heritage. They were openly rebellious against everything that smacked of injustice; and if they had faults a lack of patriotism or courage was not among them. In the light of all these factors we can hardly overestimate the decisive influence of these hardy people in the cause of freedom from the British crown.[3]

The essence of Presbyterianism in realms of polity is union of interest, confederation, and solidarity of mind and spirit. What is of vital interest to one group becomes of interest to other groups, remote though they may be. Hence, what New York Presbyterians were doing was of some concern to the Carolina Presbyterians, and vice versa. Family ties were strong, as in the clan, but these ties went beyond the local home to the local church, to the community, and to the wider area roundabout. Slowly there was fostered the idea of a Colonial unit, a place apart from the mother country overseas, and which faced its own multiple problems at home in the spirit of a progressive responsibility, which indicated growing maturity. The civil and political child was now reaching beyond early adolescence, and was soon destined to be on its own.

Presbyterians have always held three fundamental principles of life: (1) the supremacy of God; (2) the right of the laity; and (3) the solidarity of humankind. All of these tenets combine to a concept of life which may be called the divine right of man set over against the obnoxious and iniquitous idea of the divine right of kings. In essence these people expressed in deed if not in word, as Kipling sang:

> The people, Lord, the people,
> Not thrones, not crowns, but men.

Such emphases, day by day—God's sovereignty, individual responsibility, and social equality—became the molding factors in Colonial living. They were as good seed upon fertile soil to bear fruit in a Christian democracy. Elton Trueblood, in *The Predicament of Modern Man*, puts it like this:

Because every man, whatever his color, his knowledge, his station, or his financial standing, is a child of God, there is a profound level at which men are equal. They are not equal in that they have the same powers, but they are equal in that each is equally accountable. The upshot of this doctrine, perhaps the most disturbing that the human mind can hold, is that king and commoner are equally subject to the moral law. The result of this is bound to be democracy or something very much like it.[4]

At this point we might well ask what are some of the *ecclesiastical factors* which led to the so-called "Presbyterian rebellion"? Briefly, they are these:

FACTORS PROMOTING INDEPENDENCE

1. The injustices of the royal governors in showing favoritism of the crown to the Anglican (Episcopal) Church. The American Revolution was in reality a *religious* as well as a political revolution. New settlers had arrived in America, fleeing the system of prelacy in England; and as liberty-loving dissenters they had a natural apprehension toward the aggressive practices of an established state church. They felt that they, and their fathers before them, had been oppressed by a church in league with the crown, and in seeking a thoroughgoing freedom here in the New World they naturally feared the encroachments on their religious rights of the Church of England, which appeared to work hand in glove with the Tory governors. The situation did not present a great issue in some of the colonies—for example, New Jersey, Pennsylvania, Maryland and North Carolina—but it became an intense struggle in New York, Virginia, and South Carolina. Nor was it just a clergymen's battle, for the learned laity of dissenting groups joined in the clamor for freedom. In particular was this true in the case of the "Presbyterian lawyers" of New York. William Smith, William Livingston, and John Morin Scott are names that became famous in this newspaper controversy over the rights of Protestant denominations not conforming to the Church of England.[5] The impact of their logic against any ecclesiastical favoritism was a vital factor of effective influence in their day—and one which may well be remembered in ours!

In this ecclesiastical struggle it was natural that the church-establishment partisans would be regarded as sympathetic to the British crown, and those who dissented would be regarded as opposed to the crown. Thus, at the outset, a purely ecclesiastical matter came to have untold political significance, and the zeal of the Ulster-Scotch Presbyterians came to be interpreted as a kind of civil or political rebellion. The children of Scotia and of Ulster could not sanction or abide the European concept that the state and the church were so inextricably bound together that the unity, peace, and prosperity and even existence of the state depended on the church's complete accord with, and obedience to, the decrees and regulations of the state; and any departure therefrom smacked of disloyalty that was closely akin to treason. So thoroughly was the Presbyterian population identified with the pro-revolutionary party that Horace Walpole felt justified in a speech before the House of Commons with a sneering remark concerning a "Presbyterian revolution." Forceful and familiar are his words: "There is no good crying about the matter. America has run off with a Presbyterian parson, and that is the end of it." He referred, of course, to the Reverend Dr. John Witherspoon, president of the College of New Jersey (now Princeton University), and the only clergyman of the thirteen colonies to sign the Declaration of Independence.

The opposition to the Established Church resulted in some necessity for united endeavor on the part of those opposed to the Parliamentary taxation for the benefit of the Episcopalian cause. Dissenting groups held united meetings. Beginning in 1766, and annually thereafter for the succeeding nine years, a General Convention, composed of the General Association (Congregational) of Connecticut and the Presbyterian Synod of New York and Philadelphia, met to secure united action for the prevention of the establishment of Anglican episcopacy anywhere in the colonies. There was the conviction that this episcopacy was linked with a government of tyranny and therefore must not be permitted to be set up in America.[6]

Some have felt that the first suggestion of a real union of the colonies may have come in a sermon given by Dr. Mayhew of Boston at an interdenominational communion in his church. The next day he met Samuel Adams, and said, "We have just had a communion of the Churches; now let us have a union of the States!" [7] Was this not infinitely more than just a clever play on words? It would indicate that sentiments toward a possible union of colonies, early and immature though they were, were beginning to crystallize.

2. Another ecclesiastical factor in the tense situation leading to the founding of our nation—and one often overlooked—was that of the "Election Day" sermons. As early as 1633 these special sermons were begun by appointment from the governor and the Council of the Massachusetts Bay Colony for the edification of men (and women) who were idle in and around the polls. Designed to deal with spiritual things, they began to deal annually with politico-religious affairs—much the same as a modern Thanksgiving sermon today. So effective were they in molding public opinion that Edmund Burke in 1775 said that they "contributed no mean part toward the growth of the untractable spirit of the colonies." [8] Not only the presbyterian Puritan but also the Presbyterian clergy preached such thought-molding discourses. John Quincy Adams is reported to have called the American Revolution the ripe fruitage of this old custom.

We cannot overlook the fact that the union of the two Presbyterian synods, that of Philadelphia (Old Side) and of New York (New Side) in May 22, 1758, in Philadelphia, is a factor of importance in establishing strength and unity of working spirit among the democratically minded constituents of our land. United hands and hearts worked for a common goal, and the cause of freedom of worship, with the freedom of conscience, went forward apace. Educational institutions began to flourish, and, ten years after the union Dr. John Witherspoon was inaugurated as president of the College of New Jersey (August 17, 1768). The reality of an organic union in this period spoke to the populace of a new solidarity. Presbyterianism (including cognate groups) now could muster twenty-six presbyteries and classes, and 247 ministers. The impact of their united voices proved effective. Here was factual unity amidst diversity that can never be ignored, and particularly so in that day when something of a united front was the need of the hour. Without this strength and this unity of purpose the first voice of Presbyterians to dissolve all connection with Great Britain could never have been raised.

All of the foregoing has been said by way of preparation to the actual struggle itself. When hostilities broke into armed rebellion, the Presbyterians were in the vanguard of action. It was a struggle not intended at first to win separation from the crown, but to gain recognition of political and religious rights. When George Washington took command of the army in Cambridge in 1775, he did not hesitate to say, "I abhor the idea of independence." In 1775 the General Synod issued a pastoral letter indicating the prevailing spirit within the Presbyterian fold at that particular hour. One sentence reads: "Be careful to maintain the union which at present subsists through all the Colonies."

THE MECKLENBURG RESOLVES

This union was certainly not an organic union, but one of spirit and motivation. Yet contemporary with this letter there came from the sandhills of North Carolina the famous Mecklenburg Resolves [9] of May 31, 1775, passed at a meeting of citizens, all of Ulster-Scotch and Scotch Presbyterian persuasion in Charlotte. They drew up twenty resolves. One of these declared that "all laws and commissions confirmed or derived from the authority of the King or Parliament are annulled and vacated, and the former civil constitution of these colonies for the present wholly suspended." Another stated that the provincial congress of each colony under the direction of the Continental Congress was "invested with all legislative and executive powers within their respective Provinces and that no other legislative or executive power does or can exist at this time in any of these colonies." They went on to state by resolution that any person refusing to obey the Resolves was to be deemed "an enemy to his country."

We have in these resolutions and actions a forerunner of those found in the Declaration of Independence of 1776 together with the determined dedication of life to make such attitudes to lead to the founding of this nation.

PRESBYTERIANS IN THE REVOLUTIONARY WAR

At any rate the die was cast. The awful holocaust was on, and the blood of valiant men began to flow at Lexington and throughout the colonies. The Presbyterian participation in the struggle was proportionately outstanding. The ministers preached and prayed, and in many instances organized companies and regiments and led them into battle. Virtually there were no pacifists among them, no Tories in their ranks. In Pennsylvania there came such strength from the churches of the Ulster Scotch that supplied to the colonial resistance a persistence without which the cause would have collapsed.[10] Six of the early trustees of the First Presbyterian Church, Pittsburgh, became officers in Washington's army: James O'Hara, Ebenezer Denny, Isaac Craig, Stephen Bayard, John Gibson, and John Wilkins. The famous Pennsylvania Line was so gallant in action that upon it hung the success of the cause of independence—and its overwhelmingly Ulster-Scotch constituents caused "Light-Horse Harry" Lee to call it "the Line of Ireland." In the opinion of one Tory, Joseph Galloway, a member of the First Continental Congress, the underlying cause of the Revolution was the activity, solidarity, and influence of the Presbyterians. Speaking before a Committee of Parliament in 1779, he declared that about half of the American army was made up of Irish.[11]

Similar situations prevailed throughout the colonies where the patriotic fervor of Presbyterians had become legend. Pastor Caldwell, who permitted the hymn and psalm books in his church at Springfield, New Jersey (Elizabethtown), to be used as gun and cannon wadding during a battle with the British, will forever live in fame for his terse statement to the colonial troops as he carried the volumes from the sanctuary: "Give 'em Watts, boys; give 'em Watts." The same story is true of the Southland. The Carolinas were generous with Presbyterian blood. Smyth gives us a definite account of their loyalty when he says:

> The battles of the "Cowpens," of "King's Mountain,"—and also the severe skirmish known as "Huck's Defeat," are among the most celebrated in this State as giving a turning-point to the contest of the Revolution. General Morgan, who commanded at the Cowpens, was a Presbyterian elder, and lived and died in the communion of the church. General Pickens, who made all the arrangements for the battle, was also a Presbyterian elder and nearly all under their command were Presbyterians. In the battle of King's Mountain, Colonel Campbell, Colonel James Williams (who fell in action), Colonel Cleveland, Colonel Shelby and Colonel Sevier, were all Presbyterian elders; and the body of their troops were collected from Presbyterian settlements. At Huck's Defeat, in York, Colonel Bratton and Major Dickson were both elders in the Presbyterian Church. Major Samuel Morrow, who was with Colonel Sumpter in four engagements, and at King's Mountain, Blackstock, and other battles, and whose home was in the army 'till the termination of hostilities, was for about fifty years a ruling elder in the Presbyterian Church. . . . It may also be mentioned in this connection that Marion, Huger and other distinguished men of Revolutionary memory, were of Huguenot—that is, of Presbyterian descent.[12]
>
> When Cornwallis was driven back to ultimate retreat and surrender at Yorktown, all of the colonels of the Colonial Army but one were Presbyterian elders. More than one half of all the soldiers and officers of the American Army during the Revolution, were Presbyterians.[13]

The whole number of Presbyterians who performed notable service in helping the nation to be born and then to be established would very probably be very impressive could it be ascertained. It may be misleading to single out specific individuals, lest the impression be given that it is held that all Presbyterians of Revolutionary and Reconstruction days were as praiseworthy as these. We do not forget that though the Presbyterian clergy of western Pennsylvania counseled and urged against the rebellion with reference to alleged unjust excise taxes on whisky—the affair known as the Whisky Insurrection—there were many of the laity who were guilty, who acquitted themselves disgracefully. We also know that in the expedition against the British and against supposedly British sympathizers in the late eighteenth century in order to clear the western frontier of disloyal persons, there were Presbyterians who had a part in the murder of the peace-loving Moravian Indians of Gnadenhutten and other parts of eastern Ohio. Having acknowledged in small part certain Presbyterian sins, it may be allowable to record the names of such outstanding Presbyterian patriots as Richard Stockton, Elias Boudinot, Benjamin Rush, and John Witherspoon. Brief biographies of these men appear elsewhere in this volume. The sentiments expressed by Witherspoon in connection with his signing the Declaration of Independence as recorded on the pedestal of his monument erected by the federal government on a plot in front of the National Presbyterian Church in Washington, D.C., indicate the spirit which actuated the multitude of his fellow Presbyterians as they served and fought that the colonies might become the United States of America. I quote:

FOR MY OWN PART, OF PROPERTY I
HAVE SOME, OF REPUTATION MORE.
THAT REPUTATION IS STAKED,
THAT PROPERTY IS PLEDGED ON
THE ISSUE OF THE CONTEST; AND
ALTHOUGH THE GRAY HAIRS MUST
SOON DESCEND INTO THE SEPUL-
CHRE, I WOULD INFINITELY RATHER
THAT THEY DESCEND THITHER BY
THE HAND OF THE EXECUTIONER THAN
DESERT AT THIS CRISIS THE
SACRED CAUSE OF MY COUNTRY.

Needless to say, the Presbyterian churches suffered severely during the progress of the war. They were taken and turned into stables, commissaries, or shelters for the wounded. The church at Newtown had its steeple sawed off; the church at Mount Holly was burned; Princeton fell to Hessian soldiers and the church was denuded of its pews and galleries; Chestnut Level was left standing with its four walls open without a roof, while men fought for freedom. Churches in New York were possessed by the enemy and preaching forbidden. Dr. Gillett says that more than fifty churches and places of worship—a high proportion in the under-churched colonies—were utterly destroyed.

When victory came to the Colonial cause a new problem arose. So marked was the respect for our Presbyterian Church during the struggle that it was feared by some groups that it might become here what it was in Scotland, the Established Church. It is forever to the credit of the General Synod that it alleviated this alarm by passing a deliverance in 1783 setting forth with clarity its firm views on religious freedom: [14]

It having been represented to Synod, that the Presbyterian Church suffers greatly in the opinion of other denominations, from an apprehension that they hold intolerant principles, the Synod do solemnly and publickly declare, that they ever have, and still do renounce and abhor the principles of intolerance; and we do believe that every member of civil society ought to be protected in the full and free exercise of their religion.[15]

THE PRESERVATION OF THE NATION

But what part has Presbyterianism played in the preservation of our land? Has it contributed to America's continuing stream of history, and has it been a worthy tributary as the waters of the nation have flowed through the deserts of the past? Yes! By all means, yes! The zeal of the founding fathers in bringing a nation into being was not lost upon the travail of its birth, but has continued to the present. Briefly we will suggest a few factors that have helped to preserve us a nation.

1. The constitutional structure of the land. Primarily two choices confronted the land—one was a confederation of independent states; the other that of a constitutional republic. What ensued in our great Constitution was really a happy combination of the best features in presbyterianism and congregationalism. There can be little doubt that presbyterianism by its solidarity and polity in the kirk, a principle of government to be incorporated also into the American Protestant Episcopal Church, influenced the framers of the Constitution when they were seeking to erect a national organization, to the end that we have as our heritage a constitutional republic.[16] Limitations of powers are herein stated, making for a system of some elasticity, where rigidity or the pure letter of the law would prove a handicap.

2. Another factor arose from the discipline of the Presbyterian Church—and this exercised only by the voice of the people. This proved to be a marked influence toward observance of law and order. The Presbyterians were unique in this, for the Congregational churches had no connection with one another. Episcopalians were held suspect for some continued loyalty to the crown; the Dutch Reformed did not become an efficient and independent organization until 1771; the German Reformed not until 1793; the Baptists were separate units; the Methodists then were little known; and the Quakers were non-combatant and non-resistant. Hence the discipline of the church, a factor that stood well for the discipline of the Colonial army, was a much needed bond of union between large elements in population of a formerly divided people. Here an ecclesiastical republic was setting the example of law and order to a newly born political republic. It fell to the Presbyterian Church's lot, as the only fully developed federal republican institution, to lead the way. Hence our land owes much to that oldest of American republics, the Presbyterian Kirk.

SOCIOLOGICAL AND SPIRITUAL SERVICE

Surely in the fields of social and moral welfare, in developing a consciousness in society of the rights of others in the spirit of Christian brotherhood, this church has done much to preserve the nation. Harriet Beecher Stowe, Jane Addams, Charles Stelzle, John J. Eagan, and John McDowell are but five of a long list of those who have led in this field. In the fields of education, temperance, race equality, suffrage for women, slum clearance, child labor, better working conditions, pensions and social security, hospital and medical aid, and so on, this denomination has been in the vanguard, molding a better democracy where man is considerate of his fellow man.

But by far the greatest contribution has been made in the realm of the spirit. No nation can endure except it rest upon spiritual foundations—for happy and lasting is that people whose god is the Lord. The Presbyterians have endeavored to exalt the living Christ, to teach God's ways of brotherhood and peace, to foster and encourage true character and spiritual integrity in the citizenry of our land. They are not unique in this respect, for other denominations are doing the same—adhering to the motto "In God we trust."

This factor cannot well be measured. Who knows the strength given Abraham Lincoln during the dark days of the Civil War, as he attended the prayer meetings held in the Presbyterian Church under Dr. Phineas Gurley, and who can measure the impact of the Spirit of God then in preserving our nation? In gratitude our thought goes back to God-fearing founders from abroad, to Washington on his knees at Valley Forge, to Lincoln seeking power at the throne of grace, to Wilson seeking to unite humanity in a common brotherhood, to Eisenhower and his inaugural prayer.

Having mentioned two Presidents who were or are Presbyterian, Woodrow Wilson and Dwight Eisenhower, it is well to add that this communion has also given Andrew Jackson, James Buchanan,

Grover Cleveland, and Benjamin Harrison to serve in this exalted position. Presidents Abraham Lincoln, Franklin Pierce, and James K. Polk worshiped regularly in Presbyterian churches while in Washington, D.C. So also did General Ulysses S. Grant.

Through the years of this nation's history, Presbyterians have furnished their fair share of leadership in the affairs of government, of commerce, and of letters. Just to mention a few: Hugh Henry Brackenridge, Andrew Carnegie, John Milton Hay, Thomas Hart Benton, Henry L. Stimson, Will Hayes, George Westinghouse, Matthias William Baldwin, Robert Field Stockton, Louis Henry Severance, Henry John Heinz, Robert Dollar, Andrew Mellon, Henry van Dyke, Helen Gould, Cleveland Dodge, Morris K. Jesup, and Mildred McAfee Horton.

In the present federal government four members of the President's Cabinet, two associate justices of the Supreme Court, thirteen senators, forty-seven representatives, and the head of the Federal Bureau of Investigation are all active Presbyterians. After making due allowance for the deficiencies and weaknesses of any or all of these, it still remains true that here is a church which stands fast with other Christian groups in serving the nation.

In the field of letters, many of the greater of the clergy and laity produced or are now producing hymns, essays, historical treatises, poems, Biblical exegesis, sermons, scientific treatises, studies in education, in moral welfare and physical and mental health that perform a service far beyond that which the uninformed can evaluate. Some of these are listed in the Who's Who of this volume.

This entire chapter may seem to savor of denominational chauvinism. It certainly has not been written with any such spirit. The greater portion of American Presbyterianism is humbly, yet very persistently and vigorously, seeking to further visible unity among all the evangelical catholic churches. And it pursues this course not as a superior to inferiors but as a humble portion of the whole of Christ's visible body here on earth, very much in need of God's forgiving and strengthening grace.

CHAPTER VIII

Missionary Expansion at Home

In 1956 Presbyterians in the United States will celebrate the two hundred and fiftieth anniversary of organized Presbyterianism in this country. The time is therefore opportune for us to review these two hundred and fifty years of Presbyterian history in the United States and take note of some of those factors which contributed to the growth of this denomination from its humble beginnings in 1706 to its position as one of the major religious bodies of the nation.

Presbyterians were numbered among the very first of the English colonists to come to the New World. Some of the Puritans who settled at Jamestown, beginning in 1611, held Presbyterian convictions regarding liturgy and polity. Cotton Mather states that about four thousand Presbyterians arrived in New England before 1640, practically all of whom were from England. Beginning about 1660, Presbyterians from Scotland and North Ireland began to arrive. The pressure of Episcopalianism in the South and of Congregationalism in the North in New England impelled many Presbyterians to migrate to the Middle Colonies of Maryland, Pennsylvania, and New Jersey. The first presbytery, organized in 1705 or 1706 under the leadership of the Reverend Francis Makemie, was a union of the two streams of Presbyterianism which had come to this country—the English and the Scottish or the Ulster-Scots.

The seedbed of that first presbytery was in the vicinity of Philadelphia, in the heart of the Middle Colonies.

For nearly one hundred years, or from 1706 to 1802, the Presbyterian Church expanded by migration and the continuance of church loyalties, but very little by evangelization. Oppressive laws in North Ireland stimulated large numbers to migrate to America, beginning about 1710. Within ten years this had become a steady stream averaging from three to six thousand emigrants a year.[1] Some of these brought their ministers with them. Estimates regarding the number of Ulster-Scots who arrived in this country up to the time of the Revolutionary War vary from two hundred thousand to two hundred and fifty thousand. Whereas both the English and the German nationals were much divided in their religious affiliations, the Scotch and the Ulster-Scots were nearly, if not entirely, 100 per cent Presbyterian. Not only were they the most uniform in their religious beliefs, but they were also the most widely diffused throughout the thirteen colonies of any national group. Both of these facts contributed much to the expansion of the church during the eighteenth century.

EARLY MISSIONARY TECHNIQUES

An examination of the official records of the first presbytery and of the subsequent higher judicatories for the years 1706 to 1802, when the Standing Committee of Missions was organized, show that although the church had no central committee on missions with an over-all plan, yet there was a continuing recognition of a missionary obligation to evangelize the unchurched. Oftentimes the expression of this responsibility was sporadic and weak. The number of ministers was few; congregations were scattered; the people, still struggling with frontier conditions, were poor; distances were so vast when one traveled on horseback or on foot; and the techniques used to spread the gospel were often ineffective. Yet, in spite of these inherent difficulties, the church grew. While most of the growth no doubt came as a result of the accretions of Presbyterians from Scotland and North Ireland, some came as the reward of definite missionary effort.

The first Presbytery, which Makemie described as a meeting of ministers, adopted the following overture at its second recorded meeting held on March 26, 1707: "That every minister of the Presbytery supply neighboring desolate places where a minister is wanting, and opportunity of doing good offers." Here at the very beginning of organized Presbyterianism in the colonies is evidence of a sense of responsibility for evangelism which moved the ministers to go forth into "the desolate places." Only three of the charter members of the Presbytery were pastors; the other four were missionaries. Within ten years the number of ministers increased to seventeen. By 1716 the work had so expanded that the Presbytery voted to form a synod.

The first meeting of the Synod was held in 1717, and again that inherent missionary obligation asserted itself when the Synod voted to establish a "fund for pious uses." This was an omnibus fund to cover administrative expenses, the care of indigent widows and orphans of deceased ministers, and missionary benevolences. The repeated exhortations of the Synod to its churches to take annual collections for the fund served as reminders of the continuing responsibility to preach the gospel in "neighboring desolate places."

In 1722 Synod appointed three ministers to visit "Protestant dissenting families" in Virginia "and preach four Sabbaths to them, between this and the next Synod." This marked the beginning of the custom, which continued down to the establishment of the Standing Committee of Missions in 1802, of sending out ministers for one or more months each year to serve as itinerant missionaries. A study of the Minutes of the Synod of New York and Philadelphia shows that pastors of large churches were appointed to make these circuit-riding trips on the frontier as well as those from smaller churches. In 1774, for instance, the Presbytery of New York made application for men "to supply the many large and growing vacancies on the northern frontier of that province." In response to this request, Synod appointed Dr. John Rodgers, pastor of the First Presbyterian Church of New York; Dr. David Caldwell, pastor of the First Church of Elizabeth; and Dr. Alexander Mc-Whorter, of the First Church of Newark, "to supply each of them eight Sabbaths among those vacancies, and endeavor as far as their time will admit, to form them into regular congregations." [2] By such methods the Gospel was preached and churches were formed on the frontier by busy Presbyterian ministers who took a temporary leave of absence from their own parishes in order to respond to the call.

The expanding church plus the difficulties and expenses of travel made a reorganization necessary immediately following the Revolutionary War. A General Assembly with subordinate synods became a necessity. The Assembly met for the first time in 1789 with Dr. John Witherspoon as the convening officer and Dr. John Rodgers, the first Moderator. According to the records of the last meeting of the Synod, the Presbyterian Church then had 177 ministers, 11 probationers, 419 congregations, of which 215 were supplied with ministers and 204 were vacant. No statistics of communicant members were given. Dr. H. D. Jenkins, in an article in the *Interior* for May 21, 1891, stated that the church had about nine thousand members when the Assembly was organized.

Membership statistics, evidently incomplete, appear for the first time in the *Minutes of the General Assembly* for 1807, when 558 churches were reported, with a total membership of 17,871, or an average of thirty per church. If the same average prevailed in 1789 when the first General Assembly was held, then the 419 congregations reported had a combined membership of 12,570. If we strike a compromise between the estimate made by Dr. Jenkins and this latter total, we arrive at the figure of 10,785. In seventy-five years the Presbyterian Church had grown from seven ministers to 177, from one presbytery to a General Assembly with four synods and sixteen presbyteries, from three churches connected with the original presbytery to 419 congregations, and from an unknown small number of members to about eleven thousand. In addition there was an unknown number in the various branches of the covenanting bodies and in the independent judicatories in New England and in the Carolinas. However, the total membership of all bodies calling themselves Presbyterians could hardly have been more than thirteen or fourteen thousand.

EIGHTEENTH CENTURY CHURCH MEMBERSHIP PROPORTIONATELY LOW

These statistics are somewhat disturbing to Presbyterians. If from 200,000 to 250,000 Scotch and Ulster-Scots migrated to the colonies before the Revolutionary War, and if only 14,000 were members of any branch of the Presbyterian Church in 1789, then what happened to the others? What about the descendants of these immigrants? The question becomes more acute when we remember that there were English, French, Dutch, and other nationalities represented in the Presbyterian constituency, as well as those from Scotland and North Ireland. Undoubtedly some Presbyterians joined other denominations. Robert Baird, in his *Religion in America*, commenting on conditions within the first half of the nineteenth century, but bringing out a point which might have applied earlier, claimed that "the widely-extended denominations of the Methodists and Baptists are, to a great extent, composed of persons whose ancestors belonged to Presbyterian churches." [3] Even after making such allowances, the conclusion seems inevitable: the great majority of the Scotch and Ulster-Scots who migrated to this country in the eighteenth century and their immediate descendants were either uninterested in the church or unable to keep up their affiliations.

Kenneth Scott Latourette, in his recent *A History of Christianity*,

states that through most of the eighteenth century the large majority of the white population of the United States had no church
connection. According to Latourette:

> It has been estimated, although this may be excessively low, that in
> 1750 only about five out of a hundred were members of churches. The
> overwhelming proportion of the settlers came to the colonies for eco-
> nomic or social rather than religious motives. They were mostly from
> the underprivileged and by migrating to the New World sought to bet-
> ter their financial or their social standing.[4]

Latourette estimates that in 1800 only 6%₁₀ per cent of the
population had a church affiliation.[5] If this estimate be correct,
then out of a population of 5,308,483 only about 356,000 were
church members. W. W. Sweet, in his *The Story of Religion in
America,* states:

> The most recent attempt to enumerate the religious organizations in
> the American colonies at the close of the colonial period gives the total
> at three thousand and fifteen, with about one thousand each for New
> England, the middle colonies and the South.[6]

If Sweet's figures are correct, then Latourette's estimate of 6%₁₀
per cent of the country's population being church members in
1800 seems unduly large, for each of the three thousand churches
would have had to have three to four times the average membership claimed by the Presbyterian churches in 1807 to total 356,000.
All of the Protestant denominations experienced a spiritual blight
during the closing decades of the eighteenth century. The experience of the Presbyterians was common to others. L. W. Bacon, in
his *A History of American Christianity,* wrote: "The closing years
of the eighteenth century show the lowest low-water mark of the
lowest ebb-tide of spiritual life in the history of the American
church."[7]

Not only was the membership of the Presbyterian Church dis-
appointingly low in 1800; it had also by that year fallen behind

the Methodists and the Baptists in its total membership. The two strongest denominations in the country at the close of the Colonial period were the Congregationalists and the Presbyterians. According to Dr. Sweet, in his *The American Churches: An Interpretation,* the Presbyterian Church was the largest and the most influential of all the "left-wing" denominations—that is, churches having among other characteristics that of voluntary support—at the time of the close of the Revolutionary War. Coming after the Presbyterians were the Baptists and the Methodists. According to Dr. Sweet, no religious body in the United States was then "so well fitted to meet the new problems of independent America as the Presbyterians." [8] No denomination had so enthusiastically supported the War, and none was so uniformly distributed throughout the thirteen colonies and so well represented on the frontier.

The Presbyterian General Assembly of 1800 reported 449 churches, 219 of which had no pastors. This means that in the eleven-year period following the organization of the General Assembly, the denomination had increased by only thirty congregations. If the average of thirty members per congregation held true in 1800, as it did in 1807, then the denomination had only 13,470 members in 1800. [9] Notwithstanding the favored position the Presbyterians held at the time of the Revolutionary War, by 1800 this denomination had fallen to third place, numerically giving way both to the Methodists and to the Baptists. The Congregationalists fell to fourth place.

What was the cause of this numerical decline? Why did the Presbyterian Church fail to keep abreast with the Methodists and the Baptists in the expanding frontier? Was there something fundamentally wrong either with the doctrine or with the polity of the Presbyterians which made either unacceptable to the frontiersmen? Or was there some failure on the part of the church to use the right technique in its home missionary work?

THE PERIOD OF EXPERIMENTATION AND GROWTH, 1802–1837

The westward flow of population over the Allegheny Mountains began after the Revolutionary War. The federal census of 1790 indicated that about two hundred thousand, or 5 per cent, of the total population of four million had crossed the mountains. After 1800 this westward migration was greatly accelerated. During the first four decades of the nineteenth century, the population of the United States increased about 320 per cent, growing from 5,304,-483 in 1800 to 17,069,453 in 1840. During one six-year period, 1816–1821 inclusive, six new states were added to the Union.

The expanding population and the spreading frontier presented a tremendous challenge to all of the Protestant denominations. Literally, millions of people were on the move. New communities were springing up, all through the West, without the benefits of organized religion. Hundreds of communities and large areas of the country were without ministers or churches.

In 1802 the General Assembly created the Standing Committee of Missions. There were at least two good reasons which prompted this forward step. The old plan of having the Assembly direct the missionary activities of the church and of having each minister who served a term as an itinerant missionary report direct to the Assembly was time-consuming for the Assembly. During 1800–1801 sixteen Presbyterian ministers are known to have served for one or more months each on the frontier. This was 8 per cent of the total ministry of the church. Efficiency demanded that the administration of such activities be placed in the hands of a committee.

A second reason for the creation of the Standing Committee was the influence of what is called the Second Great Awakening, which began in the closing years of the eighteenth century. Out of the dark background of the spiritual depression which followed the Revolutionary War, a new stirring of religious life began to be felt throughout the nation, beginning with revivals on the frontier in Kentucky. Great camp meetings were held, beginning about 1779, in which Presbyterian ministers at first took a leading part. Paralleling the revivals in the West were new stirrings of religious life in the East. Dr. Gardiner Spring, in his *Personal Reminiscences*, states:

It was among the blessings of my childhood and youth to have heard much of those remarkable "outpourings" of the Holy Spirit which constituted the era of American Revivals. . . . From the time I entered College, in 1800, down to the year 1825, there was an uninterrupted series of these celestial visitations, spreading over different parts of the land. During the whole of these twenty-five years, there was not a month in which we could not point to some village, some city, some seminary of learning, and say: "Behold what God hath wrought!" [10]

The very appointment of a Standing Committee of Missions by the Assembly of 1802 is evidence that the leaders of the Presbyterian Church recognized the necessity of using new techniques to meet new opportunities. The appointment of this committee represented the first official action on the part of any of the Protestant churches of America to promote national missions at top denominational levels. In 1816 the committee evolved into a Board of Missions. Following the establishment of the Board of Foreign Missions in 1837, the Board of Missions became the Board of Domestic Missions. In 1870, as a result of the union of the Old and New schools, the Board of Home Missions was established, which in 1923 became a part of the Board of National Missions.

The Standing Committee of Missions was cautious about making any drastic changes in missionary techniques. The Reverend Gideon Blackburn was appointed the first missionary to the Indians, on May 31, 1803, and in all probability was the first missionary to receive an appointment for full-time service by the committee. The circuit-riding technique was continued. During the years 1802–1816, or up to the time of the organization of a Board of Missions, the Standing Committee sent out a total of 311 itinerant ministers as circuit riders, or an average of twenty-two a year. Most of these appointments were for two months. The shortness of the time, the shift of personnel, the vast distances to be covered by the slow means available, plus the absence of any strong follow-up plan, made this means of evangelism rather ineffective.

PLAN OF UNION OF 1801

Belonging to this period are several experiments in interdenominational cooperation which had both advantages and disadvantages for the Presbyterian Church. In 1801 the Presbyterians and the Congregationalists of Connecticut adopted a Plan of Union which was designed to promote cooperation between the two churches on the frontier. Later other Congregational associations of New England entered the agreement. The Plan called for ministers of either denomination to serve the members of both in the new communities arising in the West. Difference of opinion soon arose over the methods best adapted for the evangelization of the frontier. Many of the Congregational ministers favored a limited circuit and the subsidizing of a minister in a small parish, while the official Presbyterian opinion supported the old plan of sending an itinerant minister on a long trip through virgin country where he would not be able to visit any community more than once.

In defending its policy of the extended circuit, the Standing Committee stated to the General Assembly of 1811:

But while the Harvest is great, and the labourers are few, either a part of the Harvest must perish or the labourers must be left without instruction, or you Missionaries must continue to travel over wide tracts of country. On the whole, it appears best to occupy as large a Region, as may be practicable, until the increase of Missionaries, or the Settlement of Ministers in new Congregations, make it proper to alter the present plan. In the meantime, the few occasional sermons preached at each place will serve to keep alive a sense of Religion among the Inhabitants, and preserve them from falling into a State of Heathenism.[11]

After the Board of Missions was formed in 1816, the old ineffective plan of an extended circuit was abandoned. More attention was given to the techniques followed by the Congregationalists. The salary a small church was able to pay a minister was subsidized in order to provide a living salary and make possible the presence of a resident pastor.

A second major experiment which involved cooperation with the Congregational Church centered about the administration of missionary funds. In the same year that the General Assembly established the Standing Committee of Missions, 1802, the Synod of Pittsburgh formed the Western Missionary Society. The two bodies worked on fundamentally different principles. The Standing Committee assumed that participation in the missionary cause by churches or individuals was a voluntary matter. The Western Missionary Society believed that a Christian by virtue of his membership in the church was under obligation to spread the gospel. His membership in a church made him automatically a member of a missionary society.

THE WHOLE CHURCH BECOMING A MISSIONARY SOCIETY

Those holding that participation in the missionary work of the church was a matter of choice were more willing to join interdenominational societies than were those who believed that all members of the church were *ipso facto* members of a missionary society. Here was one of the main issues which precipitated the Old School-New School division of 1837. The Old School party, which was strong in the Pittsburgh area, consistently insisted upon denominational control of the administration of missionary funds, while the New School was willing to cooperate with such interdenominational bodies as the American Board of Commissioners for Foreign Missions and the American Home Missionary Society.

For about twenty years, 1817 to 1837, two schools of thought struggled for supremacy in the Presbyterian Church. In 1817, one year after the Board of Missions was formed, the General Assembly voted to unite with the Dutch Reformed and the Associate Reformed churches to form the United Foreign Missionary Society. This society merged in 1826 with the American Board with the approval of the General Assembly. This meant that the Presbyterian Church had given a semi-official approval to an independent benevolence agency over which the church had no control. Since the American Board had missions among the American Indians, its work involved missionary expansion in the homeland.

In 1831 the Western Missionary Society became the Western Foreign Missionary Society. It too sent missionaries to the American Indians. This society had the support of those who believed that Presbyterian benevolences should be under the direct and complete control of some official agency of the denomination. This issue came to a focus in the Assembly of 1837, at which time the Old School was in control. The Western Foreign Missionary Society became the Presbyterian Board of Foreign Missions. The Old School emphatically stated its position that all of its benevolence would be channeled through a church-controlled agency. The New School continued to support the American Board.

A similar story unfolds in regard to home missions. The United Domestic Missionary Society, formed in 1822 largely under Presbyterian auspices, became the American Home Missionary Society in 1826. The society included the Congregationalists and, like the American Board, was entirely self-governing. For about ten years the General Assembly gave a semi-official endorsement to the American Home Missionary Society even though this organization was doing much the same work as the Assembly's Board of Missions. The two agencies competed for the benevolences of the same churches. At the time of the 1837 split, the Old School party swung its full support to the Board of Missions, while the New School stayed with the American Home Missionary Society.

Thus these years, 1802–1837, were years of experimentation for the Presbyterian Church in the whole field of the administration of missionary funds and of interdenominational cooperation. A philosophy of missions was being slowly and somewhat painfully worked out in the field of experience.

All of the Protestant churches rode the crest of the wave during the first decades of the nineteenth century, including the Presbyterians. Assuming that the Presbyterian Church had a membership of 13,470 in 1800, we find that the percentage of its membership increase per decade for the first thirty years was about four times the percentage of population growth for the nation. The following statistics tell the story:

	PRESBYTERIAN MEMBERSHIP	PERCENTAGE INCREASE	POPULATION OF COUNTRY	PERCENTAGE INCREASE
1800	13,470		5,308,483	
1810	28,901	116%	7,239,881	36.4%
1820	72,096	149	9,638,453	33.1
1830	173,329	144	12,866,020	33.5

By 1837, on the eve of the disastrous division into Old and New schools, the church reported 2,140 ministers, 2,865 churches, and 226,557 members. There is no period of similar length in the history of the Presbyterian Church in our country when the rate of growth has been so rapid. A part of this growth resulted from the application of the Plan of Union. Dr. Frederick Kuhns, in a recent study of the subject, concludes that "not more than six hundred Congregational churches had ever placed themselves under the care of the General Assembly either before or after the schism of 1837 in the Presbyterian Church." [12] The polity of the Presbyterian denomination gave more cohesiveness and strength to the pioneer churches in isolated communities than did the Congregational. In 1852 the Congregational Church abrogated the Plan of Union. The greatest gain in Presbyterian membership during these first three or four decades of the nineteenth century came as a result of that new upsurge of spiritual power which swept the country and which is known as the Second Great Awakening.

WHY THE PRESBYTERIANS TRAILED THE METHODISTS AND BAPTISTS

And yet, in spite of all such favorable signs, the Presbyterian Church was not experiencing an increase comparable to that being received by the Methodists and the Baptists. Why did the Presbyterian Church fail to maintain its once-favored position on the frontiers of the West and the South? What was wrong with its methods of evangelism that caused the Presbyterian Church to lag so far behind its sister denominations?

Various answers have been given to these questions. W. W. Sweet, in his *Religion on the American Frontier*, advances the theory that "The Presbyterian frontier preacher tended to limit his activities to people of Presbyterian background and to Ulster-Scotch or Scotch communities," whereas the Methodists and the Baptist preachers had no similar limitations but went forth "to win people of all kinds to the Christian way of life." [13] The official records of the Presbyterian Church do not support such a theory. There were other national groups besides the Ulster-Scots and the Scotch who preferred Presbyterian polity, such as the Huguenots, the German Reformed, the Dutch Reformed, and the English. On the other side of Sweet's theory is the church historian of a century ago, Robert Baird, who, writing in his *Religion in America*, dwells on the idea that "the Presbyterian Church from the first, or nearly so, was composed of diverse elements, which could not be easily assimilated." [14] The reports of the itinerating missionaries sent out either by the General Assembly or by the Standing Committee of Missions show that all were eager to evangelize all who would listen regardless of national background or possible earlier religious affiliations.

This author wishes to emphasize two main reasons which explain the failure of the Presbyterian Church to realize the fullest possibilities of missionary expansion during the first thirty-seven years of the nineteenth century. The first was the unfortunate division of opinion within the denomination regarding the administration of missionary funds. Comment has always been made on this point. The spirit of contention which existed between the Old School and the New School in the years leading up to the division of 1837 did incalculable harm to the growth of the denomination.

The second main reason was the refusal or the inability of the Presbyterians to adapt their polity and traditions to the needs of the frontier. Presbyterian ministers took a leading part in the great camp meetings which began to be held on the western frontier about 1797. When such meetings developed unusual emotional excesses and certain objectionable physical phenomena such as the "jerks," trances, and speaking in tongues, the Presbyterians withdrew. However, other denominations stayed with this movement and profited thereby.

Both by polity and tradition the Presbyterians insisted upon an educated ministry. However, the demands of the frontier where hundreds of communities were without pastors were so insistent that other denominations, such as the Methodists and Baptists, ordained men with limited educational training and sent them out to ride circuits. Although the Presbyterians were willing to use the circuit system, they were unwilling to compromise their educational standards. They still insisted upon a full college and a full seminary training, and this took time. But the frontier could not wait.

An effort was made in Presbyterian circles to make an adjustment. The revival party in Cumberland Presbytery in western Kentucky and Tennessee asked for a lowering of educational standards in order to meet the pressing demands of the frontier. The official voice of the Presbyterian Church as expressed in the Synod of Kentucky and the General Assembly was an emphatic negative. This dissension led to the formation of an independent Cumberland Presbytery on February 4, 1810, and thus the Cumberland Presbyterian Church was born.

The Cumberland Church made adjustments to the needs of the frontier similar to those being made by the Methodists and Baptists. Men with little formal education but with a vital Christian experience were ordained and sent forth as missionaries. Many of these Cumberland preachers were self-supporting. The church spread rapidly toward the West, the Southwest, and the South. Within fifty-six years, or by 1866, the church had ninety-seven presbyteries, which means a growth of almost two presbyteries a year. After 1866 the rate of growth was slower as the frontier conditions gradually gave way to the settled communities. However, the effectiveness of the frontier techniques used by the Cumberland Church in its work of evangelization is seen in the fact that by 1906, on the eve of the union with the mother church, the Cumberland Church had 17 synods, 114 presbyteries, 1,514 ministers, 1,860 churches, and 185,212 members.

A striking parallel may be drawn between the history of the Presbyterian Church during the first ninety-six years of its organized existence, 1706 to 1802, and of the Cumberland Church during its ninety-six years, 1810 to 1906. Whereas the mother church in 1806 had, by a generous estimate, about five hundred churches and fifteen thousand members, the dissenting body a hundred years later during the same period of time had five times as many churches and twelve times as many members.

The Founding of Theological Seminaries and Colleges

The leaders of the Presbyterian Church were not unaware of the handicap under which they were working in keeping up the traditional educational standards. In 1805 Dr. Ashbel Green, chairman of the Standing Committee of Missions, submitted an overture to the General Assembly which stressed the importance and the need of getting more ministers. Everywhere the cry was being raised: "Give us ministers!" Green's overture precipitated a discussion of the whole question of theological education. In 1809 the Presbytery of Philadelphia, to which Green and several other members of the Standing Committee belonged, submitted an overture to the Assembly calling for the establishment of a theological seminary. This resulted in the founding of Princeton Theological Seminary in 1812. Ashbel Green, chairman of the Standing Committee of Missions, was the first president of the board of directors of the seminary. There is a vital link, therefore, between the missionary needs of the church and the establishment not only of the first but also of all our theological seminaries.

An interesting study could be made of the relationship of the missionary expansion of our church to the location of our theological seminaries. Statistics from the 1952 *Minutes of the General Assembly* indicate that our largest synods have within their bounds or adjacent thereto one or more of our larger theological seminaries: [15]

Synod	Membership	Seminaries
1. Pennsylvania	406,612	Princeton, Western
2. New York	284,362	Princeton, Auburn, Union
3. Ohio	202,222	Lane, Western
4. California	178,401	San Francisco
5. New Jersey	173,316	Princeton, Bloomfield
6. Illinois	170,000	McCormick, Dubuque

The total membership of these six synods is 1,414,913, or approximately 50 per cent of the total communicant roll of the entire denomination. Do not these figures prove that a vital connection exists between the proximity of the source of supply of trained ministers and the missionary expansion of the church?

In its westward march across the continent, the Presbyterian Church has ever been a college-building church.[16] We have insisted not only upon an educated ministry but also upon an educated laity. As a result of this policy, the Presbyterian Church has remained one of the most influential of all the Protestant denominations of the country. After the immediate needs of pioneer conditions were met, our sister denominations gradually accepted the higher educational standards for their ministry which have always been a part of our heritage. But, the fact remains, these other denominations were more adaptable to frontier conditions than were the Presbyterians, and as a result several of them had a greater numerical growth than did our church.

THE PERIOD OF DIVISION, 1837–1869

The United States in 1837 stood at the threshold of an era of unparalleled expansion. Between 1845 and 1867 eleven new states were admitted to the Union, and by 1870 nine territories were waiting to be promoted to statehood. Railroads were spinning their networks across the land. The first great overland emigration went out to Oregon in 1843, and in 1848 gold was discovered in California. The population of the country was greatly increased by emigration from abroad. In 1840 the population numbered 17,069,453, and in 1870, 38,558,371. During this thirty-year period, the population more than doubled.

The Presbyterian Church entered this golden era of expansion a divided church. Up to 1837 the Presbyterians, perhaps to a greater degree than any other denomination, could claim to be a national church, for they then had organized work in every state, with the possible exceptions of Maine and Rhode Island. Yet at this time of great opportunity, the disastrous split of 1837 divided the denomination into the Old and New schools, each of which claimed to be the successor of the 1837 General Assembly.

Disaster followed disaster. In 1858 the New School divided over the slavery issue, and in 1861 the Old School did the same. The two Southern branches united in 1861 to form a new denomination which continues today as the Presbyterian Church in the

United States. The two Northern branches united in 1869 to form the Presbyterian Church in the United States of America.

During the thirty-three year interval, 1837–1870, the two Northern branches of the church about doubled their strength. The rate of increase was approximately that of the nation:

	MINISTERS	CHURCHES	MEMBERS
1837	2,140	2,865	226,557
1870	4,238	4,526	446,561

Of course, it must be remembered that the Southern Presbyterian Church had drawn away many members. Otherwise the gain would have been much greater.

The New School did not grow as rapidly during this period of division as did the Old School, even though the latter lost far more to the South over the slavery issue than did the former. The New School was more stunned by the division than was the Old School, and consequently took a longer time to consolidate its forces; also, the New School found itself handicapped by differences of opinion with the Congregationalists over the administration of the funds of the American Home Mission Society. As a result the New School established its own agency to handle home mission funds in 1852. Thus by an interesting turn of events, the New School was forced to accept the same principle of denominational control of missionary funds which the Old School held. At the time of the reunion of 1869, this point, which had contributed so much to the division of 1837, was no longer a divisive issue.

To this period, 1837–1870, belong some of the most heroic tales of Presbyterian missionary endeavor to be found in our history. The Whitmans and the Spaldings, all four Presbyterians serving under the American Board, crossed the Rockies in 1836. Mrs. Whitman and Mrs. Spalding were the first white American women to cross the Continental Divide. The Whitman home at Waiilatpu and the Spalding home at Lapwai were the first white American homes in the Pacific Northwest. On August 18, 1838, the Whitmans and the Spaldings organized the First Presbyterian Church of Oregon, which was the first Protestant church to be founded on the Pacific Coast.

The first Protestant minister to settle in California after the discovery of gold in 1848 and to engage in full-time religious work was a New School Presbyterian—the Reverend Timothy Dwight Hunt, who went to California independent of any mission board. The first Protestant missionary to set foot on California soil after being commissioned and sent out by an Eastern missionary board was another New School Presbyterian—the Reverend Samuel H. Willey, an appointee of the American Home Missionary Society. Five out of the first six Protestant ministers to enter California after the discovery of gold were Presbyterians, and the first two Protestant churches to be organized in the state with resident ministers were Presbyterian. The Presbytery of San Francisco, erected September 21, 1849, was the first ecclesiastical organization to be organized on a regional basis west of the Rockies. Such evidences of Presbyterians being in the very front ranks of pioneer missionary endeavor can be repeated many times.

Among the Old School missionary heroes is Sheldon Jackson, who began his ministry with the Choctaw Indians in 1858. After working with this tribe for less than a year, Jackson transferred his activities to Minnesota and Wisconsin. Jackson was an individualist. He created his own promotional machinery and followed practices which would not be tolerated today by any well established missionary board. However, the techniques he used were most effective for his day. His vision of the importance of occupying strategic places in the growing West, especially along the sprawling railroads, was far in advance of that of the Board of Domestic Missions. He was more responsible than any other individual for the organization of the Woman's Home Missionary Society of the Presbyterian Church in 1878. Jackson saw the great possibilities of using women, and especially single women, as teachers. A great educational work followed, especially in the intermountain country where the Presbyterian schools and academies preceded public education.

Jackson was a firm believer in planting churches in strategic locations. In a day when there were few if any comity agreements with other denominations, ecclesiastical rivalries were strong. The first Protestant church to be established in a new community usually precluded the coming of another church—at least for several years. When the Union Pacific Railroad was creeping westward to join the Central Pacific in Utah, there was not, during the first half of 1869, a single Presbyterian Church between Omaha and Sacramento. Jackson saw an opportunity, and in July, 1869, organized ten new Presbyterian churches, several of which, including Cheyenne, Laramie, and Rawlins, Wyoming; and Grand Island and Fremont, Nebraska, were along the Union Pacific.

Jackson was sometimes overzealous in his ambition to place a Presbyterian church in a new community before other denominations got there, and occasionally opened himself to criticism from his contemporaries. The following items from the Minutes of the Presbytery of Montana, tell their own story:

Resolved, That the Presbytery of Montana in session at Helena, February 13–17, 1880, respectfully represents to the Board of Home Missions, that the Presbytery is strongly and unanimously opposed to having the Rev. Sheldon Jackson, D.D., Synodical Missionary of the Synod of Colorado, devote any part of his time or attention to working within the bounds of this Presbytery.

The Presbytery than gave specifications of its reasons, including the following:

In Missoula in 1872 Dr. Jackson organized a church of two members, "a freighter" named Cunningham, who was in Missoula for only one night, was induced to act the part of ruling elder for the occasion, was installed, departed from the town the next day and has never been in

Missoula since, except once last summer, when he remained in town over one Sabbath and spent the day unloading freight, not deigning to go near the Presbyterian church. The other member of Dr. Jackson's organization was a Methodist woman, who had a quarrel with her pastor. She had not the confidence or respect of the community. Of course the church died instantly. It was reorganized 1876.[17]

Jackson's zeal for establishing new churches outran his supply of men and money. The attrition rate was heavy. However, some of these pioneer churches lived, and remain today as strong units within the national body.

CONTINUED GROWTH, 1870–1952

The seventy-year period, 1870–1952, has been a time of great expansion both for the nation and the Presbyterian Church. During the years 1870–1920 the population of the country increased about 300 per cent and the membership of the Presbyterian Church about 400 per cent, growing from 446,561 to 1,803,592. The million mark was passed in 1900. Since 1920 the population of the country has increased to 150,697,361, or nearly 50 per cent in thirty years. During the same time the growth of the Presbyterian Church has been a little less then 40 per cent. In general both the population of the country and the membership of the Presbyterian Church have doubled during the past fifty years.

One factor is often forgotten in dealing with recent membership statistics, and that is the falling death rate. Although the Presbyterian Church now has twice as many members as were reported in 1900, yet this is partly because we have more old people. Life expectancy in 1900 was about forty-nine years. It is now sixty-eight, with an expectancy of seventy-one and a half for white females. About 8 per cent of the nation's population are people sixty-five years of age or older. The evangelistic index which shows the ratio of new members to the total membership has been steadily declining. If the ratio of increase of new members in effect in 1900 had been steadily maintained through this fifty-year period, the Presbyterian Church today would probably have several hundred thousand more members than it now has.

The Presbyterian Church has fewer churches than it had forty years ago, even though our membership has about doubled during that period. Back in 1912 we had 10,030 churches, whereas the last Minutes of the General Assembly give 8,636, a decline of 1,394. This means that the average size of our churches has increased from 135 in 1912 to 293 in 1952. It may be presumed that the larger church pays a better salary and conducts a more aggressive program. The traditional insistence of the Presbyterian Church on a well trained ministry finds itself in a far more congenial atmosphere in the present era of ever increasing congregations than in the pioneer period with the struggling frontier church.

In this process of eliminating the weak churches, whole presbyteries and at least one synod have lost their identity during this forty-year period. The Presbytery of San Joaquin, located in a rapidly growing area of California, reported seventy churches in 1915 but only fifty-one in 1952, a net loss of nineteen. However, the average membership of its churches for the same years increased from 84 to 244. In 1910 the Synod of Utah had twenty-eight churches in its three presbyteries. Now the Synod has been reduced to one presbytery with seventeen churches, of which six have no pastor. Similar illustrations could be given for other areas of the country. During the past five years when the membership of our denomination has greatly increased, the number of churches has remained about the same.

At least two factors explain this change. The coming of the automobile and good roads have revolutionized the life of the whole country. During the horse-and-buggy days, the radius of a church's parish might be the extent of an hour's drive, say six miles. With the automobile, that hour's drive shrinks to ten or fifteen minutes. Country churches are being closed while the urban and city churches increase in size.

A second reason is the decrease of the farm population. The introduction of modern machinery has cut down the need for farm workers. Parallel with this development has been the demand for more workers in the industrial centers. From 1900 to 1951, the farm population is reported to have declined by twenty-one million even though during the same period the population of the country has about doubled.

This reduction in the number of churches and the increase in the average size of churches has greatly affected the work of our Board of National Missions. Missionary money that once was needed to help keep a small church alive, perhaps in an over-churched community, is now available for more important projects in strategic areas. The day is gone when a new church can be organized with a handful of members and expect to get a subsidy from the board. More care is now being exercised in organizing and planting new churches, and more consideration is being given to comity agreements. All this is to the good.

The common assumption that people turn to the churches in times of depression can not be substantiated by statistics. The Presbyterian Church gained only 3,372 members in the decade beginning 1932, whereas in the ten-year period closing in 1952 the gain totaled 512,925. During the depression years the number of names placed on the suspended roll was larger than usual. However, during the same years the evangelistic index reached an all-time low, being but 3.2 in 1933, 3.3 in 1935, and 3.0 in 1938. Another factor which undoubtedly contributed to the failure of the denomination to grow during this decade was the theological unrest which resulted in a minor schism in 1936 when the Orthodox Presbyterian Church was formed.

World War II introduced a multitude of new factors which have greatly influenced our national life. Millions have been on the move. The uprooting of people always places a heavy strain upon institutional ties. The high degree of mobility has presented a new and tremendously important challenge to all of the Prot-

estant churches. The Presbyterian Church may take pride in the
degree of success it has achieved in meeting this challenge. The
following table gives a comparison of population increases in certain states for the decade beginning in 1940, as shown in the 1950
census, and the increase of Presbyterian membership in the same
states for the same period:

	PERCENTAGE POPU- LATION INCREASE 1940–1950	PERCENTAGE PRESBYTERIAN MEMBERSHIP INCREASE 1940–1950
Arizona	50.1	56.6
California	53.3	52.
Florida	46.1	71.
Oregon	39.6	36.7
Texas	20.2	14.6
Washington	37.	28.9

The rapid development of new communities has demanded a
new strategy in national missions work. A good example is to be
found in the Clairmont area in San Diego. There a community
large enough to house twenty thousand people was built in eighteen months. The Church Extension Board of Los Angeles Presbytery entered the field along with the builders. A site was
purchased and a building was erected which was dedicated in
December, 1953. In all probability it may be the only Protestant
church able to function in that community for some time to come
because of lack of other facilities. The new strategy calls for the
erection of a building and sometimes the guaranteed salary of a
pastor for a year before a church is organized and functioning.

Mention should be made of the development of freeways in our
major cities. These rivers of cement are seriously affecting the
church life of these cities as they divide the cities into irregular
geometric patterns which, from an airplane, remind an observer
of the mysterious so-called "canals" on the landscape of Mars.
These freeways can be crossed only at certain points. A new free-

way, when being built, cuts ruthlessly through old and well established parishes, making it difficult for church members to retain former connections. This is but one of the problems which confront Presbyterian leaders as they seek to follow the developments in the large cities today.

The Presbyterian Church is on the increase. Many of our long-range policies and traditions are bearing fruit. Our insistence upon an educated ministry and an educated laity has given us an envious stability. We have not lost our pioneer spirit and are as ready today to occupy new frontiers as in the days of Marcus Whitman and Sheldon Jackson. The church today is more willing to try new techniques in its missionary work than it was a century and a half ago. The area of the greatest challenge has shifted from the small frontier community to suburban developments taking place in the vicinity of large cities. Today the Presbyterian Church is giving more serious attention to the whole question of planting new churches in strategic places than ever before in its history.

If the rate of growth continues to be the same, then our church will have about three million members in 1958. And if by that time the union with our two sister churches is consummated, the total will be closer to four million.

This, then, is a brief review of the missionary expansion of the Presbyterian Church in the United States during the past two hundred and fifty years.

CHAPTER IX

Serving Overseas

THE history of American Presbyterianism serving overseas is challenging and, within the limits of this chapter, impossible. It is extensive. It has to do with the record of the global outreach of a great family of churches which has touched and is touching every continent and many of the islands of the seas. That outreach has been the means of transforming untold thousands of lives. It has helped to mold the changing patterns of some of the greatest nations and of several of the less numerous tribes and peoples. It has been made possible by thousands of missionaries, both men and women. It would not have begun or continued had it not been supported by millions in the churches from which the missionaries have gone. On the part of many that support has been casual and has entailed little or no inconvenience and but slight, if any, interest. But also for many it has involved an intelligent participation by study, continuing prayer, the sacrificial giving of money, and, for parents and families, as great and even greater sacrifice in surrendering those who have been dearest to them that the Gospel might be carried to the ends of the earth. Could the story be adequately told it would be one of the most thrilling chapters in the history of mankind.

For these very reasons the writing of the complete story is impossible. Who, even in many volumes after a lifetime of research, could compass the entire record! For a large proportion of it no written sources survive. Indeed, for much of it no author could ever give a faithful account. As Browning wrote in "Rabbi Ben Ezra":

> Not on the vulgar mass called "work" must sentence pass,
> Things done, that took the eye and had the price:
> O'er which, from level stand, the low world laid its hand,
> Found straightway to its mind, could value in a trice:
> But all, the world's coarse thumb and finger failed to plumb,
> So passed in making up the main account.

Only God knows the whole story. Only He can tell it as it should be told if it is to be full and accurate.

Yet, if the magnitude and the nature of the assignment be acknowledged, it may be feasible to note a few fairly obvious high points and outstanding individuals in the record and to venture a few generalizations. That is what I shall attempt.

EARLY PARTICIPATION IN WORK OF AMERICAN BOARD

First of all may I call your attention to the fact that Presbyterianism, broadly interpreted, had an important share in the beginnings of what we usually call the "foreign missions" of the Protestant churches of the United States. We generally and rightly date these from the Society of the Brethren which sprang from the "hay-stack prayer-meeting" of 1806 at Williams College and which was organized in that institution in 1808 with Samuel J. Mills as its central figure. After graduation from college, Mills and his fellows went to then youthful Andover Theological Seminary for their professional training, taking their society with them. There they were joined by others, including Adoniram Judson. It was their petition to clergy of New England which led, in 1810, to the formation of the American Board of Commissioners for Foreign Missions, the first organization to inaugurate the overseas missions of the churches of the United States. We do well to remind ourselves that the orthodox Congregational churches of Connecticut had a semi-Presbyterian form of organization; that their outstanding figure at the time of the formation of the American Board, President Timothy Dwight of Yale, called them and their sister churches in New England "Presbyterian"; that, led by the Connecticut churches in the 1790's, for some years the Congregational churches in most of New England sent delegates to the Presbyterian General Assembly; and that in 1801 the Plan of Union was begun for cooperation between the New England churches and the General Assembly in meeting the religious needs of westward-moving populations. Eventually the Plan of Union broke down, but while it existed it gave rise to what are now some of the strongest Presbyterian centers in the state of New York and the Middle West. At the outset many Presbyterians and Reformed, as well as those whom we now call Congregationalists, cooperated in the American Board. Even after the formation, by the Synod of Pittsburgh in 1831, of the Western Foreign Missionary Society and the creation in 1837 by the General Assembly of the Board of Foreign Missions into which the Western Foreign Missionary Society, renamed the Presbyterian Foreign Missionary Society, merged, the New School Presbyterians worked with the American Board. Partly on doctrinal and partly on organizational grounds Presbyterians and Congregationalists drew away from each other until, in 1870, with the reunion of the Old School and the New School Presbyterians, the collaboration ended. It might be said that this was because Congregationalists ceased to be Presbyterians.

At various points along the way, American Presbyterians have continued to be prominent and at times to blaze new trails in Protestant foreign missions. Arthur T. Pierson, followed by his son Delavan, both Presbyterians, for many years edited the *Missionary Review of the World*, long the one journal in the United States which sought to cover comprehensively evangelical missions. Ten years later it was edited by Royal G. Wilder, another Presbyterian. The year 1886 saw the beginning of the Student Volunteer Movement for Foreign Missions, an event which became notable in the history of the expansion of Christianity. A distinguished German student of the history of missions has declared that the initiative in the world mission then passed to the United States. It was a Presbyterian student from Princeton, Robert P. Wilder, son of Royal G. Wilder, who, supported by the prayers of his sister, headed the group at the conference at Mount Hermon which was the nucleus of the even hundred who by the end of that gathering had adhered to the declaration of purpose formulated by the group at Presbyterian Princeton: "We are willing and desirous, God permitting, to become foreign missionaries." From that group, too, came what was to be the breath-taking watchword of the Student Volunteer Movement: "The evangelization of the world in this generation." It was at Mount Hermon that John R. Mott dedicated himself to the world mission of the church and signed the Princeton declaration. Although a Methodist, it was through a Presbyterian, Robert P. Wilder, that he began the career which made him for decades an outstanding leader of the missionary enterprise. It was a Presbyterian, Luther D. Wishard, himself committed to foreign missions, through whose imagination and determination the Mount Hermon conference was undertaken. Arthur T. Pierson gave an address with the phrase, "All should go and go to all," which had much to do with the outcome. After the conference, two Presbyterians, Robert P. Wilder and John N. Forman, toured the colleges, universities, and theological seminaries recruiting for foreign missions and making of the Student Volunteer Movement something more than a temporary incident. Wilder also carried the Movement to the British Isles, thus laying the foundations for the Student Christian Movement of Great Britain and Ireland, and planted it on the Continent of Europe.

We do well to remind ourselves of the prominent part taken since 1886 by American Presbyterians in interdenominational world missionary movements. Among them we think at once of Robert E. Speer, who from the vantage of a secretaryship in the

Presbyterian Board of Foreign Missions, was outstanding in student missionary gatherings, in the Foreign Missions Conference of North America, and in meetings of the International Missionary Council. A United Presbyterian, Charles R. Watson, was long prominent in interdenominational missionary gatherings on both a national and an international scale. It is a Presbyterian, John A. Mackay, who is the third and present chairman of the International Missionary Council. It is significant that in the year in which Doctor Mackay was Moderator of the Presbyterian Church in the U.S.A., the Moderator of the Presbyterian Church in the U.S. was Doctor Frank W. Price, long a missionary in China and prominent in interdenominational enterprises in that country and in meetings of the International Missionary Council. The list might be lengthened.

MISSIONS IN MANY COUNTRIES

I must next remind you of the great variety of countries, peoples, and cultures among whom American Presbyterians have conducted and still conduct missions. Here we recall those in several of the republics of Latin America, Cuba, Mexico, Venezuela, Colombia, Chile, Brazil, Puerto Rico, Guatemala, the Dominican Republic, and in the Philippines, among peoples with a Roman Catholic background. We remind ourselves of the aid given to the Waldenses in Italy, of a noble heritage going back to the thirteenth century, of the Reformed tradition since the sixteenth century, and a small minority, often persecuted, among a Roman Catholic majority.

We note the extensive enterprises in West Africa and Río Muni, south of the Equator, among folk of primitive culture, in the Cameroons, and formerly in Liberia by the Presbyterians U.S.A., and in the Belgian Congo by the Presbyterians U.S.

We remind ourselves of the record in the Moslem world. Here American Presbyterian missions have been widely extended. They include the notable church begun and nourished by the United Presbyterians in Egypt, gathered mainly from the Copts, and the extension of the United Presbyterian Mission into Ethiopia and the Sudan. They embrace the efforts in Turkey, Cyprus, Syria, and the Lebanon, with their mixture of ancient Eastern churches, Roman Catholics of the Latin Rite, Roman Catholic Uniates and Moslems. They include Mesopotamia, thus Latin Iraq, where formerly some gains were made among the Nestorians in an attempt to quicken the remnants of that once widely spread and missionary body. Latterly, especially after the Nestorians were driven out and all but exterminated during World War I, converts have been made in Iran from Islam. These have not been in large numbers, and since World War II, especially since the dispute with Great Britain over oil, the rising tide of nationalism has brought mounting obstacles. Yet that there are scores and hundreds of Christians where once there had been none or only single individuals has been encouraging, particularly in view of the well known sparseness of accessions to the church from Islam.

In India we come to an area where Moslems are strong but, except in the present Pakistan, do not predominate. It is in the North of India, in what are now Pakistan and the Indian Union, that Presbyterians from the United States have been chiefly active. In the Punjab there was early established a mission of the Reformed Presbyterian Church. Slightly after it, there came, also to the Punjab, the first contingent of the Associate Presbyterian Synod. When, in 1858, that Synod became a constituent member of the United Presbyterian Church, the Punjab undertaking was transferred to the new body. In 1870, incorporating the enterprise in whose development Royal G. Wilder had had a large share, the Board of Foreign Missions of the Presbyterian Church in the U.S.A. extended its operations south of Bombay, into the native state of Kolhapur. American Presbyterians, including the Reformed Presbyterians, are also in what were formerly known as the United Provinces.

In Southeast Asia the sole Presbyterian mission has been in Siam, now Thailand. The Presbyterians were not the first Protestants in that country, but they entered early, in 1840, and were soon, as they have remained, the leading non-Roman Catholic mission in that land.

As we move from Southeast Asia we must not fail to note the financial help recently given by the Northern Presbyterians to the Christian cause in Indonesia.

China has constituted an important field of American Presbyterians. Both the major bodies have been represented, the U.S.A. and the U.S., especially, as was to be expected because of its size, the former. The Reformed Presbyterians were also in Kwantung Province and Manchuria. We do well to recall that the first Protestant missionary to China, Robert Morrison, although English-born and reared and of Scottish, not American, paternity, owed his early spiritual nurture to a Presbyterian church in which his father was an elder. The first American mission, in Canton, was begun by the American Board of Commissioners for Foreign Missions. In time it withdrew from that city, and American Presbyterians became its heir. They carried on the hospital begun by Peter Parker, the first medical missionary in China. Before the treaties of 1842–1844 had partly opened the country, in 1838 there arrived in Singapore, hoping to reach the Chinese in that British colony, two Presbyterian couples, among the earliest appointees of the Board of Foreign Missions newly formed by the Old School General Assembly. When the first treaties made accessible five ports for foreign residence, the Presbyterian base of operations was moved from Singapore to China proper, and footholds were gained in three of the ports—Ningpo, Canton, and Shanghai. What seems to have been the first Protestant church on Chinese soil was the one organized by American Presbyterians in Ningpo in 1845. As subsequent treaties made more of the Empire accessible to missionaries, Northern Presbyterians expanded their lines and eventually were found not only in the province of which Canton is the chief city and in those to which Ningpo and Shanghai give entrance, but also in the North, in Shantung, the native province of Confucius, in Peking, the capital, and centers in the surrounding province. These same Presbyterians entered into the lower part of the Yangtze Valley, in the province of Hunan, in Central China, and into Yunnan, in the southwest. Southern Presbyterians limited their field to East China.

As is well known, Presbyterians constitute the largest body of Protestants in tragic Korea. The Northern Presbyterians vied with the American Methodists and the Anglicans in being the first to enter that country. All three came in 1884. Southern Presbyterians arrived eight years later, in 1892. While Australian and Canadian Presbyterians also came, the large majority of the missionaries have been from the United States, and more from the Northern than from the Southern Church.

American Presbyterians were among the first to take advantage of the opportunities afforded by the Townsend Harris treaty of 1858 which made possible the beginning of Protestant missions and the renewal of Roman Catholic missions in Japan. It was in 1859 that the first missionaries arrived. One of these was J. C. Hepburn, who had formerly served in China under the American Board, but who came to Japan under Presbyterian appointment. The first Protestant church in Tokyo was Presbyterian, organized in 1873. That same year a presbytery was brought into being. Cumberland Presbyterians and Southern Presbyterians also shared in planting Christianity in Japan. Along with Methodists, Congregationalists, and Anglicans, American Presbyterians have been chiefly responsible for the numerical growth of Protestantism in the Land of the Rising Sun.

Are Characteristic Patterns Discernible?

In all this wide variety of countries, peoples, and cultures where Presbyterians have joined in planting the church, are any characteristic patterns discernible? Have Presbyterians tended to appeal predominantly to any one class, or to emphasize any one method? In general, the great contribution of Scottish Presbyterian missions has been in the field of education, and especially of higher education. When we think of the achievements of the Presbyterians of Scotland, after David Livingstone, who, incidentally, was sent not by the Presbyterians but by the London Missionary Society and was not primarily a churchman, there come to mind Alexander Duff and the precedent which he set for higher education in Protestant missions in India. We also think of Madras Christian College, so largely the lengthened shadow of the great Scottish missionary William Miller; of John Wilson, first vice chancellor of the University of Bombay, where Wilson College bears his name; of Hislop College in Nagpur; and of Lovedale and Fort Hare in South Africa. We recall the historic emphasis of Presbyterianism upon an educated ministry and its corollary, the fact that in the United States Presbyterianism has not been the church of the masses but has ministered, in general, to those to whom an educated ministry speaks, those of middle and upper incomes.

It has been Methodists and especially Baptists who have had, in times past, the lower income and less educated elements of the older American stock, both white and black. Has this been true of the overseas outreach of American Presbyterianism? Has there been a corresponding social stratification of the churches in Latin America, the Philippines, Africa, and Asia? Have the converts and Christian communities gathered by American Presbyterians conformed to the pattern of the Presbyterianism of the United States?

There has been some correspondence. The mass movements of the underprivileged in India—the outcastes and the tribal peoples of the hills—have been affected much more by Baptists and Methodists than by Presbyterians. Presbyterian missions in Africa south of the Equator, among the Negroes of primitive culture in that region, have not been as extensive as those of Methodists and Baptists.

However, the parallel to the situation in the United States has by no means been exact. We need to remind ourselves that in India the United Presbyterians have won many from the outcaste Chuhras and from the Megs, lowly weavers. We also must recall that much of the field of American Presbyterians in India is predominantly Moslem and that, by whatever denomination, conversions from Moslems are few. The Moslem lands in western Asia and North Africa are not a fair test, for here there have been relatively few Methodist and almost no Baptist missions and the main numerical gains of Protestantism, as of the Roman Catholic Church, have been from the old Eastern churches. Burma and Thailand also do not fit the American precedent. In Burma the major mission is that of the American Baptists. They have had only a few thousand converts from the dominant people, the Burmese Buddhists, who are fairly highly civilized. The large majority of their gains have been from those of primitive and near-primitive culture, notably the Karens. But in Thailand, where American Presbyterians are the largest Protestant mission, they have had even fewer accessions from the Buddhists than in Burma, and their major gains are among the Lao, who are nearer to the primitive stage of culture than are the Thai. In China and Japan, in both of which American Presbyterians, Methodists, and Baptists are represented, there does not seem to be the same social stratification in these denominations that were allegedly found in the United States.

Korea certainly does not present a parallel to the United States. Here Baptists are not represented, but American Methodists have been strong. American Presbyterians have had more than half of the Protestant missionary body, but the fact that almost three-fourths of the Protestant communicants have been Presbyterians seems to disclose a greater popular appeal of the latter than of the Methodists. The difference may in part be due to the method adopted at an early stage in the Presbyterian mission, and in general continued. It is associated with the name of John L. Nevius. Nevius was a Presbyterian missionary who came to China in 1854 and who spent most of a long life in Shantung Province. He was the vigorous advocate of a method of spreading Christianity and planting the church which is associated with his name. This called for a way of making Christianity and the church the property of the people of the country from the very first—from the beginning to have the church attain the standard which is generally regarded as the object of missionary effort; namely, to bring into being churches which shall be self-supporting, self-propagating, and self-governing. The Nevius program entailed encouraging each Christian to win his neighbors to the faith, and while doing so to support himself by some occupation rather than to depend on a subsidy from the foreigner, to insist that from the start all churches be self-sustaining and not rely on foreign funds or leadership, and that church buildings be erected in an indigenous style of architecture and only as the nationals themselves are able to pay for them. Much emphasis was placed upon Bible schools for training the laity, so that every Christian, and not just the clergy, would be an informed and earnest missionary. Some foreign funds might be employed, but they were to be kept to a minimum. Nevius was not able to obtain the consistent following of this method by Presbyterians in China, but in 1890, when he was in late middle life and when the Korean mission was young, he came to Seoul and so persuasively presented his convictions that, in the main, they were adopted. The results are seen in the characteristics of Presbyterianism in Korea.

While the Presbyterians of the United States have paid more attention to evangelism and the bringing into being of Christian communities than have their Scottish brethren, and have not placed relatively so large an emphasis upon education, especially higher education, they have not neglected the latter. One of the most remarkable aspects of their record overseas has been the colleges and universities which they have brought into being, either singlehanded or in cooperation with other denominations. In Latin America we remark especially what has been accomplished in

Brazil, notably in Mackenzie College in São Paulo, and we recall that the Protestant schools, particularly those of the Presbyterians, have had a profound effect upon the educational system created by the government. The Philippines have Silliman University, now interdenominational with Presbyterians as major participants. In Africa south of the Sahara we remind ourselves of the college recently begun in the Cameroons. We recall the system of schools which the United Presbyterians have created in Egypt in connection with their mission, culminating in a college at Assiut. We are aware, too, of the American University at Cairo, undenominational but frankly Christian, chiefly the creation of Charles R. Watson, son of one of the outstanding members of the United Presbyterian mission.

India has Forman Christian College, at Lahore, named for its first head and beginning in 1888, with James C. R. Ewing as its distinguished principal. One of the best known educators in India, Ewing won the respect both of Christians and of non-Christians and was vice chancellor of the government Punjab University. At Allahabad, through the initiative of Sam Higginbottam, a remarkable agricultural institute was developed, outstanding in its class in all India. At Miraj, in the native state of Kolhapur, a remarkable medical center with hospital, leper asylum, and medical school arose through the vision and creative energy of William Wanless. Forman, Allahabad, and Miraj are associated with the Northern Presbyterians. The United Presbyterians have Gordon Mission College.

On the eve of 1914 Thailand saw the founding by American Presbyterians of Bangkok Christian College.

In China American Presbyterians have had a notable part in education, particularly higher education. Lingnan University, earlier incorporated as the Christian College in China, eventually undenominational, was begun on the initiative of the American Presbyterian Mission in that city. With it are inseparably associated the names of two Presbyterian missionaries, its first president,

Andrew P. Happer, who raised most of the initial funds, and B. C. Henry. Northern and Southern Presbyterians joined in maintaining a college at Hangchow. Presbyterians shared in the maintenance of the interdenominational Nanking University. Its School of Agriculture and Forestry, for a time the best in China, had an American Presbyterian, John H. Reisner, as its first dean. After putting the institution on its feet, Reisner withdrew to make it possible for a Chinese to take over, and became the chief creator and the head of the Agricultural Missions Foundation in New York which has had as its purpose, as its name indicates, the promotion of assistance by missions to agriculture and rural life throughout the world. American Presbyterians joined in forming Ginling College, for women, at Nanking. American Presbyterians were prominent in the interdenominational Shantung Christian University, later Cheeloo University. Outstanding in the merger which brought it into being was a famous school developed at Tengchow by the American Presbyterian Calvin W. Mateer. An American Presbyterian, Henry W. Luce, had a large share in effecting the union which brought Cheeloo into being. He helped raise funds for it and also for the larger Yenching University, on the outskirts of Peking. Yenching, interdenominational, had as its first president a Southern Presbyterian, J. Leighton Stuart. For a time Luce was vice president. Modern China has had no more notable educator, Chinese or foreigner, than Stuart. As we all know, he courageously remained through the Japanese occupation, frankly critical of it, and ended his active career as American Ambassador to China.

In Japan American Presbyterians have had a major share in Meiji Gakuin. To those who know its inner history it is an open secret that it was the unpublicized vision and determination of a secretary of the Presbyterian Board of Foreign Missions, John Coventry Smith, which saved the Japan International Christian University in a critical hour before it had even opened its doors.

Presbyterians have had an outstanding part in the founding and maintenance of the two leading Christian colleges in Korea, the Union Christian College at Pyeng Yang and the Chosen Christian College at Seoul. The present president of the latter institution, a Korean, George L. Paik, owes his conversion to a Presbyterian school and had most of his formal education in Presbyterian schools in Korea and the United States. The Severance Union Medical College in Seoul had as its head a Northern Presbyterian, A. O. Avison.

Educational, Language, and Other Problems

One of the continuing problems of Protestant missions is theological education. In solving it American Presbyterians are probably neither far behind nor ahead of the average. The difficulties are in part social. In most lands in which Presbyterian missions operate, the Christian ministry is without precedent and is not held in honor. Difficulties are also economic. For the most part the younger churches founded by missions are unable or unwilling to meet the cost of supporting a highly educated ministry. The kind of ministry to which we have been accustomed in Europe and the United States entails a standard of living and an average income much higher than that found among the large majority in Asia and Africa. This makes possible the maintenance of well educated ministers for individual parishes. Naturally in the churches which they have helped to bring into being missionaries have tended to reproduce the pattern with which they are familiar. Experiments have been made in a different organization of the churches which could utilize both men of lesser training and those with more prolonged education, but thus far without entire success. Moreover, language constitutes a major obstacle. In no language of Asia and Africa does there exist the wealth of theological literature that is found in English. In some tongues the amount, apart from the Bible, is so scanty as to be negligible. But if theological students are given sufficient English to be able to use it with facility, they have difficulty in communicating in their mother tongue to their parishioners what they have learned. In general, theological schools are behind other main branches of education undertaken by missionaries. Yet the problem has been recognized and valiant efforts have been made to solve it. In this, Presbyterians from the United States have had an outstanding part. To name only one of many, Frank W. Price, whom we have already mentioned, labored intelligently and heroically to train men for the rural ministry in China until war and Communism forced him to desist.

We must note, too, that American Presbyterians, in common with men and women of other denominations, have devoted much effort to providing the peoples among whom they have lived with Christian and other literature in the vernaculars. The translation of the Bible is foremost. In whole or in part it has been put into more than a thousand tongues. On occasion this has involved, as a preliminary, the reduction of a language to writing. More languages have been given a written form by Christian missionaries than by all other agencies combined. In it American Presbyterians have had a part.

Along with missionaries of other communions, American Presbyterians have sought to bring into being autonomous churches. We have noted the success of this effort in Korea. It has also been seen in most other areas in which these Presbyterians have worked.

PARTICIPATION IN UNION ENTERPRISES

American Presbyterians have participated largely in interdenominational enterprises. They have joined in comity agreements which have prevented competition and duplication of effort and which have promoted the inclusion of an entire population. We have noted their collaboration in interdenominational colleges. They have cooperated with other communions in the preparation of the ministry, as in Nanking Theological Seminary and in Yenching. They have been prominent in national and regional Christian councils. For example, Robert E. Speer had a leading part in bringing into existence the Committee on Cooperation in Latin America and was long its chairman. E. C. Lobenstine, of the Northern Presbyterians, was one of the first secretaries of the National Christian Council of China, and Robert P. Wilder, also of that church, was the first secretary of the Near East Christian Council. In 1924 the Reformed Church in the U.S., the Reformed Church in America, and the Presbyterian Church in the U.S.A. merged their work in Iraq in the united mission in Mesopotamia.

We may note in passing something of the part that other members of the family of Presbyterian and Reformed Churches have had in the Ecumenical Movement. Thus William Paton, of the English Presbyterians, was a secretary of the National Christian Council of India and went from there to be a secretary of the International Missionary Council and later, concurrently, of the World Council of Churches while it was in process of formation. W. A. Visser't Hooft, of the Dutch Reformed Church, at one time general secretary and then chairman of the World's Student Christian Federation, has from its inception been the general secretary of the World Council of Churches. As the associate secretary of that body, Robert Mackie of the (Presbyterian) Church of Scotland came to the post from the World's Student Christian Federation. The first American secretary of the International Missionary Council was A. L. Warnshuis, of the Reformed Church in America. American Presbyterians are in good company with other members of the Reformed faith when they share in cooperation with other communions.

Perhaps we should also remark here the large place which Presbyterians from the United States have had in the World Council of Churches. The president's house on the campus of Princeton Theological Seminary was the scene of one of the earliest meetings preliminary to the formation of that body. William Adams Brown was one of the outstanding leaders in the World Conference on Faith and Order and was the first chairman of the American

LAYMEN

Harriet Beecher Stowe

Stonewall Jackson

Robert Field Stockton

John Wanamaker

LAYMEN

Henry J. Heinz

Andrew Carneg

Mrs. W. C. Wins-
borough

Marcus Whitman

Mildred McAfee Hor

SCHOLARS

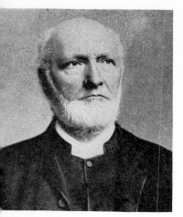

ilip Schaff

Charles A. Briggs

James Woodrow

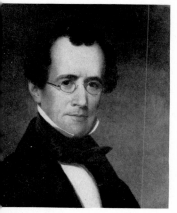

hn W. Nevin

Elias Compton

SCHOLARS

Archibald Alexander

John T. Pressl

Charles Hodge

Henry Ruffner

William J. Hollar

committee for the support of the World Council of Churches. H. P. Van Dusen, now chairman of the Board of Foreign Missions of the Presbyterian Church in the U.S.A., has been the first chairman of the Study Commission of the World Council of Churches. In addition to being chairman of the International Missionary Council, John A. Mackay is a member of the Central Committee of the World Council of Churches.

Under these circumstances, it is not strange that the subjects of this treatise have been prominent in movements for the organic union of churches. So far as I am aware, in every area where such a union has been effected of different denominational families of what we call the "younger churches," and where Presbyterians have been represented, at least some of the latter have entered into the union. In some places not all of them have joined. For conscientious reasons some have held aloof or, having once joined, have withdrawn. In some of the unions there have been no Presbyterians in the region or country involved. That, for instance, is the case in Ceylon, where a union is in process of achievement. In the area served by the Church of South India none of them are represented, but the churches affiliated with the Church of Scotland and with the Reformed Church in America are there and through the South India United Church, of which they were constituent members, have entered into the more inclusive body.

The united churches in which American Presbyterians have joined can be quickly named. The Church of Christ in China, the largest Protestant body in that country, the first general assembly of which met in 1927, has had the Presbyterian Church in China as its nucleus and its chief constituent. In the Church of Christ in Japan, whose formation, in 1941, was expedited by the political situation, the majority of former Presbyterians are members. In 1934 the Church of Christ in Thailand came into being, with Presbyterians constituting the majority of its membership. It was in 1929 that the United Evangelical Church of the Philippines was born, made up of Presbyterians, Congregationalists, and United

Brethren, and with a Filipino as the first moderator. Somewhat earlier, in 1924, the United Church of North India brought together Presbyterians and Congregationalists. In Iran plans, not yet consummated, have been discussed for uniting all Protestants. The majority are Presbyterians and Anglicans.

This enumeration of the organic unions with which American Presbyterians have been pioneers indicates the fulfillment of a slogan only lately coined, "A call to mission and unity." Within the last two years several ecumenical gatherings have been challenging themselves and their constituencies with this summons. Its purport is that the church universal has mission and unity as inseparable in its commission from its Divine Lord. It must offer the gospel to all mankind. If it is to do this effectively, it must attain the only true Christian unity, that of love. If, divided, it seeks to witness to the gospel to all men, its witness, a witness to the self-giving love of God in Christ, will be handicapped by its failure fully to exemplify that love and by its denial in life of the power of the gospel to which it professes to bear witness. If it gives itself primarily to attaining unity, that unity will be merely that of an ecclesiastical structure which, concerned with its own existence, will fail to disclose Him Who so loved the world that He gave His only Son.

This means that the entire church must be a missionary society and that in giving itself to that purpose it must show forth in its life the love which is at the heart of the gospel. In its initial circular letter to the churches, the Western Foreign Missionary Society declared that the church in "her organization" should be "a society for missions to the heathen." In its first annual report the Board of Foreign Missions of the Presbyterian Church in the U.S.A. declared that it is "the duty of every individual christian . . . to aid in making known the gospel to all the world" and that the church should be "a missionary community." Across the years American Presbyterians and the churches planted by them have been drawing closer to other Christians in the fulfillment of this purpose.

THE PURPOSE OF TRUE UNITY

All of us, whatever our confessional attachments, need to remind ourselves that the essence of Christian unity is love, and that it does not necessarily express itself through any one pattern or group of patterns. Neither cooperation between autonomous churches nor organic union in one visible church is the final answer. Within the bodies thus created there may still be jealousies, rivalries, party strife, and even hatred. Organization can facilitate true unity and probably is a necessary expression of it. But it cannot ensure true unity. Moreover, the experience of the past century and a half has proved that the growing unity which these years have witnessed is a concomitant and an outgrowth of the missionary motive. It is as Christians seek to obey their Lord's commission to be his witnesses to the ends of the earth and to make disciples of all the nations that they draw together in one or another visible expression of the unity which is through him and discover that to a greater extent than they had realized the grounds for that unity already exist. They then become aware that the prayer "that they all may be one . . . that the world may believe" states succinctly two inseparable facets of the life to which they are called through the gospel. Fortunately, that awareness has not been confined to any one denomination. But of it the majority trend in American Presbyterianism is a leading example.

CHAPTER X

Wrestling with Human Values:
The Slavery Years

T HE history of the Christian Church has too often been written in terms of theological controversy. Latterly Dr. Latourette has shown how it may be exhibited within a framework of missionary expansion. Yet possibly the true genius of our faith is best revealed in battles waged against moral evils that curse society, and defile the image of God in man. These struggles have been as often civil wars within the Christian brotherhood as they have been foreign campaigns against the outside world. Begun as a kind of guerrilla warfare by a few prophetic souls who had glimpsed new meanings in the gospel, or had awakened to a new conscience concerning ancient evils, they have brought the whole fellowship at last to higher levels of conviction, of practice, and of testimony; but not without some shedding of blood and toll of tears. A new conscience concerning war is even now emerging within Christendom, voiced as yet only by prophets crying in the wilderness.

Of all these moral struggles which so definitely mark the real epochs of Christian history, none has been so significant of the gospel leaven at work, and none so universal in its final grip upon the Christian conscience, as that against human slavery. There is one chapter in the story of that conflict that has never yet been put into print, one that is of particular concern to the Presbyterian fellowship; and only a little less directly of interest to Christians in all the world. It shows certain corrupting influences at work which still threaten, perhaps always will threaten, the health and purity of the body of Christ. We shall here attempt to present that missing chapter in American Presbyterian church history. It undertakes to trace the rise, development, victories, and final re-absorption of the Free Presbyterian Church in America.

An Infant Evil Grows into a Giant Curse

Chattel slavery is a very ancient evil. In the first century the slave population of Rome outnumbered the free. But until modern times it was primarily a way of controlling war-conquered peoples. The slaves of the Roman regime were mainly of a kindred race and color, and slavery did not subject men to the horrible indignities and disabilities which race prejudice has added to African slavery. But war as such had little to do with the slave trade developed and sanctioned by the English, French, Portuguese, Spanish, and Americans in the seventeenth, eighteenth, and early nineteenth centuries. The primary motive was economic gain. Minor contributory motives were a desire for social prestige and the continuance of an English cavalier style of living.

When, after an attempt to make slaves of Indians had failed, those first twenty Africans were bought at Jamestown in 1619, the extreme need of labor to clear land and produce food made their coming seem even to the more decent or pious a kind of special providence. The Colonial cavaliers looked upon these strange creatures as not quite human. Very few if any of them had any conscience in the matter. From that small beginning, slowly the traffic grew. The Negro slave population increase was at a somewhat more rapid rate than that of the whites. Over against the white population was an ever mounting traffic in slaves, brought by the ships of four or five nations either straight from the west coast of Africa, or through the West Indies. This earlier traffic was not to Southern ports only. The purchasers of slaves were New Englanders almost as many in numbers as the Carolinians. At the opening of the Revolution, after 156 years of experience with it, slavery was being practiced in New England, New York, New Jersey, and Pennsylvania. The system was recognized and protected by law in every one of the colonies. Slaves were owned by many Christian men, even by the clergy. At least three of the pioneer Presbyterian preachers who crossed the mountains into western Pennsylvania brought slaves with them, or acquired some soon after. It was in 1780 that the Keystone State enacted legislation for the gradual elimination of slavery; yet almost forty years later some aged Negroes were still being held as property in western Pennsylvania owing to the provisions of last wills and testaments.

Certain background facts, fully dealt with and documented in general histories of the period, need only to be recounted here.[1]

First, slavery did not prove generally profitable in the North, where labor demands were being met by voluntary immigration, and, during Colonial days, by a system of short-term indentured labor. There was, and is even now, very little direct immigration into the Southern states, except for the Mexican influx into the Southwest.

Second, from the opening of the eighteenth century, slavery was more and more concentrated in the Southern states or colonies, and already in the Continental Congress it was found to have become a sectional issue.

Third, when the Declaration of Independence was adopted slavery was legal and protected by positive statutes in every one of the thirteen colonies.

Fourth, when the founding fathers declared that all men are created equal and are endowed by their Creator with certain unalienable rights, among them life, liberty, and the pursuit of happiness, apparently only Jefferson and certain Baptists were thinking of Negroes as men. The Congress cut out of his first draft of the great Charter of Freedom his reference to the evils and dangers of the slave trade.

Fifth, down to the 1820's there were almost, if not quite, as many voices lifted in the South as in the North against the moral evils of slavery.

Sixth, the Industrial Revolution and certain inventions which followed close upon it radically altered the relation of the Negro slave to the prosperity of the cotton-growing states. Great spinning and weaving mills were set up in England and in New England which created a demand for more cotton than was then being produced at prices which made the expanding of the acreage grown most desirable. Then the application of steam to ocean travel, and the consequent rapid expansion of the tonnage capacity of sea-going vessels, opened the way to get the cotton quickly and cheaply to northern and transatlantic ports. In those same few years the processing of cotton for market was greatly speeded by the introduction of the cotton gin and of machinery for baling and compressing. Thus was erected what may in a parody not altogether pointless be dubbed the "Holy Cotton Empire." Thus also, even as now, the labor problem became the crucial issue in a changing and expanding economy.

Seventh, the slaveholding population was very small both in the border states and in the deep South. It has been estimated that even in 1860 there were not more than 2,300 large slaveholders— families owning 100 or more slaves; and that, leaving the white mountaineers out of account, fewer than one-fourth of the white families in the slaveholding sections had any property interest in Negroes. "About 77,000 owners had only one slave each, and 200,000 more owned fewer than ten slaves each." [2] This means that some 10,000 families constituted the ruling South in economic, social, and political life. An oligarchy was being built up, contrary to the genius and ideals of American life. Under it the

non-slaveholding population was deteriorating economically, intellectually, and even physically. More than half a million white
illiterates were reported in the slave states in the census of 1850.
The very soil was being impoverished and abused, with little attempt to build it up again. This led the planters to put their profits
into more land and more slave labor rather than into buildings,
machinery, and permanent improvements. Slavery was pushing the
life of all but the favored few downward in a vicious spiral. The
Southland seemed headed toward a new phase of feudalism. Not
until after 1830, did the curse of slavery begin to be apparent. Then
the forces began to accumulate which in our Presbyterian family
led finally to the emergence in 1847 of the Free Presbyterian
Church.

THE BACKGROUND AND SETTING OF THIS DRAMA

Two kinds of crises have repeatedly confronted the Christian
Church. Some have arisen out of theological controversies, some
out of moral conflicts. Sometimes, to be sure, the two have been
tangled together in one knotty problem, as in the Protestant Reformation. Sometimes the issue has been clearly and simply one
of doctrine, as at Nicaea, and again at Chalcedon. Sometimes again
the conflict has been over moral standards and human rights.
With such a problem the Presbyterian Church in America wrestled
long and awkwardly during the four decades preceding the Civil
War.

A few gross sins the Christian Church has always unequivocally
condemned, and for these it has barred offenders from the Lord's
table. Murder, adultery, theft, slander—concerning these, practice
might sometimes waver; mental condemnation never did. But
what about such sins as buying, selling, holding, and breeding
human beings as chattel slaves? Concerning this evil it took our
Presbyterian Church a long time to learn to speak with one clear

voice of condemnation. The General Synod of 1787 and the General Assemblies of 1793 and 1795 frowned upon it, and came little short of putting it among the heinous, deadly sins, as we shall soon see. When we come to 1845, we find the General Assembly refusing to entertain the idea that slaveholding might be a bar to Christian communion, but not by a unanimous vote. That day and that action began the movement which concerns us here; namely, the schismatic movement, as it was promptly branded, which opened a new rift within our communion, and a war which reached its climax only at Appomattox. Since then, no man anywhere who aspires to be called a Christian, no man who condemns murder and adultery as violations of Divine law, will dare to defend human slavery on moral grounds. Does any one suppose that had been the case before? The evidence proves the contrary. In the actions of numerous presbyteries, north as well as south, and in the printed sermons of Presbyterian preachers in the South during the forties and fifties are scores of elaborate defenses of slavery from Holy Writ. Nor was it all in the South. In June, 1861, after the War Between the States had actually begun in western Pennsylvania, the Reverend Samuel Willson preached in the Norwich Church a sermon in which he argued from Scripture that slavery, equally with the family, is an institution of divine origin and sanction. A physician in the village was tried and suspended by the session for disturbing the peace of the church by criticizing the sermon.[3] An example at the other extreme is another western Pennsylvanian, a farmer, Robert Welsh. In 1848 he wrote to his friend Jacob Slagle of Washington, Pennsylvania, a letter[4] full of misspelled words and hot indignation, in which he denounces slavery as man-thievery, accuses slaveholders generally of fornication with slave women for the breeding of more plantation workers, and calls it blasphemy against God who has created all men in His own image, for one man to hold another in bondage as a mere thing, a piece of property, subject to barter.

The Economic Complications of This Moral Problem

In the face of such extreme differences of opinion, or in spite of them, we shall probably agree that Christians ought to find it easier to see eye to eye on a question of right and wrong than on one involving theology and philosophy. And if the great majority of our church leaders held for forty years a position on a moral question which today no one in any church would espouse, there are likely to be found some ulterior motives or external pressures to account for it. Of that also, more anon.

Let us go back to examine the records, trace the growth of this issue, and witness the deterioration of the conscience of the church concerning it. We might go all the way back to New Testament times, even to Paul's letter to Philemon, from which pro-slavery Christians misappropriated so much comfort. Let it suffice us to begin with early American colonial days when slaves, plundered and shanghaied from the West African coast, were being sold in America to meet what seemed then a vital need for more and cheaper labor. A few voices were raised in protest even then. The first on record were not those of New Englanders with their hypersensitive consciences, nor of psalm-singing Scots and Ulster men, nor even of Quakers. The first pronouncement on record is that of a little congregation of Pietists of the Reformed faith in Germantown, the group which later developed into what we know as the Market Square Presbyterian Church of Philadelphia.[5] That was soon after the middle of the seventeenth century. William Penn in 1682 brought strong convictions against slavery and propagated them diligently among his fellow migrants and his converts. John Woolman, the Quaker saint, made some of his missionary journeys into anti-slavery crusades, winning many friends and more enemies thereby. There is evidence that down into the first decade of the nineteenth century there were large numbers of intelligent people below Mason and Dixon's Line who were convinced that the slave system was an evil both morally and economically and must be abolished sometime, somehow, though no one seemed to know just how it could be done. When the Declaration of Independence was written, and again when the Federal Constitution was framed, Thomas Jefferson wished to put into them the guarantee of freedom for black as well as white. But he was in a hopeless minority. Most of the founding fathers, north as well as south, had not yet learned to call the Negro human when they declared that all men were created free and equal. Among the Christian forces, not only Friends but Mennonites, Moravians, Calvinists of New England and the Middle Colonies, a new conscience was beginning to stir. In our own Presbyterian communion it found utterance in three official statements.

First, the Synod of New York and Philadelphia in 1787 went on record thus:

The Synod, taking into consideration an overture respecting slavery, determined as follows: viz—The Synod of New York and Philadelphia does highly approve of the general principles in favor of universal liberty that prevail in America and the interest which many of the states have taken in promoting the abolition of slavery.[6] Yet inasmuch as men introduced from a servile state to a participation in all the privileges of civil society without a proper education and without previous habits of industry may be in many respects dangerous to the community; therefore they earnestly recommend it to all persons belonging to their communion to give those persons who are at present held in servitude such good education as may prepare them for the better enjoyment of freedom. And they moreover recommend that masters, whenever they find servants disposed to make a proper improvement of the privilege, would give them some share of property to begin with; or grant them sufficient time and sufficient means of procuring by industry their own liberty, at a moderate rate; that they might thereby be brought into society with those habits of industry that may render them useful citizens. . . . And finally, they recommend it to all people under their care, to use the most prudent measures, consistent with the interest and state of civil society, to procure eventually the final abolition of slavery in America.

That is a broadminded statement of emerging Christian convictions, made almost on the eve of the creation of our federal government. Note that the word "abolition" is used twice, without apology or embarrassment, a word which sixty years later was to be as much feared and hated and shunned as the word "communism" is regarded by us today.

In response to repeated overtures, the General Assembly in 1793, and again in 1795, took action on the same subjects in such words as these—I quote the 1795 resolution replying to an overture from Kentucky, in which the issue of Christian communion with slaveholders was directly posed:

The following overture was brought in by the committee of bills and overtures, viz—"a serious and conscientious person, a member of a Presbyterian congregation, who views the slavery of negroes as a moral evil highly offensive to God, and injurious to the interests of the Gospel, lives under the ministry of a person, and amongst a society of people, who concur with him in sentiment upon the subject upon general principles, yet for particular reasons hold slaves, and tolerate the practice in others. Overtured:—ought the former of these persons, under the impressions and circumstances above described, to hold communion with the latter?" Whereupon, after due deliberation it was

"Resolved, that as the same difference of opinion with respect to slavery takes place in sundry other parts of the Presbyterian Church, notwithstanding which they live in charity and peace according to the doctrine and practice of the Apostles, it is hereby recommended to all conscientious persons, and especially those whom it immediately respects, to do the same. At the same time, the General Assembly assure all the churches under their care, that they view with deepest concern any vestiges of slavery which may exist in our country, and refer the churches to the records of the Assembly, published at different times, and especially to an overture of the Synod of New York and Philadelphia published in 1787, and republished among extracts from the minutes of the General Assembly of 1793 on that head, with which they trust every conscientious person will be fully satisfied.

"Resolved, 2nd, that Mr. Rice and Dr. Muir, ministers, and Mr. Robert Patterson, ruling elder, be a committee to draft a letter to the Presbytery of Transylvania on the subject of the above overture, and report in the afternoon."

The Bills and Overtures Committee in 1795 consisted of thirteen
ministers and six elders, of whom five ministers and two elders
were from the South, and at least seven of that committee were
themselves slaveholders. The resolutions were adopted, but the
letter the subcommittee brought in was warmly debated, and parts
were stricken out. The letter as approved and sent reads thus:

> To our Brethren, members of the Presbyterian Church under the care
> of Transylvania Presbytery, Dear Friends and Brethren: The General
> Assembly of the Presbyterian Church hear with concern from your
> commissioners, that differences of opinion with respect to holding com-
> munion with those possessed of slaves agitate the minds of some among
> you, and threaten divisions which may have the most ruinous tendency.
> The subject of slavery has repeatedly claimed the attention of the Gen-
> eral Assembly, and the commissioners of the Presbytery of Transylvania
> are furnished with attested copies of these decisions, to be read by the
> Presbytery when it shall appear to them proper, together with a copy of
> this letter, to the several churches under their care. The General As-
> sembly have taken every step which they deemed expedient or wise to
> encourage emancipation, and to make the state of those who are in
> slavery as mild and tolerable as possible.[7]

The letter concludes with a brief homily on peace and concord.

So in 1795 there appears a distinct awareness of sectional differences, an attempt to delay action on what is recognized as a moral
curse, and to salve conscience with injunctions to religious nurture
of those in bondage. Strangely enough, this first raising of the
question about communion with slaveholders came from a slave
state.

We pass over two eventful decades during which the tensions
kept growing and the Assembly kept avoiding further action. In
the minutes of the Assembly of 1815 we find this deliverance:

> Although in some sections of our country, under certain circum-
> stances, the transfer of slaves may be unavoidable, yet they consider the
> buying and selling of slaves by way of traffic, and all undue severity in
> the management of them, as inconsistent with the spirit of the Gospel.
> And they recommend to the Presbyteries and Sessions under their care,

to make use of all prudent measures to prevent such shameful and unrighteous conduct.[8]

We come now to the Assembly of 1818. Its action was more
incisive, and to it the Presbyterian friends of freedom harked back
in later years as the storm clouds thickened. That deliverance was
written by President Ashbel Green of Princeton College, the second
man on the small committee being one of the strong anti-slavery
men of the Chillicothe Presbytery, most vocal of all our church
courts in its year-after-year protests against the whole slave system,
and the church's compliance in it. This again I must quote in full
for a proper understanding of what happened later. It is the strongest of all official Presbyterian pronouncements on the subject.

We consider the voluntary enslaving of one part of the human race by
another, as a gross violation of the most precious and sacred rights of
human nature, as utterly inconsistent with the law of God, which requires us to love our neighbor as ourselves, and as totally irreconcilable
with the spirit and principles of the Gospel of Christ, which enjoin that
all things whatsoever ye would that men should do to you, do ye even so
to them. It is manifestly the duty of all Christians who enjoy the light
of the present day, to use their honest, earnest and unwearied endeavors
as speedily as possible to efface this blot upon our holy religion, and to
obtain the complete abolition of slavery throughout Christendom and,
if possible, throughout the world.

John Rankin reports that this was adopted by the Assembly with
practical unanimity. Members both north and south voted for it;
and hence it is evident that abolition sentiment was in 1818 predominant in the Presbyterian Church.

Now begins a tale of moral tragedy that seems almost to support
a theory of economic determinism. Things were happening outside the walls of our churches, the poisoning effects of which crept
through their walls. The perfecting of Whitney's cotton gin, and
its general introduction throughout the cotton-growing states, were
in themselves a second industrial revolution. This was followed
soon by baling machinery, then by compresses to prepare the bales

for export. By swift stages cotton outran tobacco and all other crops in the acreage planted, and in the man power required for this increased production. Slave labor became correspondingly profitable. New England and Old England alike expanded their manufacturing facilities. The price of cotton soared.[9] For more than a generation before the Civil War the great money power of this nation lay in the South among the cotton planters and exporters. Northern business became increasingly subservient to this power. National charities, church benevolences, the mission enterprise, all leaned heavily upon the South. Therefore the pressure to avoid anything that would antagonize the South and cut off these prolific sources of revenue became terrific. In a word, the weight of our Presbyterian Church as a body was thrown against the agitation of the slavery question, and toward apology for and compromise with the whole hideous system.[10] Our Presbyterian Church and several others which were strong both in the North and South were in real danger of selling their souls for the sake of slaveholders' gifts to fill the treasuries of their benevolent agencies. At practically every Assembly between 1818 and 1845 anti-slavery overtures were handed in, sometimes dozens of them, and again and again they were stifled in committee and never came to the floor. In the latter year, it is estimated, between 77,000 and 80,000 slaves were owned by Presbyterian communicants, in cases not a few, by our ministers. Ministers were preaching from their pulpits in justification of slavery from God's word, sometimes, as we have seen, even in the North. There appears to be no instance of that type of preaching before 1820.

At last, in the General Assembly of 1845, in a blanket response to all the anti-slavery overtures before them, the Bills and Overtures Committee brought in the following resolution, which was adopted by a large majority:

Resolved, first, that the General Assembly of the Presbyterian Church in the United States was originally organized, and has continued the bond of union in the church upon the conceded principle that the existence of domestic slavery, under the circumstances in which it is found in the southern portion of this country, is no bar to Christian communion.

Second, that the petitioners who ask the General Assembly to make the holding of slaves in itself a matter of discipline, do virtually require this judicatory to dissolve itself, and to abandon the organization under which by the divine blessing it has so long prospered. The tendency is evidently to separate the northern from the southern portion of the church, a result which every good citizen must deplore, as tending to the dissolution of our beloved country; and which every enlightened Christian will oppose, as bringing about a ruinous and unnecessary schism between brethren who maintain a common faith.[11]

Here is no recognition whatever of a moral issue, only a nervous concern for peace, prosperity, and union. Someone might well have risen up in that Assembly to say what a good Virginian did say most pungently on a later occasion in the face of a moral issue less sharply drawn than was this: "The right is more precious than peace." Indeed, a little group of country commissioners did say it that day, by voting a vigorous *No!* to the resolution, then filing their solemn protest because the Assembly had virtually nullified the witness borne in the Assembly of 1818. A few of them went a step further, a fateful step, when they declined the jurisdiction of the General Assembly and walked out. Long they had struggled within the church in obedience to their convictions. Some of them had spoken openly against secession in their own churches and presbyteries, as had John Rankin. They were all conservatives in theology, and absolutely loyal to the gospel and to our Presbyterian standards. But this Assembly action spelled for them the loss of their last hope of doing anything within the church. They interpreted the resolution as proof that the ecclesiastical leaders were in moral retreat. The overwhelming majority vote seemed to them to bring the church to the brink of moral apostasy. And so they walked out and went home.

Among these men were James Robertson of New Lisbon Presbytery, their leader and spokesman on the Assembly floor (a doughty old warrior born and educated in Scotland, and already a leader in the Underground Railroad); also A. S. McMaster of Beaver Presbytery and Elder Ezekiel Miller of Allegheny Presbytery. The others were mostly Ohio men. Of course, these were not the only men ready for secession. They were the only ones present in the Assembly with courage enough to do it on the spot.[12]

When they went home and reported to their presbyteries and to their congregations, there was of course rejoicing among some that now the die was cast; among others grief and hot indignation at such an act of rebellion and schism. Few congregations were of one mind in the matter, and several were split at once. A few pastors resigned their charges. A few carried their congregations with them. These declined the jurisdiction of their presbyteries and became independent. This sifting process went on for two years before anything was done to bring the scattered and lonely congregations and ministers together. All that has been related so far, it must be remembered, took place within the Old School ranks, and affected chiefly a few presbyteries in western Pennsylvania, Ohio, and Indiana.[13]

In the New School Assembly the story is somewhat different, and the storm did not break until 1846.

It is generally supposed that the disruption of 1837 was largely caused by the controversy over slavery. The facts will not substantiate this. The slavery issue entered into it in some sections of the church, especially in southern Ohio. But it was not the central issue.[14] Perhaps at the beginning there were more abolitionists in the New School branch than in the Old, but there were many in both. On the other hand the outstanding leaders of both parties were lukewarm, to say the least.

The following appears in the narrative adopted by the New School Assembly in 1838: "A zeal for universal freedom, supposed by some to be indiscreet, seems to be gradually changing to an enlightened and appropriate sympathy for the oppressed, and augmented prayer in their behalf." That was a very lovely way of saying nothing. At the same time it betrays a desire to sidestep the moral issue. The New School Assembly of 1839, after playing hide and seek with the matter for two days, finally accepted this innocuous proposal from the pen of George Beecher:

Whereas certain memorials have been sent up to this Assembly from several presbyteries, desiring some action on the subject of slavery; and whereas these memorials have been read and freely discussed by this body; and whereas this Assembly is made up of members from different portions of our extended country, who honestly differ in opinion, as well in regard to the propriety as to the nature of the ecclesiastical action desired in the case,—wherefore, Resolved, that the Assembly does most solemnly refer to the lower judicatories the subject of slavery; leaving it to them to take such order thereon as in their judgment will be most judicious, and adapted to remove the evil.[15]

The next New School action worth our attention came in 1846. To that Assembly were presented overtures, nearly all of them urging a stronger pronouncement against slavery, from four synods, twenty-nine presbyteries, and two congregations; also from two fraternal bodies, the General Congregational Associations of Connecticut and Massachusetts. Among these bodies were the Synod of Ohio and the presbyteries of Erie, Meadville, Grand River, Cleveland, Athens, Portage, and Trumbull. Thus the upper Ohio Valley was well represented. Out of these came three divergent reports from the Bills and Overtures Committee, presented respectively by Dr. Ezra Stiles Ely, W. H. Beecher, and George Duffield. A motion came from the floor that any action by this Assembly was inexpedient. On this the roll was called, this consuming the better part of two days, being resumed at intervals eleven times. But the result was not announced. Possibly the roll call was not even completed. Finally, after several motions had been rejected, Dr. Duffield's report was adopted by a vote of 92 to 29, and is as follows:

The General Assembly, having duly considered the subject of slavery, presented to their attention in the various memorials forwarded from presbyteries, synods, etc., adopt the following as the expression of their judgments.

1. The system of slavery as it exists in these United States, viewed either in the laws of the several states which sanction it, or in its actual operation and results in society, is intrinsically an unrighteous and oppressive system, and is opposed to the prescriptions of the law of God, to the spirit and precepts of the Gospel, and to the best interests of humanity.

2. The testimony of the General Assembly from 1787 to 1818 condemns it, and it remains still the recorded testimony of the Presbyterian Church of these United States against it, from which we do not recede.

3. We cannot therefore withhold the expression of our deep regret that slavery should be continued and countenanced by any of the members of our churches; and we do most earnestly exhort them, and the churches among whom it exists to use all means in their power to put it away from them. Its perpetuation among them cannot fail to be regarded by multitudes, influenced by their example, as sanctioning the system portrayed in and maintained by the statutes of the several slaveholding states wherein they dwell. Nor can any mere mitigation of its severity, prompted by the humanity and Christian feelings of any individuals who continued to hold their fellowmen in such bondage, be regarded either as a testimony against the system, or as in the least degree changing its essential character.

4. But while we believe that many evils incident to the system render it important and obligatory to bear witness against it; yet we would not undertake to determine the degree of moral turpitude on the part of individuals involved in it. This will doubtless be found to vary in the sight of God according to the degrees of light and the circumstances pertaining to each. In view of all the embarrassments and obstacles in the way of emancipation interposed by the statutes of the slaveholding states, and by the social influences affecting the views and conduct of those involved in it, we cannot pronounce a judgment of general and promiscuous condemnation, implying that destitution of Christian principle and feeling which would exclude from the table of the Lord all who stand in the legal relation of masters to slaves, or justify us in withholding our ecclesiastical fellowship from them. We rather sympathize with and would seek to succor them in their embarrassments, believing the separation and secession among the churches and their members are not the methods that God approves and sanctions for the reformation of His church.

5. While therefore we feel bound to bear our testimony against slavery, and to exhort our beloved brethren to remove it from them as

speedily as possible, by all appropriate and available means, we do at the same time condemn all divisive and schismatic measures, tending to destroy the unity and disturb the peace of our churches, and deprecate the spirit of denunciation, and that unfeeling severity which would cast from the fold those whom we are rather bound, by the spirit of the Gospel and the obligations of our covenant to instruct, counsel and exhort, and try to lead in the ways of God, and toward whom, even though they may err, to exercise forbearance and brotherly love.

6. As a court of our Lord Jesus Christ, we possess no judiciary authority. We have no right to institute and prescribe tests of Christian character and church membership not recognized and sanctioned in the sacred Scriptures, and in our standards by which we have agreed to walk. We must therefore leave this matter with the sessions, presbyteries and synods—the judicatories to whom pertains the right of judgment—to act in the administration of discipline as they may judge it to be their duty, constitutionally subject to the General Assembly only in the way of general review and control.[16]

Mr. McLain, a commissioner from the Presbytery of the District of Columbia, gave notice of protest by himself and others. Of the twenty-nine who voted against the above, twenty-one can be identified as from the South.

This action was, to be sure, much stronger and more nearly acceptable to an abolitionist than that of the Old School Assembly of 1845. Ten years earlier it might even have suited John Rankin, for then he had argued strongly against dividing the church on this issue.[17] But now he and others not a few were persuaded that the slavery power had such a stranglehold on the church that its witness was growing weaker and weaker. Probably they were correct in that. We cannot imagine Ashbel Green back in 1818 writing what the New School Assembly voted for in 1846. In 1849, as if to confirm the opinion of John Rankin, the New School Assembly voted down flatly a resolution to the effect that "slaveholding is a sin against God and man, and should be treated by the church as are other gross immoralities."[18]

But Rankin and Dyer Burgess were not there to vote, nor was any commissioner from the New School Presbytery of Ripley. Certain acts of the Synod of Cincinnati in 1847 were to them the last straw.[19] As a presbytery, they declined the jurisdiction of the Synod and the General Assembly, and went out into the wilderness to begin a kind of guerrilla warfare on their own. Into some of the complications to the events that followed we cannot enter here. Concerning some of them no documentary evidence has been unearthed. Suffice it to say that early in the year 1847 these protestants against the Synod of Cincinnati and the New School General Assembly organized themselves into the Free Presbytery of Ripley, and invited all who shared their repugnance to communion at the Lord's table with defenders of the slave system to join with them.[20] We do not know how many ministers and congregations were included at the outset; but among them were John Rankin, their acknowledged leader; Dyer Burgess, Adam B. Gilleland, J. R. Gibson, George Poage, J. Smith Poage, J. P. Hill, Jesse Lockhart, Victor M. King, and Samuel A. Van Dyke. Among the congregations were Ripley, Red Oak, Strait Creek, Russellville, Mount Leigh, Winchester, Hillsboro, Frankfort, and Felicity.

They invited others to join them, and others did. Among them was one who was to play a leading part in the movement, Joseph Gordon.[21] He was a graduate of Washington College and Western Seminary, was licensed by Coshocton Presbytery, and after two years of successful mission work in that area was called to a professorship in Franklin College at New Athens, Ohio. The Presbyterian Church of New Athens had been formed a few years earlier out of the Crab Apple Church—the pastor, Jacob Coon, and a large minority of the membership having withdrawn from Crab Apple because their anti-slavery convictions were not shared by the majority. The sentiment in New Athens, both among the Presbyterians and the Associate Reformed, was strongly abolitionist. They invited Gordon to supply their pulpit along with his college work. After a few months they gave him a unanimous call to become their pastor. Signifying his purpose to accept, he transferred himself to the care of St. Clairsville Presbytery, and under their

direction completed his trials for ordination, all of which were
unanimously sustained. Presbytery met at New Athens for his ordination and installation. The local congregation was assembled,
and the solemn service was about to begin, when a member of
Presbytery threw a bombshell into their midst by arising and an-
nouncing that Gordon had published in a Cadiz newspaper slanderous statements against the General Assembly of 1845, concerning
the action we have already reviewed.[22] He moved that the ordination be arrested until Presbytery should investigate the matter.
They demanded that Gordon repudiate his article and apologize
to Presbytery for his statements. He replied that his statements
were not made in malice against any man, but were directed only
against a specific act, and that he could not retract them. They
refused to ordain him, and revoked his license. Immediately the
New Athens Church declined the jurisdiction of St. Clairsville
Presbytery, and stood by Gordon to a man. He had already had
some correspondence with John Rankin, who when he heard what
had happened invited Gordon to come to Ripley and apply for
ordination to their new Free Presbytery. This he did. A few weeks
later, in October, 1847, Rankin came to New Athens and met there
with Gordon and three other men who had already withdrawn
from the Old School Church. Together they organized the Free
Presbytery of Mahoning, the one which covered most of our upper
Ohio Valley territory. The three men were James Robertson of
Hanoverton, who had been floor leader of the abolitionists in the
Assembly of 1845; A. B. Bradford of Darlington, Pennsylvania; and
S. A. McLean of Clarksville, Pennsylvania. A few months later,
partly by division of Ripley, a third Free Presbytery of Hillsboro,
sometimes called Highland, was formed. In 1848 these three pres-
byteries united in organizing the Free Presbyterian Synod of Cin-
cinnati, or as they later called it, the Free Church Synod of the
United States.

So much for the organized beginnings. The movement grew. The
Fugitive Slave Law gave it a great impetus, until there were little

Free Church congregations scattered here and there all the way from Lancaster County in eastern Pennsylvania out to Central Iowa. The names of ten presbyteries have been found. Perhaps some others besides Hillsboro-Highland had two names.[23] We are sure of seven presbyteries, Ripley, Mahoning, Central Ohio, Highland, Cincinnati, Illinois and Iowa, or Northwest. How many congregations there were we do not know. We have a list of sixty-five, but it is not complete. Of the ministers, we have sixty-four of them identified. We have the names of about nine hundred individuals who were members of these little groups, but that again we know is far from complete. They came from both Old and New School branches, more than two-thirds of their ministers were from the Old School. With only two or three exceptions their churches were in small villages or in the open country. Some of them, such as New Castle Central and Worthington, Pennsylvania, began as Free churches. Some were minorities, as at Martinsburg and Savannah, Ohio; others were majorities, as at Darlington and Clarksville. Some, such as New Athens, Ohio, and Sand Creek, Indiana, had gone as a whole into the Free Church fold. Some were colonies of abolitionists from the East, as at Aledo, Illinois, and Kossuth and Quasqueton, Iowa. But all alike had, just as did the Free Church in Scotland in 1843, for the sake of a principle forsaken old friends, surrendered property, assumed heavy financial burdens, and gone out into the wilderness in protest against a hideous evil, against which within the church of their fathers they had long lifted their voices in vain.

The Free Church, whatever the origins of any of its ministers, was staunchly orthodox.[24] They refused to have anything to do with Garrison and the other New England abolitionists, because they believed these were breaking away from their Christian moorings. They were evangelistic in their ministry, and some of their pastors led fruitful revivals. They were ardent advocates of total abstinence without exception. They were against oath-bound secret societies, as were all the Associate, Reformed, and Seceder bodies of that day, and many other Presbyterians. But their one distinctive conviction was expressed in their slogan: "No Christian fellowship with slaveholders, whose gross sin is compounded of theft, murder and adultery." [25]

Wherever a Free Church was found, somewhere in its membership was sure to be found also a station of the Underground Railroad. John Rankin had a hideout for runaway slaves in the attic of his house on the hill above Ripley, and there Eliza of *Uncle Tom's Cabin* and her baby found refuge after they had crossed the Ohio on the broken ice. James Robertson maintained a hiding-place in his home at Hanoverton, and the tunnel is still there that connects the cellar of his house with the cellar of the house across the street. Elder James Gaston at Clarkson, Ohio, had a secret cellar under his house. It is still there. From it a tunnel leads out into a coal mine nearly a quarter-mile away. So too with Elder John Porter Shannon of the Free Church at Keene in Coshocton County, and with the home of Dr. Benjamin Mitchell, long pastor at Mount Pleasant, Ohio.

These Free Church people were scorned and ridiculed and persecuted in many ways by their neighbors, but they did not stand entirely alone. Not only the Quakers, but the Mennonites, the Moravians, the Wesleyan Methodists, the Seceders, and two synods of the Associate Reformed Church took exactly the same ground, making slaveholding a bar to Christian fellowship.[26] Not only so, but they were in correspondence with Presbyterian bodies in Canada, Ireland, and Scotland, and with the Congregationalists in England, all of whom commended their action and encouraged them in their witness. Some of these also sent to the Old School Assembly protests against its 1845 action—protests which were treated with scant courtesy.[27]

These Free Church folk were crusaders, but they were not organizers. They might have grown much stronger if they had given more attention to organizing and building up their churches. Most of these were too weak to support a pastor alone. Many were so isolated as not to be easily grouped. They never had an adequate supply of preachers; and some of these, like Rankin, gave far more time to lecturing against slavery than to the care of their congregations. Their meetings of Presbytery and Synod were not well attended. Their records were carelessly kept, and apparently carelessly preserved, for few of them have been found. It is likely that their neighbors found them sometimes hard to live with. Crusaders usually are. They were schismatics, no doubt, and for many ardent churchmen that is the major anathema.

Yet they cannot be lightly dismissed with such criticisms. Few and feeble they were and full of human frailty; but they represent the birthpangs of a new conscience within the American Presbyterian Church. They were God's trumpet to arouse and recall a church that was guilty of moral backsliding, and was in grave danger of selling its soul for gain. Both Old School and New School became shamefully afraid to do or say anything which might alienate the South, upon which they were depending so heavily for the support of all their enterprises.[28] As it turned out, all their anxiety on that score was in vain. The South was alienated in any event. And they could not blame the Free Church for what came. In 1857 the New School Church split north and south. Most of us have forgotten that. In 1861 all the Southern synods withdrew to form the Presbyterian Church in the Confederate States of America, and a few months later welcomed with open arms the Southern New School Church, which a little before they had deeply distrusted as unorthodox. These withdrawals they did not call schisms. Then, almost overnight, both Northern branches were ready to speak out against slavery, for they had nothing more to lose.

We record here an incident of the Civil War which in itself has nothing to do with the Free Church or its distinctive principles, but is a parable of what this Free Church was and did.

In the battle of Corinth a certain regiment of Wisconsin infantry was under fire for the first time. They were ordered to advance and hold a certain ridge. Their color sergeant was a fresh young college boy named Jerome Davis, later to become a great Congregational missionary to Japan. Sergeant Davis marched on ahead with his flag as ordered, till he gained the ridge. Crouching down behind a stump he looked back. The regiment was not there. Far down the slope he saw their ragged line, wavering and threatening to break as the bullets whined about them and a few men fell. But Sergeant Davis held his ground. In a few minutes an orderly came crawling forward on his stomach. When near enough he shouted in a lull of the firing, "Sergeant Davis, bring back the colors!" Davis shouted back: "The colors are where they belong; bring up the regiment." This they did, helping to win the battle.

The Free Church carried forward the flag of a zealous Christian morality under fire. They kept shouting back: "This is where the colors belong, the banner of the Son of God, the Brother of all men. Bring up the regiment!" Tardily, stumblingly, the regiment did come up to the colors. And today there is probably not a Christian in America who would deny or dispute what the Free Presbyterian Church stood for, the conviction that human values outrank all other values, and that therefore the enslavement of one man by another is among the gross sins from which followers of Jesus must keep themselves clean.

What became of the Free Church? When the war was over its work was done. Its sons had fought almost to a man in the Union Army. Its daughters had given themselves to teaching and relief work among the freed slaves even in the midst of the war. It had never retreated with the flag. Gradually it gave up its separate existence. Its Synod did not meet after 1863. There were some presbytery meetings as late as 1865. A few congregations maintained their separate existence even down to 1870. But gradually they disbanded and went back into the congregations from which they had withdrawn. In a few cases they became United Presbyterian. Even more of their ministers went into this same church. So far as is known not one of them ever thought it necessary to apologize for having been a Free Presbyterian.

Today they are all but forgotten. Many of the Presbyterian ministers of this generation do not know that there ever was such an organization as the Free Church. Yet their story is a part of the record of American Presbyterianism. Their two presbyteries of Mahoning and Central Ohio covered the territory of the upper Ohio Valley. They helped to give our Presbyterianism a moral earnestness it has never wholly lost. The evils against which they protested in the form of their expression in that day were set aside. But there are other evils against which the conscience of our church is not yet aroused: the liquor evil, the gambling evil, the divorce evil, the drug scourge, the hideous evil of militarism. And the church is in danger of having its lips sealed and its hands tied by the same sinister forces that brought our beloved church in the forties and fifties of the last century near to the abyss of apostasy. The Free Church sounded a trumpet call that still needs to be heard and heeded: "Be ye clean, that bear the vessels of the Lord."

CHAPTER XI

Events and Trends—Early
Nineteenth Century

AT the opening of the nineteenth century the portion of American Presbyterianism included by the General Assembly organized in 1789 had expanded west of the Allegheny and Blue Ridge mountains to a very considerable degree.[1]

By treaties with the Indians, southwestern Pennsylvania was opened for comparatively peaceful settlement after 1768 and, after 1795, the northwestern parts of the same state could be occupied. Into these areas, and spilling over into the Ohio country, also down the Ohio River as far as the Mississippi, came tens of thousands of the Ulster-Scotch and the Scotch from eastern Pennsylvania, Maryland, and Delaware, also directly from northern Ireland and Scotland. From the same eastern portion of the middle states, and by way of ports of entry farther south, there came additional thousands of the same nationality to go into the central valleys of Virginia, thence on south and west, mostly through the Cumberland Gap, into Kentucky and Tennessee.

Across New York State, some to settle there, others to migrate on to the Western (Connecticut) Reserve of Ohio, still others to continue on to Indiana, Michigan, and Illinois, came thousands of Congregationalists from Connecticut and other New England states—most of whom were presbyterially inclined.

In western Pennsylvania the Germans, Reformed Church or Lutheran, took up residence. At the same time, the Ulster-Scotch and the Scotch came in great numbers. The tens of thousands swelled to a few hundred thousand before the new century had advanced far. Normally all of the Scotch, whether from northern Ireland or from Scotland, would either be Presbyterian or would be very open to recruiting by the representatives of this denomination.

STRICT CONSERVATISM BRINGS TROUBLES

But the Presbyterian leaders in certain presbyteries and synods already established belonged almost wholly to the conservative, strict subscriptionist party as found along the Atlantic coast and in the parent countries. They had an unbending attitude with respect to the admission to the ministry of only college or university graduates with special training in theology. They also were steeped in the most severe forms of Calvinism with its double reprobation features. From these severe forms, they could not and would not recede when challenged by revival leaders in the Cumberland country of Kentucky and Tennessee. As the inevitable result of these two instances of rigid attitudes, the Presbyterian Church, instead of forging ahead as the leading communion in these frontier areas, finally took fifth place. The Methodists, the Baptists, the newly formed Disciples of Christ, and the Cumberland Presbyterians moved ahead. All of these and other denominations were advanced, the latter two founded, as the result of the Awakening of 1800. This Awakening began as early as 1795 and continued almost unabated, if the work of Charles G. Finney and the Laymen's Revival of 1847 are included, until 1860.

As for the Presbyterian portion of this Awakening,[2] the difficulties resulting from conservative, strict subscription stands on the part of certain leaders in the Synod of Kentucky, who, in turn, influenced the General Assembly, finally caused the formation of the first presbytery of the Cumberland Presbyterian Church in

1810.[3] Not until 1902–1903 did the Presbyterian Church U.S.A. modify the Westminster Standards by taking out the "fatalistic" feature, thus making it possible for the Cumberland Church, in most part, to unite with it.[4]

What a happier history for Presbyterianism had the change of 1902–1903 been made in 1802–1803! As for the ordination of men to the ministry who are neither college nor seminary graduates, there are now ways and means to make exceptions when it is apparent to all the church courts concerned that the candidate has such graces and accomplishments as constitute the equivalent of the standards thus relaxed.

THE PLAN OF UNION OF 1801
AND RESULTING SCHISM

Let us return to an examination of another lamentable incident resulting in another schism—this in connection with the migration of the Connecticut and other New England Congregationalists across New York State, into northwestern Ohio, into Indiana, Michigan, Illinois, and parts still farther west. In the year 1801, the "Plan of Union," [5] as of that year, was adopted as a mode of operation as between the Connecticut Congregational Association and the Presbyterian General Assembly. By this Plan it was provided that as new churches might be founded thereafter, each local group would have the right to decide whether it would be presbyterian or congregational, and it could call as its pastor a clergyman from either presbyterian or congregational sources. As it worked out, most decided to be Presbyterians, preferring the connectional feature as that best suited for the frontier. But most of the clergymen were of Congregational origin, hence there arose what the rigidly minded Scotch and Ulster-Scotch Presbyterians called "Congre-Presbyterianism," a spurious mongrel church, so they said, heterodox in many particulars. Finally those rigidly minded succeeded, in the General Assembly of 1837, in having all of the presbyteries and synods that were products of the Plan declared legally out of the church. This ruling was based on the point that the Plan of Union had never been overtured down to the presbyteries and therefore had never received the required favorable vote to make it legal. There was a secondary matter which, though important as a principle, would not necessarily have brought about the exscinding of the New School presbyteries and synods. This was the principle that the whole church should itself be a foreign missionary society. At that time the New School Presbyterians were sharing in the far-flung missionary efforts of the American Board of Commissioners for Foreign Missions, a union society. The Old School side could not conscientiously share in such a united effort.

Once again, as in the schism of 1741–1758 and in the schism of 1810, the rigid subscriptionists, made up mostly of those who had maintained close ties with the similarly minded of the Presbyterians of Ireland and Scotland, accomplished the breaking up of the church. It should be made plain that among those who were quite ready for liberty within evangelical bounds, there was a very large percentage of the Ulster-Scotch and of the Scotch. Hence the foregoing observations are not made with prejudice; they are made simply to state a historic fact.

The Auburn Affirmation

When, in the twentieth century, the Auburn Affirmation [6] was formulated and signed, it was a revival of that hitherto oft expressed yearning that Christians be permitted to have a degree of liberty within the recognized bounds of evangelical, catholic, protestant Christianity. Not all of the opponents of the Auburn Affirmation chose to go into schism following several years of rather bitter wrangling culminating in contests in succeeding General Assemblies.

We have traced the foregoing events as trends even as they extended themselves into this present century. Let us now return to examine another event and trend of great significance in connection with which a few outstanding intellectuals were the principal actors.

THE CHURCH AND SACRAMENTS

The general harmony and cooperation of all evangelical churches, with which the nineteenth century had opened, began to break up in new denominational and sectional consciousness and jealousy. The largest of the American reformed churches, the Presbyterian, was now split into New School and Old School. The system of home missions cooperation with the Congregationalists broke down. The terrible tensions over slavery and the national union split the churches yet again.

Less influential in its own day than these controversies was still another, which may, on the other hand, have more direct significance for us in the twentieth century. All across Christendom in this generation there occurred a revival of interest in the church, not just as an institution but as a religious reality, closely associated with a revival of interest in sacramental worship. We see it in Eastern Orthodoxy with Khomiakov, in the Roman Church in Möhler, in Anglicanism with Newman and Pusey, Coleridge and Maurice, in Lutheranism in Löhe, Schartau, and Grundtvig. And in the United States, it was the Reformed Church which presented the most substantial theological formulation of the movement, although the American Episcopalians also shared. It is this American Reformed expression of the churchly and sacramental revival that I now set forth. It was called the Mercersburg movement from the name of the theological seminary where its leading theologians taught. Of its direct institutional results there is only the liturgy of the present Evangelical and Reformed Church, but the writing and debates of the original controversy often seem more relevant to our problems today than do the dissensions of Old School and New School, pro-slavery or anti-slavery. For in our day, too, there has been a great renaissance of religious and theological interest in the church and sacraments and their basis in Christology. These are some of the knottiest problems of the contemporary ecumenical movement. There are many to agree with Nevin and Schaff that the most important issue of the day is the nature of the church.

The Mercersburg movement began with a challenge to the re-vivalism which was sweeping nearly all evangelical Protestantism in the United States in the second generation of the nineteenth century. The so-called "Anxious Bench Controversy" concerned the "new measures" then being used so dramatically by Finney and his imitators. In it Nevin set forth the most searching attack on the dangers of such methods which had yet been heard. And much of American Protestant history since bears out his charge that there is a hidden affinity between emotional revivalism and rationalistic moralism.

One may also say of the movement what has been said of the Tractarian movement in Anglican history: that it burst the bounds of a theological tradition which had become ingrown and provin-cial. John W. Nevin and Philip Schaff declined to work within the well worn grooves of New England theology or Calvinist scholas-ticism, and they brought American theology once again into touch with the active currents of thought in Great Britain and on the Continent. It may be fairly said, I think, that at least on some issues and at times they left Reformed ground or Protestant ground altogether. But in fighting for their right to represent a high-church understanding of the Reformed tradition they raised some grave questions about the validity of the kind of churchmanship then prevailing in Presbyterian and Reformed circles and broadened and deepened the whole consciousness of the meaning of the Re-formed doctrines of faith and order.

I wish to discuss only one phase of the debate in this controversy; namely, that which dealt with the Reformed doctrine of the Lord's Supper and the church. The antagonists were two of the ablest Presbyterian theologians of the period, Charles Hodge, editor of

the *Princeton Review*, and John W. Nevin, chief contributor to
the *Mercersburg Review*. The principals were closely related in
background. Both were the products of American Presbyterianism
in the conservative Scottish tradition. Both had studied and then
taught Old Testament studies at Princeton Seminary—Hodge
first, for he was five years older. Nevin took over Hodge's classes
for two years when the latter went to Europe for advanced study.
Then through the decade of the thirties while Hodge taught at
Princeton, Nevin was professor at the Western Theological Seminary in Pittsburgh. At that stage he was so strenuous an opponent
of rum and slavery as to be described by some influential persons
as "the most dangerous man in Pittsburgh." While suspected of
some New School sympathies, his theology was still apparently the
scholastic federal theology he and Hodge had alike studied from
the manual of Turretin at Princeton. And according to his son,
Hodge always thought of Nevin as his greatest student.

In 1840, however, Nevin moved from the Pittsburgh Seminary
to the seminary of the German Reformed Church at Mercersburg.
At the beginning his move had no theological significance, and
apparently President Alexander of Princeton encouraged him to
make it with the view that this was simply a transfer from one
branch of the Reformed Church to another. In the line of his new
obligations Nevin began to preach and write his way through the
Heidelberg Catechism. Coming to it fresh in the maturity of his
powers, he rediscovered its merits for the German Reformed Church
and became a chief means of restoring it to use and honor. But
also he became increasingly aware that the theology of the Heidelberg Catechism was not at all points identical with that of the
Westminster Confessions. Heidelberg was less scholastic, simpler,
more religious and more churchly. It was less emphatic on some
points, such as predestination, which Nevin, and later the Reformed churches generally in the nineteenth century, were increasingly less concerned to put at the center of things. As Nevin
explored further the history and the thinkers of the German Re-

formed Church, he gradually came around to the view that here was a distinct tradition or school of Reformed theology to be set beside that of Zwingli and Calvin. And he bestirred himself to make other Presbyterians and Reformed in America come to terms with a Reformed theology which differed from that of the Scots or Swiss or Dutch on significant points.

In his studies in German theology, however, Nevin was not merely a traditionalist, not merely oriented to Melanchthon, Ursinus, and Heidelberg, as Hodge was merely oriented to Pictet and Turretin. While at Pittsburgh he had begun to read the theologians of modern Germany. Professor Moses Stuart of Andover had introduced the work of German Biblical scholars to America and had stimulated the interest of both Hodge and Nevin as to what could be learned from them. The greatest intellectual event in Nevin's Pittsburgh career, however, was his discovery of Neander, the father of modern church history. It was Neander who changed his outlook from the static concepts of Princeton scholasticism to envision the Christian movement in history as a living, growing, developing force. Neander had been converted from his original Judaism by Schleiermacher, and here too Nevin found a fresh grasp of the Christian faith as a life, rather than merely as a set of propositions to be believed or disbelieved. Schleiermacher also placed as the fulcrum of his theology the person and work of Jesus Christ rather than the divine decrees, or sin and atonement in the abstract. From him nearly all nineteenth century German theologians had learned to make their theology Christocentric. Nevin and Mercersberg were to follow here too, although American theology generally did not do so until near the end of the nineteenth century. And with these Germans Nevin had a philosophical sympathy. Even at Princeton, where the empirical philosophy of Locke and the Scottish school of Reid and Stewart were dominant, Nevin had felt an affinity with the Platonizing theologians of the seventeenth century, Leighton and Howe. This leaning toward Platonic idealism made the general German temper of the day congenial to him, while for Hodge, who neither liked nor understood it, it was all misty "transcendentalism." The Mercersberg men, in contrast, were to form a significant bridge for the transmission to America of the great thinkers of modern German philosophy, especially Hegel and Schelling, as well as theology proper. And half of Nevin's first theological work was to consist of an attempt to restate Calvinist ideas in modern philosophy and psychology.

Neither sixteenth nor nineteenth century German influences, however, can adequately explain the most characteristic concerns of Nevin, his high views of church and sacraments. None of the Germans he had read satisfied him on these subjects. Where did he derive these ideas? He tells us that his first glimpse of what the "church spirit" really meant was obtained unexpectedly in Pittsburgh from looking into a volume of the Oxford Tracts given him by a friend. While in no sense converted by the book, he first sensed then the profoundly earnest religious problem with which the authors were wrestling. Later he was to follow Newman's course and writings with the greatest interest and sympathy, and corresponded with R. I. Wilberforce, an able theologian of the Oxford Movement. But with due acknowledgment of stimulus from this direction, Nevin must be said to have largely evolved his high-church visions himself. He starts, not with the Oxford men, from problems of church and state and clerical authority, but from the religious center, the sacraments. And one can watch the whole system unfold itself in his mind over a period of six or eight years. This working out of the inner logic and coherence of his viewpoint makes the reading of him most interesting.

The first extended presentation of Nevin's theology came in his little volume of 1846, *The Mystical Presence, A Vindication of the Reformed or Calvinistic Doctrine of the Holy Eucharist.* While he did give considerable space to his own theological reformulations, Nevin's main intent was to define what the Reformed view of this subject had actually been and to challenge the Reformed of his own day to face their standards on this subject. Nevin's contention was that "the modern popular view of the Lord's Supper is chargeable with a serious defection from the original Protestant orthodoxy." [7]

The seriousness of such a situation, in Nevin's view, could not be evaded on the ground that the view of the Eucharist was a rather special and secondary point in theology.

> As the Eucharist forms the very heart of the whole Christian worship, so it is clear that the entire question of the Church, which all are compelled to acknowledge the great life-problem of the age, centers ultimately in the sacramental question as its inmost heart and core. Our view of the Lord's Supper must ever condition and rule in the end our view of Christ's person and the conception we form of the Church. It must influence at the same time, very materially, our whole system of theology, as well as all our ideas of ecclesiastical history.[8]

Nevin's summons to the American churches thus swept the whole range of what we now describe as the domain of "faith and order."

> Our sect system must be considered, in its very nature, unfavorable to all proper respect for the sacraments. . . . In proportion as the sect character prevails, it will be found that Baptism and the Lord's Supper are looked upon as mere outward signs, in the case of which all proper efficacy is supposed to be previously at hand in the inward state of the subject by whom they are received. . . . It is particularly significant moreover in the aspect now considered, that the *Baptist* body, as such, is numerically stronger than any other denomination in the country. But the baptistic principle prevails more extensively still; for it is very plain that all true sense of the sacramental character of baptism is wanting in large portions of the church, where the ordinance is still retained. . . . Along with this, of course, must prevail an unsacramental feeling, by which the Lord's Supper also is shorn of all its significance and power. Methodism, in this way, may be said to wrong the sacraments, (as also the entire idea of the *Church*,) almost as seriously as the Baptist system itself.[9]

"Methodism itself can hardly be said to make less account of the sacraments, practically or theoretically," than does American Lutheranism.

It is notorious that the American Lutheran Church, under its principal and most influential exhibition at least, has given up altogether the sacramental doctrine of Luther, and along with this, (for the two things can never be sundered,) the original genius and life of the Lutheran Confession.[10]

Even those denominations among us which represent the Reformed Church by true and legitimate descent, such as the Presbyterian in its different branches, and the Reformed Dutch, show plainly that they have fallen away, to some extent, from the original faith of the church. . . . Not only is the old doctrine rejected, but it has become almost lost even to the knowledge of the church. When it is brought into view, it is not believed, perhaps, that the Reformed Church ever held or taught in fact, any doctrine of the sort; or if it be yielded at length, that Calvin and some other maintained some such view, it is set down summarily as one of those instances in which the work of the Reformation appears still clogged with a measure of Popish superstition. . . . Even in the Episcopal Church, with all the account it professes to make of the sacraments, few are willing to receive in full such representations of the eucharistic presence, as are made either by Hooker or Calvin.[11]

And by way of illustration Nevin produced a catena of distinguished Congregationalist and Presbyterian theologians: Jonathan Edwards, Samuel Hopkins, Edward Bellamy, Timothy Dwight, John Dick, Ashbel Green, Albert Barnes.

Nevin gives a hint of the personal agony roused in him by the contemplation of this "apostasy" of the Reformed, including the Presbyterian, churches. This history, he says, poses a question

which is perfectly legitimate and of immense practical importance; which it becomes the friends of the *Reformed* Church to look steadily in the face. If Calvinism—the system of Geneva—*necessarily* runs here into Zwinglianism, we may, indeed, well despair of the whole interest. For most assuredly no Church can stand, that is found to be constitutionally unsacramental.[12]

In contrast to this prevailing unchurchly and unsacramental view of religion, Nevin set forth in about fifty pages the Reformed doctrine of the Lord's Supper as taught by the theologians and the confessions of the sixteenth and early seventeenth centuries. This exposition we do not have space here to analyze. On the whole it would, I think, now be acknowledged a balanced and penetrating account, but, as we shall see, American Presbyterians found it hard to believe in Nevin's day. It will be enough for our purposes at the moment to note the specific points on which Nevin contrasted the classical Reformed and Presbyterian doctrine with that prevailing in his day. The crucial point was the conviction of the Reformed fathers that in the action of the Lord's Supper we are brought face to face in a real way with the person of our Risen Lord, and draw life and power from Him. This communion is in His flesh and blood, that is, His concrete incarnate human character, though now glorified and immaterial. In this conception the sacrament has an objective force, independent of our faith, although received only by faith, and is literally a great mystery, not to say miracle. It constitutes a specific and distinctive form of communion with our Lord, different from all other means of grace. The "modern Puritan," in contrast, admits a communion in the Supper at the most in the *divine* nature of Christ or His Spirit only, by which is generally meant simply a quickening of the appropriation by faith of the benefits of Christ's atonement, which is no mystery, but an understandable psychological process and in no way different from the exercise of faith in any other means of grace. In this contrast Nevin was able to show also the agreement of the writers of the early church with those of the Reformation against the "Puritan" view.

So much for Nevin. The case for the defense was taken up rather surprisingly by Nevin's former teacher, Charles Hodge of Princeton. For the first few years of the new movement at Mercersberg, Princeton had looked on with mild benevolence. The Princeton men also felt reservations about revivalistic excesses. The *Princeton Review* had published favorable reviews of Schaff's *Principle of Protestantism* and *What Is Church History?* and reported Nevin's *Catholic Unity* accurately without comment. Then there had been silence from Princeton for two years, although a review of *The Mystical Presence* was to be anticipated. Then at last, in 1848, Hodge declared himself in opposition in a long review article.

There are several curious aspects to Hodge's review of Nevin's *The Mystical Presence*. He begins by confessing that he had let the book lie on his desk for two years without reading it, and only when he had occasion to define what the Reformed doctrine on the Lord's Supper was, had he managed to wade through it. Perhaps the occasion was the prompting of some clergy that he should refute Nevin. But in any case Hodge had already said something significant about the place of church and sacraments in his theology when he confessed that he found it took some external necessity to force him to read books on such themes.

There was also an ungracious, one might almost say, unfair character to Hodge's treatment of Nevin. He set out to prove "that Dr. Nevin is tenfold further from the doctrines of our common fathers, than those whom he commiserates and condemns." He had some significant observations to make about Nevin's theological reconstructions, but these we must here overlook and confine ourselves, as we have done in Nevin's case also, to the historical portions of the argument. Here Hodge shows himself very reluctant to give credit where credit is due. He provided a substantial parade of sources for the Reformation doctrines, all with an air of setting Nevin straight, and yet with very few exceptions he owed his authorities to Nevin and exhibits no general grasp of the historical question in his own right. Similarly in his systematic exposition of the *differentiae* of the Reformed view he contrived to convey the same tone of censure of Nevin in setting out points which Nevin had already made with equal care and with more fullness. He credited Nevin with extraordinary versatility in deserving at one time the epithets Sabellian, Eutychian, Romanist, Socinian, mystic, and rationalist.

Hodge's method of historical argument was to rearrange Nevin's authorities in three groups: the Zwinglian Swiss documents (including the Anglican, which Nevin had pointed out as lower in sacramental doctrine than almost all early Reformed Confessions);[13] the distinctly Calvinist theologians and Confessions of various countries, Scottish, French, and Belgic; and a third group influenced by both Reformed fathers, but agreeing, as Hodge read them, with Zwingli in essentials.

The two former schools differed on their understanding of participation in the body and blood. They were agreed that this meant appropriation in faith of Christ's sacrifice, the breaking of his body and the shedding of his blood, in atonement for our sins. Did it mean also the reception of new power from communion with Christ's glorified body?

Both views are expressed in the public confessions . . . but if a decision must be made between them, the higher authority is certainly due to the doctrine of sacrificial efficacy first mentioned.[14]

And with regard to the question whether our union with Christ involves a participation of his human body, nature, or life, Hodge dogmatically excluded any such possibility.

Apart from the relative weight of the historical authorities, Hodge cites two theological arguments for preferring Zwingli to Calvin:

It is difficult to reconcile the idea that a life-giving influence emanates from the glorified body of Christ with the universally received doctrine of the Reformed Church, that we receive Christ as fully through the ministry of the word as in the Lord's Supper.[15]

And secondly,

All the Reformed taught, Calvin perhaps more earnestly than most others, that our union with Christ since the incarnation is the same in nature as that enjoyed by the saints under the old dispensation.[16]

But if that union takes place only in virtue of the human incarnation of Christ, it could not have been possible to Jews before Jesus Christ. These two considerations, Hodge urged, indicate that Calvin's doctrine of the Eucharistic presence really was not an integral part of his theology, but rather a concession to the Lutherans. And this supposition seemed borne out by the fact that Calvinistic scholastics such as Beza, Turretin, and Pictet gave up the conception entirely.

Hodge had not a word to say about that quarter of Nevin's work devoted to the "modern Puritan" theology. Here his sympathies obviously lay. But perhaps he would have been embarrassed as an Old School Presbyterian to come to the defense of New England Congregationalists and Albert Barnes, to say nothing of the string of German "neologists" Nevin had classed with them.

Nevin could hardly be expected to yield tamely to Hodge's extraordinary definition of the Reformed tradition by the exclusion of Calvin and Calvinist confessions. The September, 1850, *Mercersburg Review* carried over one hundred pages in rebuttal. Nevin was now fortified by Ebrard's second volume on *The History of the Dogma of the Lord's Supper*,[17] which supported his historical contentions on every point in the most elaborate account written, to that date, of the eucharistic controversies of the sixteenth century. Nevin noted that Ebrard had attempted to rescue Zwingli from the Zwinglians, a point on which he himself reserved judgment. But in any case he pointed out that the earliest Swiss formulations had all been superseded under the influence of Calvin's riper thought, and that it was indefensible historically to set them up as parallel authorities to the thought of Calvin or the great confessions of the fifties and sixties, as Hodge had tried to do. And as for Hodge's third group of confessions, the Zurich Consensus, Second Helvetic and Heidelberg Catechism, Nevin showed that, read in their historical context, they taught the Calvinist rather than the Zwinglian view. This long historical essay of Nevin's has proved sufficiently substantial so that a writer of our day on "The Protestant Doctrine of the Lord's Supper" has found it worth while to reproduce some twenty pages' worth of Nevin.[18]

Hodge had appealed to certain apparent internal contradictions in Calvin's thought as a ground for rejecting his view of the Eucharist. Nevin also noticed a tension, but drew from it the opposite conclusion. In his case the incompatible element was predestination. He wrote of Calvin:

> The sacramental interest and that of the decrees, in his system, are not free from some inward conflict, and . . . the one has a tendency continually to overthrow the other. Hence it is, no doubt, that in those sections of the Reformed church where the doctrine of the decrees has been regarded as the main interest in theology, the original Calvinistic view of the sacraments has fallen more and more into the shade, so as to be frequently of no authority whatever. And yet the doctrine of the decrees as held by Calvin never belonged at all to the constitution of the Reformed Church as such; whereas the sacramental doctrine entered in truth into its distinctive character as a confession.[19]

Nevin claimed Calvin's authority for his views of church and sacraments, but admitted some dissatisfaction with Calvin's theories of the decrees. Hodge's position was just the contrary.

Ten years after *The Mystical Presence* Hodge published a *Commentary on the Epistle to the Ephesians.* Nevin reviewed this commentary at considerable length since it touched so frequently on his favorite topic of the doctrine of the church. He found Hodge's whole reading of the Epistle vitiated by his low and un-Biblical view of the church. Hodge pressed a distinction of the visible and invisible church which was not to be found in the letter itself. By Hodge, however, they are so radically separated as to have no relation to each other. Both of them, moreover, were deprived of all real social and corporate character. The invisible church was just a collective term for the aggregate of all elect souls. The visible church was just the aggregate of those who profess the true religion, and in no sense, as the Epistle holds, the home of the Spirit, and itself the medium of salvation.

Looking back over this debate we note much of interest. Nevin had uncovered the inner logic of Calvinist scholastic orthodoxy in its rejection of the original Reformed view of church and sacraments. The unchurchly attitude of pietist evangelicalism and of

rationalism had been widely recognized, but the tendency of orthodoxy, as represented by Charles Hodge, in this direction was
less obvious and thus perhaps more dangerous to the church.
Nevin's influence on the American Reformed churches cannot yet
be estimated. At least he succeeded in opening up again very practical as well as historical issues for Reformed and Presbyterian
churchmen, issues which stand high on our present schedule of un-
finished business. As representatives of American Presbyterianism
participate in the modern ecumenical studies in the doctrine of
the church, it will be of great interest to note whether this portion
of the visible church adopts the sacramental doctrine of the church
or tends still further in the direction of the conception that the
visible church is a loose association of unrelated individuals without
corporate power to mediate grace.

CHAPTER XII

Some Trends and Events
Since 1869

THE doctrine of the church—that is to say, a church's theory about itself—is the joint product of that church's Christian heritage and of its modifying environment. Where the doctrine of the church is vitally and realistically formulated it is therefore in part a condensed or sublimated history of the church. One could almost read a church's history backward from the implied changes in this doctrine. But we shall not attempt to read church history backward; it is difficult enough to read it forward. Instead, let us scan certain broad areas of the history of the Presbyterian Church in the U.S.A. since the reunion of 1869, noting the trends in these areas, and especially the implication of these trends for the doctrine concerning the nature of the church.

EXPANSION AT HOME AND ABROAD

The first area which we scan is the area of missionary expansion. During most of the nineteenth century Americans seemed to be on wheels moving westward. By a leap, settlement moved from the Mississippi River to the Pacific Ocean. The golden spike, completing the transcontinental railroad that bound together the Atlantic and Pacific coasts, was driven just a few days before the reunion of the Old School and New School Presbyterian churches. The need of ministering to the rapidly growing Western settlements was a principal motive of Presbyterian reunion and a chief task of the reunited church.

Sheldon Jackson—who like another Westerner, Stephen A. Douglas, could well be called a "little giant"—was the very embodiment of the Presbyterian home missionary spirit. He established preaching points along new railroads or wagon routes. He secured special railroad rates for commissioners for the 1871 General Assembly at Chicago, or for the 1874 Assembly at St. Louis to visit Denver. He sent names of deserving home missionaries to potential Eastern supporters. He collected some $10,000 in a year and a half for his "raven fund" and he founded and sent to every Presbyterian minister his *Rocky Mountain Presbyterian*. He recruited new home missionaries on his periodic visits to the seminaries. After he had completed one life work in the West, he then accomplished another in Alaska.

A kindred spirit was Henry Kendall, co-secretary of the Home Board. Like Sheldon Jackson on the field, Henry Kendall on the staff lived, ate, slept, and dreamed home missions. He was a true missionary statesman who had no use for pinch-penny policies that would rob the church of its future in the West. When the situation seemed fully to warrant it, he could be as daring an advocate of expansion as Jackson himself.

A favorite child of the church was its foreign missionary movement. When this was attacked on a very few occasions, the church rallied to its support with fervor. To many Presbyterians Dr. Robert E. Speer seemed the embodiment of the Presbyterian foreign missionary spirit. Eloquent in address, wise in committee, prolific in authorship, he was one of the outstanding leaders of the world missionary movement.

During the period under view the church's chief glory, under

God, and its most notable historical achievement, was its missionary expansion at home and abroad.

Educational Advances

A second area of Presbyterian life which we scan is that of education. Parochial schools were tried by Presbyterians in certain areas in the two decades before reunion, but these were dying out soon after reunion. Presbyterians were not denominationally minded enough to maintain so costly a system. In any case they were firm in their endorsement of the public schools.

By 1869 Sunday schools were well past the experimental stage. With a few in the church, by a strange inversion of causal relations, there was questioning whether instruction given by the Sunday school was responsible for the decline of religious instruction in the home. However, the church overwhelmingly endorsed and promoted the Sunday school. Soon after the turn of the century the General Assembly was told that the majority of new church members was being received from the Sunday schools.[1] While catechetical instruction and Sunday-school libraries declined,[2] such new developments as "Children's Day" and "Rally Day" blossomed forth.

Soon after reunion the General Assembly first noted with approval the holding of communicants' classes in local churches.[3] During the twentieth century these increased greatly.

Although "Father Endeavor Clark" cannot be claimed by Presbyterians, the Christian Endeavor movement spread rapidly within the church.[4] In the nineteenth century the General Assembly refused to act on requests to found a parallel Presbyterian movement, but more recently, reflecting the growing churchly consciousness of the times, this has been successfully done with the establishment of the Westminster Fellowship.

Before the turn of the century lamentations were heard that

church attendance of young people was declining. A "children's sermon" was presently introduced into some services.[5]

In the twentieth century daily vacation Bible schools and week-day church schools, especially the former, became an important educational activity in some churches.

The Presbyterian Church has had one notable academy, the West Nottingham, at Colora, Maryland. On the level of higher education the church has been showing growing interest in its denominational colleges, putting forth special effort in the face of increasingly strong secular forces which would remove American colleges from church relationships. The church has been giving increasing attention to theological education, with relations between the church and its seminaries becoming closer. Both parties appear to be more aware of their need of each other and of their mutual responsibilities. The Council on Theological Education has brought the seminaries closer together and has also made the church more conscious of their needs and purposes.

Social Concern

Another important area of Presbyterian activity during the period since 1869 has been the area of social concern. The theological heritage of Presbyterians lends itself to social application, with its emphasis on God's sovereignty and universal concern coupled with an emphasis on God's holiness and transcendence that operates against easy complacence with things as they are.

During the eight and a half decades under view, American population was not only expanding, but the nation was also undergoing qualitative changes of vast importance, as industrialization became accelerated and great polyglot metropolitan areas arose on the Atlantic seaboard, in the Midwest, and, later, on the Pacific coast. A new immigration, preponderantly from eastern and southern Europe, together with Americans leaving their farms, swarmed into the overcrowded cities.

As industrial problems arose, Presbyterians, like most other churchmen of the period, ignoring the reasons for the discontent of workingmen and seeing only the strikes that disrupted the peace, were at first quite unsympathetic toward labor.[6] But by the turn of the century Presbyterians were among the foremost in their concern for the problems confronting industrial workers. In 1903 the church created the Department of Church and Labor, originally the Workingmen's Department. Labor Temple in New York has been a distinguished effort to bring Christian principles to bear on the situation. Charles Stelzle, whose autobiography *Up from the Bowery* tells his story, was a mechanic who heard and answered the call to serve industrial workers as a Christian minister. He was a notable leader of Presbyterian efforts in the labor field. More recently the Department of Church and Industry has been serving in this area.

The decades immediately following the Civil War saw much discussion in the religious press by Presbyterians and others as to how to "reach the masses." [7] One effort to meet the situation was the development of "institutional" churches. The Bethany Church in Philadelphia, in which John Wanamaker was a ruling elder, organized Bethany College, which later became the Wanamaker Institute. In Chicago the Presbyterian neighborhood houses have been a notable institutional undertaking.

The new immigration, predominantly non-Nordic and non-Protestant, proved difficult to assimilate. Institutional churches, special evangelistic meetings, foreign-language churches, and other methods were used to reach these peoples, but with somewhat limited success. At least a partial explanation is perhaps to be found in the vigor with which church leaders sometimes denounced the newer type of immigration. Presbyterians, like most other Protestants of the period, were not fully able, even in their own minds, to bridge the sociological and cultural gulf that separated them from the newer arrivals.

Rapid concentration of wealth and conglomeration of uprooted peoples caused many an American city to fall easy prey to political corruption in the period after the Civil War. Presbyterians, along with other Protestants, at times showed intense, even if sporadic, interest in municipal reform. The sensational anti-Tammany crusade of Dr. Charles H. Parkhurst, pastor of the Madison Square Presbyterian Church in New York, was nationally publicized. During the Presidency of Theodore Roosevelt and the muckraking era, Presbyterians sometimes set themselves to scouring a city hall.[8] But too often, with reform achieved, zeal cooled and corruption returned.

The rapid growth of cities was accompanied by the depletion of many rural areas. Stimulated by the zeal for conservation of natural resources during the Presidency of Theodore Roosevelt, Gifford Pinchot surveyed the problem of rural depletion. The Presbyterian General Assembly of 1910 directed that the church study religious aspects of the situation. Dr. Warren H. Wilson for the Presbyterians made important sociological and religious analyses of the rural problem, and through the Country Life Department developed a constructive approach to the situation.

PROBLEMS OF PEACE AND WAR

Perennial problems of peace and war were frequently to the fore during these years. Amid the dispute with Great Britain during Grover Cleveland's administration over the boundary of Venezuela, the Presbyterian General Assembly shared the widespread anxiety over possible war and exchanged friendly greetings with certain Scottish Presbyterian judicatories. Not satisfied with this gesture of international good will, the Assembly for several years sent birthday greetings directly to Queen Victoria, receiving a courteous acknowledgment from her private secretary.[9] It was not stated whether this action was to be classified as ecclesiastical, political, or merely personal.

In the decade before the Civil War exponents of America's

"manifest destiny" were becoming increasingly vocal. During President Grant's administration there was renewed talk of pushing into the Caribbean. In less than a decade after the "frontier" was formally declared ended, the United States was embroiled in the Spanish-American War and launched on at least a temporary program of overseas expansion. While the famous "yellow press" was demanding that the United States go to war with Spain, many Presbyterians urged restraint. After war broke out they supported the government; some endorsed the new program of expansion overseas. One report to the General Assembly spoke of the "peace-speaking guns of Admiral Dewey." [10] A little later the Assembly endorsed the Hague Conference movement.[11]

The Presbyterian General Assembly, in the language of the Westminster Confession of Faith, supported participation of the United States in the First World War as a "just and necessary" war, and many individual Presbyterians, after the fashion of those years, were quite unrestrained in their zeal for the fray. Postwar years saw a reaction toward pacifism, in which many Presbyterians were conspicuous, followed by a more restrained and sober endorsement of American participation in the Second World War. One dares to hope that out of the fluctuating echoing of national chancelleries and newspaper headlines there is developing among the American churches a more seasoned approach to the baffling problem of peace and war, in which a particular war or a particular peace will not be absolutized, but all will alike be seen in relation to the role which the United States should be expected to play in world affairs, with ample recognition that great political issues are seldom in sharply contrasting black and white but are at best fraught with a degree of moral ambiguity.

The causes of temperance and Sunday observance, which had been the classic centers of Protestant social concern next to slavery, continued as objects of Presbyterian interest in the period after the Civil War.[12] In the so-called "communion question" total abstinence influences pressed for unfermented "wine" in the Lord's

Supper.[13] The General Assembly, consulted in the matter, diplomatically replied that "the General Assembly has always recognized the right of each church Session to determine what is bread, and what is wine." [14] A prominent Presbyterian was reported to have boycotted for a time the communion table on the ground that Scripture had been doubly violated in removing the yeast from the wine and putting it into the bread.

This expanding interest in social concern had obvious implications for the doctrine concerning the nature of the church. It enlarged the conception of the church's responsibility and mission, emphasizing the fact that the church regarded itself as having some responsibilities to society as a whole, and not merely to the inner spiritual life of its own members. At the same time such activities point the church to the task of analyzing more fully than it has yet done the relation between social ethics on the one hand and the distinctive character of Christian faith and Christian fellowship on the other.

Organization and Promotion

The fourth area of Presbyterian life since 1869 is that of organization. At the outset of this period financial promotion was greatly improved by the creation of the Committee of Benevolence and Finance, whose name later changed and whose functions gradually developed.[15] After the turn of the century there was created the Executive Commission which later became the General Council. The increasing emphasis on the duty of proportionate giving to support the church's expanding activities found appropriate expression in the insertion of a new chapter into the Directory of Worship entitled "Of the Worship of God by Offerings." Starting with the "Reunion Fund" which, with a goal of five million dollars, raised over seven million, Presbyterians in this period had numerous special fund campaigns, most of them notably successful.

The church's vigorous and increasing activity in such fields as missionary expansion, education, and social concern necessitated during these eight and a half decades a tighter integration and increasing strength of organization with steadily increasing emphasis on executive functions. The movement exactly parallels the growing powers of the United States federal government. Powers of government in church and state were expanding for the same reason—there were tasks that had to be performed, and this required an organization strong enough to promote, direct, and exercise the necessary responsibility. The time of the General Assembly meetings necessarily came to be less devoted to deliberation and more devoted to promotional and organizational matters. The power and influence of the church boards as agents of the General Assembly to perform the activities needing to be done grew apace. The duties and powers of stated clerks—particularly in the General Assembly and the presbyteries, the most active judicatories above the session—expanded to meet the new needs. New executive offices—superintendent, executive secretary, and the like—were created.

All this activity has had profound implications for the doctrine of the church which are yet to be fully evaluated by theologians. Running through such activism is often the implication that the church is primarily a voluntary society, chartered to do business for the Lord; and also the intimation that anything that hampers the church's work should be eliminated or reduced. But there have been operating in this recent period other tendencies also which balance these contractual and pragmatic conceptions with more organic principles. The intense activity of the period, with resulting development of executive power, has perhaps made possible authoritarian tendencies in the area of the church's spiritual and theological life, which happily have not as yet materialized.

THEOLOGICAL CHANGES

A fifth area of the church's history is the extremely important area of theology. At the same time that social change was sweeping the United States, a new cultural climate was forming. Charles

Darwin's *The Origin of Species*, published in 1859; the development and dissemination of Biblical criticism; the increasing tendency to hold optimistic views about man were among the factors
challenging the old theology. Drs. A. A. Hodge and B. B. Warfield,
in an article on "Inspiration" in the *Presbyterian Review* in 1881,
asserted the absolute inerrancy of the original Bible manuscripts.
Some challenged this theory as an innovation, but presently the
General Assembly embodied it in formal resolutions and made it
the virtual basis on which Professors Charles A. Briggs and Henry
Preserved Smith were suspended from the ministry.

In 1902–1903 the Northern Church, in its negotiations with the
Cumberland Presbyterian Church with a view to union, amended
the Westminster Confession of Faith by adding two chapters:
XXXIV, "Of the Holy Spirit," and XXXV, "Of the Love of God
and Missions"; also a Declaratory Statement. Chapter XXXV, thus
adopted, reads as follows:

I. God in infinite and perfect love, having provided in the covenant
of grace, through the mediation and sacrifice of the Lord Jesus Christ,
a way of life and salvation, sufficient for and adapted to the whole lost
race of man, doth freely offer this salvation to all men in the Gospel.
II. In the Gospel God declares His love for the world and His desire
that all men should be saved, reveals fully and clearly the only way of
salvation; promises eternal life to all who truly repent and believe in
Christ; invites and commands all to embrace the offered mercy; and by
His Spirit accompanying the Word pleads with men to accept His
gracious invitation.
III. It is the duty and privilege of every one who hears the Gospel
immediately to accept its merciful provisions: and they who continue
in impenitence and unbelief incur aggravated guilt and perish by their
own fault.

The Declaratory Statement includes the following paragraphs:

FIRST, With reference to Chapter III of the Confession of Faith:
that concerning those who are saved in Christ, the doctrine of God's
eternal decree is held in harmony with the doctrine of His love to all

mankind, His gift of His Son to be the propitiation for the sins of the whole world, and His readiness to bestow His saving grace on all who seek it. That concerning those who perish, the doctrine of God's eternal decree is held in harmony with the doctrine that God desires not the death of any sinner, but has provided in Christ a salvation sufficient for all, adapted to all, and freely offered in the Gospel to all; that men are fully responsible for their treatment of God's gracious offer; that His decree hinders no man from accepting that offer; and that no man is condemned except on the ground of his sin.

SECOND, With reference to Chapter X, Section III, of the Confession of Faith, that it is not to be regarded as teaching that any who die in infancy are lost. We believe that all dying in infancy are included in the election of grace, and are regenerated and saved by Christ through the Spirit, who works when and where and how He pleases.

The United Presbyterian Church of North America in 1925 adopted a complete revision of the Westminster Confession, which revision included teachings similar to those adopted by the U.S.A. Church. The Presbyterian Church U.S. in 1942 added to its Confession of Faith Chapters IX and X, the latter introducing Arminianism as was done by the Church U.S.A. with its new Chapter XXXV.

Except possibly with the retention of "the security of the saints," by the United Presbyterian Church, all three of these divisions of American Presbyterianism have now officially omitted the causal foreordination, predestination, election features of Calvinism and have included the offer of Christ's atonement to all men, such changes bringing these denominations into accord with the Arminianism of the Remonstrants at the Synod of Dort. Changes similar to these have been adopted by various Presbyterian bodies abroad, as, for example, by the United Presbyterian Church of Scotland in 1879 and by the Free Church of Scotland in 1892. The Presbyterian Church U.S.A. in its Declaratory Statement of 1902–1903 wrote, as you will note, that the change (to Arminianism) was "in harmony with" the Calvinism of the unmodified Confession. This was to forestall a victory in the courts by the opponents of the change who might win, as did similar opponents in Scotland in 1900 when they succeeded in getting the Law Lords to declare the resultant Arminian Church not to be the legal successor to the former Calvinistic Church.[16] [17]

By such changes the Arminianism of the Remonstrants of the Synod of Dort and of *The Marrow of Modern Divinity* finally won permanent recognition in the three largest divisions of American Presbyterianism. This change to Arminianism had already taken place in much of Scottish Presbyterianism—in the United Presbyterian Church in 1879, in the Free Church in 1892, and in the United Free Church in 1900.

With the twentieth century, discussions in the church broadened out to deal with questions other than the Biblical one alone. In 1910 and again in 1916 and 1923 the General Assembly undertook to name five doctrines and to declare these "essential and necessary" articles of the faith. The constitutional propriety of this was challenged, and in 1926 and 1927, under the leadership of a distinguished Special Commission of Fifteen, the Assembly declared that the General Assembly cannot thus designate any doctrine as "essential and necessary," for to do so is virtually to amend the Constitution, an act which requires the concurrent action of Assembly and presbyteries.

During these extended theological discussions, some wrote as though the church were a voluntary society created by contract by those who happened to agree in their theological views. The action which the church finally took seems clearly to point toward more organic conceptions of the nature of the church, that the church is not built on formal theology alone, but is an organism involving the church's total life. While it was never the accepted Presbyterian view that theology was the church's sole *raison d'être*, there has perhaps been a shift of emphasis rendering theology somewhat less central to the conception of the church than it had been.

PUBLIC WORSHIP

Still another area of the Presbyterian Church's life in this period is the area of public worship. Early Calvinistic worship cannot properly be characterized as "informal." The ideal was more positive, based on an emphasis on God's utter spirituality. In the Puritan controversy with Anglicanism, worship became characterized by a chaste austerity. Under the influence of the American frontier, revivalism, and other forces, worship declined to informality, almost to slovenliness.

By the middle of the nineteenth century there were among Presbyterians discernible stirrings toward the improvement of worship. Charles W. Baird, in his *Eutaxia*, published in 1855, said that early Reformed worship was liturgic. Dr. Charles Hodge, reviewing the book, favored the idea of a Presbyterian worship book. Dr. Samuel M. Hopkins of Auburn Seminary, in an article on "Presbyterian Cultus" in the *Presbyterian Review* in 1882, urged reform of worship. In 1897 there was organized in Dr. Henry van Dyke's home a Church Service Society to promote the idea of improved worship among Presbyterians. A milestone was passed when the General Assembly of 1903 created a committee, of which Dr. van Dyke was chairman, to prepare a Presbyterian Book of Common Worship containing forms for voluntary use.[18] The book, revised in 1932 and 1944, has contributed much to ideals of worship within the church.

The relation between the doctrine of the church and the function of worship is of course a reciprocal one. As the consciousness of the church as a Christian community increased in some Presbyterian quarters in the nineteenth century, the demand for a worthier worship grew apace; and as worship was emphasized and improved in the twentieth century it contributed to a deepened appreciation of the "church" as a mystical body.

INTERDENOMINATIONAL COOPERATION

The last area of recent Presbyterian history to be scanned here is the area of interdenominational cooperation and union.

Many forces during the last eight and a half decades have been urging toward larger unities. Written large over recent economic and political history in the United States is the prevailing movement toward increasingly large aggregations which appear in the economic sphere as corporations and trusts, and in the political sphere as constant accretions to the power of the federal government. Similarly, the increased activity of the various denominations at home and abroad pointed toward the desirability of greater unity of effort. Theology was moving toward a greater emphasis on the voice of the Universal Church and the Christian consensus. In aspects of Western culture there seemed to be tendencies away from extreme forms of individualism toward more organic views.

From the beginning of the post-reunion period there were Presbyterian voices which urged greater Christian unity. Notable among these was Dr. Charles A. Briggs, better known by some in his other activities. He had a strong sense of the Universal Church. He thought that a new creed would aid Christian unity. Biblical theology, to which he was devoted, he saw also as contributing to Christian unity by showing the diversities of the primitive Christian Church within its unity.[19] Dr. Charles Hodge in an address at the meeting of the Evangelical Alliance in New York in 1873 set forth in notably broad terms the Calvinistic conception of the church and of Christian fellowship.[20]

On the most readily attainable level of Christian unity, Presbyterians were active in many Christian cooperative movements, often acting merely as individuals. During this period, too, comity developed in cities, in states, and in the national and foreign fields.

Federative movements among churches in their corporate capacity developed greatly during this period. A prominent Presbyterian minister, President James McCosh of the College of New Jersey, played a leading part in organizing the Alliance of Reformed Churches.[21] At the meeting in 1905 to prepare for the projected Federal Council of Churches of Christ in America, the stated clerk of the Presbyterian General Assembly, Dr. William Henry Roberts, presided. In the recent organizing of the National Council, Presbyterians have shared conspicuously in the leadership. In order to facilitate the formation of federated congregations, the Presbyterian Church amended its constitution.[22]

Presbyterians have been active, too, in seeking organic unity with other churches. There have been frequent negotiations from the beginning of our period to the present, with one or more of the Reformed churches at a time. There have twice been extended negotiations with the Episcopalians, and in 1918, amid wartime enthusiasm, the Presbyterian General Assembly proposed the organic union of the evangelical churches of the United States. There have been several notable successes to date in the area of church mergers. At the outset of the period was the memorable union of the Old School and New School Presbyterian churches. In 1906 came union with the Cumberland Presbyterian Church, and in 1920 union with the Welsh Calvinistic Methodist Church. Presbyterians, too, have been active in the Ecumenical Movement. The creation of the Committee on Church Cooperation and Union by the General Assembly of 1903 was a notable milestone in the growth of Presbyterian interest in Christian unity.[23]

TOWARD A UNIVERSAL CHURCH

The extensive Presbyterian interest and activity in church cooperation and union pointed toward fresh thinking concerning the ultimate nature of Christian community and of the Universal Church. It opened the way for more daring experimentation with the old Calvinistic theory that the visible church, too, is universal.

Do recent events in Presbyterian history argue for the doctrine that the church is properly "Catholic"? Of course, the propriety of using a term in any particular connection depends on the sense in which it is employed. It is not necessary to quarrel about terms. But let us be assured that the unity and larger conceptions about the church toward which the church seems to be moving lie not in the past but in the future. The church will never surrender the priceless insights that have come to it from the Protestant Reformation. Led by God's living Spirit, drawing on the richness of that particular form of the Christian heritage which is ours, and responsive to some of the best of the creative forces in our environment, let us go forward. Let us go forward courageously, and let us go forward together.

CHAPTER XIII

Today and Tomorrow:
The Road Ahead

GLADYS SCHMITT *

Everybody has doubtless pondered much on what is wrong with man in the twentieth century; and some of you have surely come to the conclusion that there is need for a spiritual revival, for something to transcend the growing materialism. The situation today—spiritually or mentally or psychologically speaking—is not so different from the situation when Jesus initiated and spread the first great revival of the spirit that the world had seen in centuries. We—like those wretches in the late Roman Empire—weary of our comforts and of the limitations of our spiritual boundaries, are "hovering between two worlds, one dead, the other powerless to be born."

The spiritual revival begun by Christ and His apostles did not break totally with tradition. It found the living core at the center of an old tradition; it saw, with new insight, what had been said to the soul of man in the Law and the Prophets; it accepted the moral obligations therein with honor and with a full sense of responsibility. We talk much today of a revival of religion. Our

* From an address by this noted historical novelist and Professor of English at the Carnegie Institute of Technology at the Friday evening banquet of the Historical Symposium of Oct. 2–3. See Introduction.—ED.

267

churches are more crowded than they have been, and we have more books and movies that draw the attention of millions to material which springs out of the Biblical field. In five or six years, we have seen on the screen the story of David and Bathsheba, the story of Samson and Delilah, the story of John the Baptist, the story of the Crucifixion.

The fact that we are dealing with such material in the popular arts *is* something to congratulate ourselves about. The Bible is our great heritage, and great art could surely spring from it—has sprung from it in medieval times and in the Renaissance. The Greeks, who produced a splendid and still-contemporary literature, had a much less rich and splendid heritage than ours to transform into art. Yet who, today, seeing *Salome* or reading *The Robe*, could say to himself that the source was done justice by the product derived from it?

Sophocles and Aeschylus and Euripides, taking material trivial in comparison with ours, turned out gems of rare depth which still burn with a fiery intensity. We do not have their equivalent in current literature or on the screen.

If you were to ask the publishers and producers who are turning out the current Biblical romances why they nourish us on such shallow stuff, they'd give you a ready answer: they'd tell you the spiritual and intellectual capacities of the American audience are such that a higher standard is a money-losing proposition.

I have never had as low an opinion of the American public's spiritual and mental capacity as all that. And I think, if the conjecture is not statistically unsound, it is certainly entirely un-Christian. According to what smattering of theology I have read, the human soul is not to be considered idiotic and beyond improvement. It is considered God's most exquisite creation, capable of redemption and of understanding divine mystery. And whether it is a money-losing proposition seems to me a secondary consideration.

What I am writing is simply this: the kind of art that has celebrated Biblical history in the present decade—and threatens, according to the *New York Times* theater section, to celebrate it, to the aggrandizement of the box-office, for a good while to come —does not do justice to that great source which all of you know far better than I.

It is a sorry business to see a saint's life turned into a juvenile. It is regrettable that the Crucifixion should be secondary to a love affair. It is—well, a little discouraging—to see John Baptist walk wanly through several reels for the sole purpose of giving an actress a reason for screaming at his head brought in on a platter. The Christian field—and I have come, perhaps a little arrogantly, to consider it my field, too—is so rich in real drama, profound tragedy, authentic glory, that I mourn to see it used so wretchedly.

What I am trying to make plain is this: Wouldn't it be possible for you religious leaders—experts in the field—to use influence to induce all of us in the arts to put your material to better use? I do not mean that I want pictures and popular books to be duller— in fact, in their inane attempt to be always entertaining, it seems to me they have grown horribly dull. The life of Isaiah, the sins of Jezebel, the doubts of Thomas—these are not dry and scholarly matters. These are the very stuff of human experience, such matters as could make the most sated audience sit on the edges of their chairs, the weariest reader shed tears.

There are hundreds of stories in Biblical history which carry in them the core of true drama—the everlasting struggle between good and evil, the never ending war between the soul and the world. But it is a long, long time since we have seen one of them presented in an art form that did not detract from it.

If the artist is to bear his part in the modern spiritual revival— and you will remember that the artist was no mean colleague in the days when he adorned your altars with masterpieces and composed your canticles and wrote your miracle plays—he must be conscious of his obligations to his materials. He must use those things you have found and sorted out for him honestly, reverently, in justice and in truth, knowing always, in his conscience, that no box-office success will ever cleanse him of any violence he has done to his original, always comparing what he has done with what he might have done, always saying to himself that he is taking into his hands the most valuable spiritual source that we have, always recognizing that what he does with one of the Gospels or a section of Kings will be reflected in thousands of minds and hearts.

The spiritual truth is a profound and elusive truth. A man must have terrible honesty to find it for himself and terrible self-discipline, once he has found it, to transfer it in art to anybody else. The intent is much. The poorly drawn little cards we used to get for attending Sunday school without absences were, I am sure, much closer to the religious spirit—because of the piety, no matter how sentimental, of those who drew them—than the most colossal major production thrown onto the most expensive three-dimensional screen.

I have heard people question, after seeing a Biblical film, the authenticity of a sword or a lute or a headdress. I have not heard them say: "But was that *all?* Those stupid lines—are we to presume that John Baptist said them?" I have not heard them say, "Take away the crowns and the coiffures and the drapery and the twenty-five elephants, and tell me what the whole thing was originally about—the struggles and the sufferings and the triumphs and the redemption of the human soul."

And what I fear most is that a generation nourished on such tawdry stuff will come to the original—if they trouble to come to the original at all—only with a sense of disappointment, wanting the elephants, wanting the crowns and the gauze, wanting the 3-D screen, and feeling a vague insufficiency at finding only man and God. When that comes to pass, the very roots of our spiritual revival will be cut away. It will be too late, and we will not have another chance.

The spirit of Christianity and the Christian tradition are com-

MOLDERS OF THOUGHT

Charles Stelzle

James D. Moffatt

John McNaugher

James A. Kelso

Eugene C. Caldwell

Benjamin Rush

John Ha

Elias Boudinot

Henry L. Stimson

John Foster Dull

PRESIDENTS

Andrew Jackson

James Buchanan

Woodrow Wilson

PRESIDENTS

Grover Cleveland

Benjamin Harrison

Dwight David Eisenhower

pletely antithetical to the splendid, the colossal. The story of Israel was played in part in wandering nomad poverty and in part in little desert towns. The very meaning of "Christianity" in its early phases is unpretentious simplicity. The story of Noah needs no set but an expanse of water and a poor ark, and no props but a branch of olive. The story of Mary Magdalen could be played out in low-ceilinged houses, and asks for nothing but a few benches and tables, a few jars and dishes, a sparse garden in the wilderness, and a rough-hewn tomb.

I hope against hope to see the day when the shouting subsides and the gauze is stripped away. And I believe that man is better than men think—that most of the benighted, searching children of the twentieth century would come gladly, very gladly, even if there were no palaces and no elephants and no 3-D screen, if they could be assured of seeing the only real drama—the drama of men in search of themselves and each other and God.

FRANK H. CALDWELL

The first observation to be made is that for the church the road ahead is a way backward which is really a way forward.

This is not a time in which to attempt a comprehensive appraisal of the effects of the Protestant Reformation upon the church. But, among others, one very obvious and significant effect was to give the church a thrust, with the power of theological-ecclesiastical jet propulsion, down the road of fragmentation and division.

In a careful analysis of that thrust, it would probably be valid to say that some sociological and political tailwinds reinforced the power exerted in this direction by a revitalized theology and a multiplied polity. But, whatever be the church historian's analysis and description of the forces and his evaluation of the several consequences, the fact looms large that one major consequence has been the progressive fragmentation of the church in what has come to be known as the scandal of Christianity.

Now, division of the church, in and of itself, need not be condemned as altogether evil. There is good ground for the conviction that the Protestant Reformation was of God, and there is indisputable evidence that much good, both within and without the numerous churches spawned by the Reformation, has been the fruit of that movement. But the recognition of the divine origin of the Reformation, and the appreciative acknowledgment of the good which has grown out of it, still do not warrant a complacent attitude toward some of the evils which have also been rooted in this movement. It has become almost axiomatic that many sins are but the perversion of basic virtues, but such sins are not to be condoned and perpetuated merely because of their virtuous basis.

It is not surprising, therefore, that as the evils of multiplied divisions of the church have become more and more apparent as obstacles to the effective witness of the church, an ecumenical movement has arisen in the providence of God to manifest itself in two conspicuous forms. One is the form of self-criticism, cooperation, and the discussion of union by denominational groups at both the national level and the world level. Such conferences as Madras, Oxford, Edinburgh, Amsterdam, and Oslo; and such cooperative organizations as the National Council of Churches and the World Council of Churches are eloquent witnesses to the fact that most of the major denominations in the Protestant tradition are feeling with increased acuteness their need for each other in order to be what God would have His Church be and in order to do what God would have His Church do. The other conspicuous form of the ecumenical movement is the re-union of families of churches, and in some instances, as in the cases of unions in India and in Canada, the union of churches having decidedly different traditions and forms of government.

The movement toward closer cooperation and union is a "backward" movement in at least two significant respects. It turns back to a reexamination and a reappraisal of the Reformation spirit and theology. And it turns back in its effort to reverse the process by which liberty, turned into license, has divided, and divided, and divided the body of Christ until, in these United States alone, there are over two hundred and fifty separate religious bodies, most of which call themselves Christian churches. In the name of conservatism, or fundamentalism, and as champions of the inerrance of the Scriptures, the thought and spirit of the twelfth chapter of First Corinthians is often denied, or defied, so as to leave the impression that the body of Christ is not intended of God to be one body, but many separate bodies. But a spirit of repentance is at work. Men have been cut to the quick with an acute sense of the sin of schism. Many are under deep conviction that

as the body is one, and hath many members, and all the members of the body, being many, are one body; so also is Christ. For in one Spirit were we all baptized into one body, whether Jews or Greeks, whether bond or free, and were all made to drink of one Spirit. . . . And the eye cannot say to the hand, I have no need of thee; or again the head to the feet, I have no need of you.

Yet such a twofold backward movement is only superficially backward. Like the look that a driver takes in a rear-view mirror, it is a means of pressing more surely forward from the churches to the church. The weakness of the ecumenical movement is the pride, the prejudice, and the inertia of those who think of their respective denominations as "doing all right" and who can see no point in disturbing the comfortable *status quo* with vexing problems of cooperation and union. The strength of the ecumenical movement is that the sense of greatest compulsion to be the church, rather than an aggregation of voluntary Christian associations magnifying small differences into formidable confusion, has come from the mission fields abroad.

The three strongest bodies of Presbyterians in this country are now in the final stages of discussion of a Plan of Union which is scheduled for votes by the respective General Assemblies in 1954. While any body of Presbyterians is resourceful enough and sufficiently endowed with the highly fissionable materials of "Adamic energy" to be able to blow any plan of union to pieces, it seems increasingly evident that provisions of the proposed Plan of Union itself are not the issue. The real issue is whether constitutional majorities in these Presbyterian bodies believe it to be the will of God that the brokenness of the body of Christ be perpetuated, or that these closely related families, with one heritage, one system of doctrine, and one pattern of polity, should take one significant step toward a full-orbed answer to Christ's own fervent prayer that His disciples might be one.

Whatever the result of this particular vote, much has already been accomplished by the printing and wide distribution of more than seventeen thousand copies of a specific Plan of Union which is the result of some fifteen years of diligent work, and which is the only such detailed and comprehensive plan to be developed for these three bodies in almost a century of their separate existence. Moreover, some of the most ardent leaders of the opposition to Presbyterian union frankly admit that such a union is apparently inevitable sooner or later, and that the most they can hope for is some further delay of its consummation.

Those who believe that the ecumenical movement is an expression of the will of God are confident that, in this respect, the road ahead for the church is a way of reversal of the post-Reformation process of fragmentation—a reversal which is really a gloriously forward way.

A WAY TO RENEWED VITALITY AS THE FELLOWSHIP OF REDEMPTION

A second observation concerning the church and the road ahead is that it should be, and there seem to be indications that it may be, a way to renewed vitality as the fellowship of redemption.

In comparatively recent years, idolatrous ideologies, such as Communism, Fascism, and Nationalism, have captured the minds of multitudes and added their pressure to that of mankind's sense of disillusionment with the erstwhile prevalent confidence in automatic progress toward utopia. This faith, or mood, which was perhaps at its zenith in the decade of the 1920's, suffered two terrific blows in the twenty years immediately following "the jazz age." One was the great depression. The other was World War II. Out of the rubble which those two sociological atom bombs made of "escalator religion," came a widespread mood of disillusionment. At the same time came the tensions of "the cold war" between the East and the West. Back of the military race for air supremacy, the testing and stockpiling of atom and hydrogen bombs, and the sickening "police action" in Korea, it becomes increasingly apparent that fundamentally the conflict in which we find ourselves is a conflict of ideologies.

In a recent conversation with an alert and discerning reporter who is assigned primarily to the writing of religious news, he told me that, in his judgment, the comparatively large church attendance and increasing church membership of the past five to seven years is less an evidence that people *have found* in the church what they are looking for than that they are looking in the church for what they have not yet found anywhere.

"They are shopping," said he, "and if they don't find something to buy, in my judgment, one of these days there is going to be the greatest falling away from the church that we have seen in many a year."

In this groping which the reporter calls "shopping," people are feeling for Christian convictions which have at least three characteristics.

One is that they be convictions which, in their essence, are the self-authenticating Word of God. Apparently, some people will continue as in the past to derive such assurance from the basic concept of a one-and-only church which has been appointed of

God to provide His children with authoritative and infallible guidance in matters of religion and morals. To some others, such assurance will still come in terms of a traditional concept of the Bible which assumes, among other things, that language is static rather than dynamic.

Many others, however, recognize that a word is dynamic, whether it be the word of man or of God. Its locus is not on a printed page or in the ether as sound waves, but in persons, or beings, capable of at least the rudiments of thought or meaning. Only the *symbols* of language are to be found on the pages of a book or in the ether as sound waves. The word—the idea, the thought, the meaning— is a mental creation which occurs *in persons* when they react, or respond, to the stimuli of visual or oral symbols of language.

Through the centuries, multitudes have found in experience that the collection of symbols embodied in the Scriptures of the Old and New Testaments are unique in their capacity so to stimulate meanings in the minds of men which are cleansing, uplifting, re-creative, and redemptive in effect, that it is no wonder that we refer to the Bible as the Word of God. Undoubtedly, we shall continue so to speak of the Bible.

But it will be lamentable if we encourage ourselves or others to think of the Word of God as a static collection of black marks confined between the covers of a book. The Word of God is eternal, to be sure. But the Word of God is always contemporary. It is forever a new creation *in persons* by the Spirit of God. Such a view of the Word of God is not sheer subjectivism which permits of the interpretation of just any moral or religious intuition as God's truth. The intelligent Christian will test his convictions by what Theodore M. Greene has called "the criteria of the reality of any 'object' of experience"; namely, coerciveness, coherence with total experience, and public verifiability.

In his Yale Lectures on *Preaching the Word of God*, Morgan Phelps Noyes recalls how, during the London Blitz, the Scottish church of St. Columba was destroyed by bombs. On the following

Sunday morning, a member of the congregation went to the spot where the church had stood. Only a portion of the wall remained. On it the minister had placed a notice indicating where the morning service would be held. Beneath the notice somebody had written the verse which appears in Latin around the burning bush on the seal of the Church of Scotland, *"Nec tamen consumebatur."* Observes Noyes:

> The man who wrote that notice believed that the church is more than stone and bricks and mortar. It is more than organization and ritual and schedule of services. It is the faith and life of men and women to whom the Word of God has come with power, and through whom that word is mediated to the world.

As the church attains this ideal, the wistful "shoppers" to whom our reporter friend referred will find in such a fellowship of redemption that for which they are groping.

A second characteristic of the convictions which will be found in this renewed fellowship of redemption is that they lay claim upon the allegiance of the whole man—his thought, his affection, and his volition.

Some forms of Christianity seem to produce in man a sort of psychological "fission" in which feeling explodes in a standard "mushroom" pattern of action. Such an experience is usually accompanied by verbally uniform propositional beliefs which are embraced with almost fanatical zeal. The resulting pattern of Christianity seems to fall short of full-orbed Christian faith by virtue of two major defects. One is the conspicuous absence, or weakness, of trust (partly in God, but especially in fellow Christians) as an essential ingredient of faith. The other is the corollary attitude and action of non-fellowship with other Christians whose trust is grounded in somewhat different verbal expressions of belief. This is the nub of the theological problem, not only of union, but also of such cooperation as is sought in organizations like the National Council of Churches and the World Council of Churches.

On the other hand, some other forms of Christianity address

themselves to man so exclusively in terms of his capacity to reason and think that they practically ignore the significance of feeling in relation to the kind of loyalties and volitional commitments and activities which are involved in full-orbed Christian faith. We Presbyterians, along with some other communions which insist upon comparatively high educational standards for the ministry, have tended to starve to death the emotional lives of people by virtue of our primary concern with their intellects.

Although I have used the familiar threefold division of man in terms of his capacity to think, to feel, and to will, I am quite skeptical as to the validity of such a division even for purposes of analysis. For what else is volition than the fusion of thought and feeling in terms of action?

Whenever the church is renewed as a fellowship of redemption, it becomes creative of convictions which are expressive of the whole Gospel of the grace of God laying claim to the clearest perceptions of man's intellect and the deepest feelings of man's heart, fusing them into the decisive act of commitment and the continued activity of faithful abiding in Him.

Yet a third characteristic of the Christian convictions to be found in the church as a renewed fellowship of redemption is that they bring to man Christ's peace, as contrasted with the world's peace.

In introducing this thought in a context in which it cannot be adequately elaborated, it should be made clear that there is no intention to belittle the reality and seriousness of widespread mental illnesses, to depreciate the insights and techniques which are the fruits of modern psychology and psychiatry, or to disparage the development of pastoral counseling. The church can ill afford to be unconcerned with mental illnesses or to be reluctant to utilize proven techniques because of their secular origins.

But the church has a more *inclusive* mission than the healing of those who may appropriately be diagnosed as the "mentally ill." The church has a mission of reconciliation and redemption in relation to the deep and universal contradiction in *man as man*. Furthermore, the *objective* of the mission entrusted to the church is not simply the "peace of mind" which comes with the resolution of a few tensions, conflicts, hostilities, and fears, so that persons are rendered sufficiently comfortable and "adjusted" in their social context to be able to carry on without the imminent threat of suicide, murder, theft, rape, and sadistic cruelties of various degrees of refinement.

Including these objectives, but going beyond them, the church has a mission as the fellowship of redemption to be the kind of "social focus" of God's redeeming power and grace in which such a radical change may come to man that he knows in his own heart and life the incomparable peace of Christ.

Language cannot precisely define the characteristic qualities of this peace. It can only suggest them. Salvation, reconciliation, redemption, wholeness, at-homeness with God, forgiveness, assurance —these are among the various familiar terms which have been used to suggest both the vital relationship and the qualities of "the peace of God which passeth understanding."

As the church proceeds along the road ahead, there are movements and directional signals which seem to give grounds for a lively hope that, in terms of ecumenicity, it is proceeding on a way backward which is really a way forward from the churches to the church; and to a renewed vitality as the fellowship of reconciliation. In such a fellowship may be found convictions which, in their essence, are self-authenticated as the living Word of the living God; which lay welcome claim upon the whole of man; and which bring with them the wholeness of the peace of Christ.

JOHN A. MACKAY

Whither are we bound in Presbyterianism and in the Reformed family of churches? As we face tomorrow, what are the prospects that lie before us? What are the aspirations and hopes that should inspire us? What are the decisions we should make?

Let us get ourselves into perspective for the forward view, for the next steps. It is important to remember that Presbyterianism is two things. It is, first, a definite *theological outlook*; it is, secondly, an *ecclesiastical structure*.

I. PRESBYTERIANISM AS THEOLOGICAL OUTLOOK

It is fair to say that the Reformed Christian tradition to which the Presbyterian churches belong has been deeply interested in doctrine, in theology. There is a sense in which, more than all the great Christian traditions, Presbyterianism has taken seriously the injunction that God should be loved with the *mind* as well as with the heart. Ideas have played an important role in the history of Presbyterianism, and must continue to do so. In an era when anti-intellectualism is becoming a potent reactionary force, there sounds a clarion call to Presbyterians to brace themselves to clarify the great ideas of the Christian faith, and to defend and proclaim them with militant ardor.

THE CHURCH

In that most massive and incomparable body of Christian truth, Calvin's *Institutes of the Christian Religion*, which structurally is an expanded commentary on *The Apostles' Creed*, there is a conception of the Christian Church which is sublimely Biblical and which is of crucial importance in this revolutionary time. The Christian Church in Calvin's view is basically a *community* of those for whom Jesus Christ is Lord, the Body of which He is the supreme and only Head. This community is the "theater of God's glory," that is to say, it is the sphere, the arena, where the splendor of His character breaks forth and where His mighty works take place more than in any sphere or segment of secular history. But this community, to be true to its nature, must never seek to become an end in itself, or to live for its own sake. It must become, Calvin contends, an instrument of God's glory. The Christian Church is most truly the church when it allows itself to be used by God as His agent to bear witness to His truth and to execute His redemptive will. As such, the Christ is the true bearer of history and the community of destiny.

It is also of supreme importance at the present time to emphasize the truth that the Christian Church has *a prophetic mission to fulfill in human history and society*. It must look at everything in the light of God. In this light it must discern and interpret the meaning of the times. It must unmask and oppose all alien patterns of human behavior which violate the revealed righteousness of God. It must refuse to become subject to any human attempt to set up a rival to Deity, whether that rival be a man, a government, or an ideology.

The human situation today calls upon Presbyterians to reaffirm and reinterpret certain very basic aspects in the Reformed heritage of faith which belong to the very core of the Christian revelation.

THE MAJESTY OF TRUTH

Emphasis needs to be placed upon the *majesty of truth*. Truth is no mere bird to be chased and caught, to be encaged and, perchance, set free again, for the pure thrill of resuming the pursuit. Truth is no mere badge to be ostentatiously worn as a proof of orthodox standing. No, truth is the belt that girds the Christian, that braces him for action. It is an unfurled banner which rallies him into the service of One who is Himself the Truth. For the Christian religion, truth is personal. It involves a given. Jesus Christ is the Truth, and no one can be His follower unless he gives utter allegiance to Him and follows Him on the road of life with calm mien and crusading heart.

In keeping with our tradition, we Presbyterians need to proclaim that truth has fallen upon evil days in the house, in the hands, and on the lips of those who should be its friends. In what we nowadays call the "cold war," truth has become subordinate to propaganda. It is no longer judged by the reality it contains, but by the discomfiture it may cause. According to the standards of this war, if there are true things which might be said in fairness and justice to our enemies, or in order to explain in a sympathetic way why they are what they are and do what they do, those things must remain unsaid. They must remain unsaid because truth is to be regarded as traitorous if it should give "aid and comfort to our enemies." So, too, dissent from a thesis which is officially considered to be a pillar of security can be denounced as treason. Alas, we have been passing through a time when the only thing that seems to matter is to make your case, get your man, blackguard your foe.

Two things are happening which should give deep concern to all thoughtful people. A calm analysis of the human situation in the light of history, and a basic study of the causes which have produced the satanical attitudes and fanatical moods which mark our time, are not encouraged. On the other hand, we witness the attempt to solve by material power what can only be solved by the successful propagation and acceptance of true ideas. Let this never be forgotten: it is ideas, mistaken and perverse ideas it is true, but none the less ideas, which have given Communism its revolutionary crusading power in the world of today. It is only ideas, ideas which are clearly grasped and become incarnate in spiritual crusaders, that can match the militant ideology of our adversaries.

THE VOCATION OF MAN

A second emphasis which is very basic in our Reformed heritage is *the vocation of man*. The question about man is the great question of our time. What is man? What is human life for? When can it be said that a man is a true man, or that life is being lived with a true, rich humanity? This is the crucial concern of contemporary culture.

In our Presbyterian heritage of faith there is a marvelous little compendium of Christian truth called the *Westminster Shorter Catechism*. Its first question runs thus: "What is the chief end of man?" That is the basic question of our time and of all time. What is the supreme object or goal of human life? The answer given to that question is a classic: "Man's chief end is to glorify God and to enjoy Him forever." To glorify God means to make Him manifest. It means to unveil in thought and behavior the splendor of God's character, to serve His redemptive will, and in so doing to enjoy His fellowship on life's road until the sun goes down. To unveil the splendor of God, to further the purposes of God, to enjoy the communion with God both now and forever— there is nothing grander than that. Nothing is more important in our time than to translate into concrete terms in our churches, and in the whole secular order, what it means for man to "glorify God and to enjoy Him forever."

The clue to the meaning of man's vocation is found in the words and life of Jesus Christ Himself. In His great prayer in the Upper Room, the night before He was crucified, Jesus said, "I have glorified Thee on the earth, I have finished the work that Thou gavest me to do." In what He had said and done our Lord had made God manifest to men. He had been the servant of God, the instrument, the agent of God's redemptive will for mankind. To take seriously the meaning of man's vocation as God's servant, as it was illumined by Jesus Christ, is to affirm that man is truly man when he unveils God in his thinking and doing, that is, when he is God-like. But to be truly God-like is to manifest self-giving love. That being so, the self-centered man or woman is subhuman and is not really alive. The only people who are truly human are those who in the spirit of sons, and with the devotion of servants, are dedicated to God in such a way that they are willing to serve God and His purposes. Man is truly man when he is God's man. He is truly free, not when he gives the rein to his own self-will, but when he is God's captive, when he is the servant of the Highest, when, in the words of that medieval saint, he is willing "to be to the eternal Goodness what his own hand is to a man." Man without God ceases progressively to be man, as contemporary civilization has shown. Failure to take God into account, the attempt on man's part to establish his own order in accordance with his own standards leads inevitably to anarchy or to tyranny. For the affirmation that man exists to glorify God is equally opposed to totalitarianism and to libertarianism. It is opposed to totalitarianism because it exalts unreserved allegiance to God above every human loyalty. It is opposed to libertarianism because it affirms that human freedom does not mean that any man is the lord of his life in such a way as to be free to do whatever he wants, even when his actions do not appear to circumscribe the liberty of other people. "Make me a captive, Lord, and then I shall be free." That line, written by a great Presbyterian hymn writer, presents the precondition of true spiritual freedom.

THE RULE OF GOD

An emphasis upon the rule of God is also native to our Presbyterian heritage. The sovereign rule of God is the controlling factor in history. There is an everlasting righteousness which God has written into the constitution of the universe. There is an eternal purpose which governs human history; there is an ultimate order to which all human planning and purposes must relate themselves or suffer utter frustration. The American-born poet T. S. Eliot has caught a Biblical insight into this divine order in these words of his:

> Those who put their faith in worldly order
> Not controlled by the order of God,
> In confident ignorance, but arrest disorder,
> Make it fast, breed fatal disease,
> Degrade what they exalt.*

* From *Murder in the Cathedral* (Harcourt, Brace and Company, Inc.) Used by permission.

If Presbyterianism, which has always taken seriously the reality of God's sovereign rule, is to exercise its prophetic function today, it must unveil the inner meaning of God's order in certain great emphases which have contemporary relevancy. Here are some affirmations which must be literally thundered into the ears of the men and women, and very especially the rulers, of our generation:

1. *Each human individual is sacred and must be treated as such.* He must be granted the inviolable rights and privileges which belong to him as one who is loved by God.

2. *It never pays to be vindictive.* This is true in the relations between persons. It is equally true, and even more true, in the relations between nations. No nation is wise enough or good enough to assume unconditional control over any other nation. Only Almighty God has the right to demand unconditional surrender on the part of any man, group, or nation.

3. *Ideas can never be adequately dealt with by mere police or military measures.* The terrible ideas which have plunged mankind into this tragic era must be met by better and truer ideas. These counterideas must be presented by men and women whose lives incarnate what they believe, and who are capable of passionate crusading action to put their ideas into practice.

4. *It is always right to confer with those with whom we differ even though their behavior has been dastardly and the process of consultation imposes a severe strain upon patience and forbearance.* In all human relations, moreover, there is a place for the dimension of grace. Mercy and forgiveness, when applied at the appropriate moment, can have far-reaching political consequences. There is no greater illusion than the idea that material might can solve problems where an ultimate clash of ideas and attitudes is involved. Wrong ideas and wrong attitudes must be changed. The people who have these ideas and manifest these attitudes may need to have their power curbed. But they must not be made the objects of total destruction. "Vengeance is mine, I will repay, saith the Lord."

II. Presbyterianism as Ecclesiastical Structure

Let us now leave the thought aspect of Presbyterianism and turn to its organizational aspect. The supreme organizational expression of Presbyterianism in the world of our time is known by the name of "The Alliance of Reformed Churches Throughout the World Holding the Presbyterian System" (that is, the Presbyterian order). This organization, popularly known as the World Presbyterian Alliance, was founded in 1875 and is the oldest of the so-called ecumenical confessions. It was the earliest form of what is coming to be called ecumenical confessionalism. Certain things of great importance are happening in Presbyterianism throughout the world which have a very decided bearing, not only upon interchurch relations within Presbyterianism, but also upon the future of the ecumenical movement today.

1. The first thing worthy of note is that *American Presbyterians are engaged in a quest for church union.* I am thinking in particular of the three denominations which are represented in this gathering; namely, the United Presbyterian Church, the Presbyterian Church in the U.S., and the Presbyterian Church in the U.S.A. A plan of union has been drafted. Let me offer some reflections regarding this plan and its prospects.

In all questions concerning union the supreme thing that matters is the will of Jesus Christ, the Head of the church. Does Christ will that these three Presbyterian churches, which are virtually identical in organization, and are equally loyal to the same basic, constitutional standards, should become organically one? Speaking personally, I would say this. Our three churches have a common heritage to inspire them. They confront a national situation which demands a common Presbyterian approach to evangelism and to the application of Christian faith to life. The world situation demands corporate planning and action, if the missionary witness of Presbyterianism is to be effective in our time.

We must recognize, however, in all candor and charity, that fears are current in some quarters regarding the projected union. Some beloved brethren have a theological concern. They charge that in the church to which I belong there are many heretics. Speaking from an intimate knowledge of our church I can say this: Never did the evangelical fires burn more warmly or more brightly than today. Never was John Calvin's crest, with its flaming heart in the open hand, and the words, "My heart I give Thee, Lord, eagerly and sincerely," more creatively operative in our church than in these last years of the New Life Movement which that crest inspired.

In some quarters I have found congenital prejudices against union. Some of these prejudices conserve the scars of history, and some project the shadows of a particular social philosophy. I know one presbytery whose members were frank enough to state that they did not want their presbytery to formulate the reasons for its opposition to union because those reasons might be answered! I have sensed in some quarters a very genuine fear of ecclesiastical absorption. The feeling exists that the smaller bodies might be engulfed by, or disappear in, the larger. This fear has no foundation. It is hard for me, who grew up into manhood as a member of a minority group politically and ecclesiastically, to take this apprehension seriously. At a time when Scotland had only a tenth of the population of England, the country gave five Prime Ministers to the British Parliament. In that same period, England gave only two Prime Ministers, and Wales gave one. That is to say, the two smaller countries gave three-fourths of the leadership to the British Empire. If it is true that I am today a minister of the largest member of the Presbyterian family of churches, I grew up in, and was both converted and ordained in, one of the very smallest. Think, too, that Presbyterians, who are a minority in the church life of our country, exercise a very decisive religious influence. What would undoubtedly happen in the event of union is this. Every gift, every talent, every dynamic personality, every spiritual vision in the smaller churches, would make a very creative contribution in and through the united church.

I have also heard the fear expressed that in the united church power would be too highly centralized, as it is alleged to be in the church to which I belong. I want to say frankly that in our church power is not highly centralized. The General Council of our church, which coordinates the work of the boards and agencies and endeavors to think through the church's problems, is subject to the superior will of the General Assembly. The organization of the council is thoroughly representative and democratic. Our church, moreover, is committed to the principle of regional synods, a principle whereby deal more adequately with the religious situation in those areas. that have common problems, can be integrated in such a way as to deal more adequately with the religious situation in those areas. General Assembly action on this subject is being held in abeyance pending the result of the union negotiations. What is really happening in our denomination is a trend toward the decentralization of power.

2. *Presbyterians are also in quest of ecumenical unity.* This they pursue at two levels, (*a*) at the confessional level, and (*b*)at the interconfessional level.

a) The World Presbyterian Alliance is the symbol and agent of ecumenical Presbyterianism. The Alliance serves the cause of understanding among the Reformed and Presbyterian churches of the world. It is of supreme importance that we Presbyterians should know what the Reformed heritage is, and what it has to offer for our guidance today, as well as for the guidance of the Church Universal of Jesus Christ.

The Alliance serves, moreover, and I trust will serve in the future still more effectively, the cause of Presbyterian solidarity throughout the world. There are some Reformed churches in our country, and in other countries, which do not belong to the Alliance. We who are members of the Alliance need them, and they need us.

They need to be drawn out of their isolation, while we need to sense their concerns and to avail ourselves of their insights and ardor. Not only so, but through the Alliance, Presbyterian churches, which have tended to be too national or racial in spirit, will be helped to transcend themselves through the influence of the World Alliance. It is, moreover, one of the glories of our Presbyterian Alliance that it disavows any thought of becoming an end in itself. It does not exist to propagate Presbyterianism in the world, but the holy Christian faith through the Presbyterian medium. Ecumenical Presbyterianism stands for, and desires to be the servant of, the Church Universal, which is the Body of Christ.

b) What now of our Presbyterian relationship to ecumenical Christianity? From the time of John Calvin, who was the most ecumenical figure in the era of the Protestant Reformation, Presbyterians have been committed to Christian unity. The great Reformed Confessions, and the Westminster Confession of Faith in a very special manner, take seriously the "Communion of Saints." Of the three Reformation Communions, Anglicanism, Lutheranism, and Presbyterianism, it is only among the Reformed churches that it is constitutionally in order for a minister, on his own authority, to invite all Christians, for whom Jesus Christ is Lord and Saviour, to sit down at the Lord's table.

There is a sense in which Presbyterianism, by its nature and tradition, stands at the very heart of the ecumenical movement. This is so because in our heritage of faith Christian unity is dynamic in character; it is unity under the lordship of Jesus Christ. The unity which is native to our Presbyterian heritage, and toward which the churches of Christ throughout the world should aspire, is one in which church structure must never be regarded as an end in itself but be always subordinate to the will of Christ, the Head of the church. Just as the church can never be an end in itself, so no form of ecclesiastical structure can be regarded as the one indispensable form of church organization. That being so, Presbyterians will always be opposed to any kind of unity which would absolutize structure in any form whatever, and still more to any attempt to create a super-church on the Roman Catholic model. Happily, the World Council of Churches, largely through Presbyterian influence, has gone on record as saying, "We disavow any thought of becoming a single unified church structure, independent of the Churches which have combined to form the Council, or a structure dominated by a centralized administrative authority."

Presbyterians, moreover, with their conception of dynamic unity, can never be satisfied with a unity based on a common devotion to merely ethical principles. We believe that the basis of every true ethic, as of all Christian behavior, must be ultimately theological in character.

True unity must be unity in the Saviourhood and Lordship of Jesus Christ. There must be no doubt about Jesus Christ, or about ultimate allegiance to Him. At the same time, Christian unity must be much more than unity in faith. It must also be unity in work. Those who give their allegiance to the same Lord must act together. They must seek every opportunity to cooperate in common tasks, and to manifest that kind of solidarity in cooperative action and church relations which is worthily expressive of the Body of Christ. I am personally committed to the proposition that the Holy Spirit has not exhausted the possible forms of church structure. What Christians need to do is to think and live, and work and pray, together to the greatest degree possible. Then, on the road of obedience, and under the guidance of the Holy Spirit, there will emerge the most appropriate structural form whereby to express Christian unity in Christ's Church Universal. Presbyterians have thus a crucial role to play in the thought and life of the ecumenical movement.

Let me conclude with this word. There are Presbyterians today, and I would class myself among them, in whose spirit something paradoxical is taking place. On the one hand we can say, unequivocally and unashamedly, "We never felt ourselves to be *more* Presbyterian than we do today." But then we go on to add, "We never felt ourselves to be *less* Presbyterian than we do today." Both affirmations are true. We are less Presbyterian than ever before because we never, for a moment, allow ourselves to believe that Presbyterianism exhausts the Christian religion, or that all Christians, in order to be truly loyal to the Christian faith and life, must think as we do. On the other hand, we were never more Presbyterian than today because we believe that there are insights in our Presbyterian heritage of faith, and attitudes in our Presbyterian tradition of life, which the Church Universal needs in this tremendous hour.

*Rising above all bigotry and party spirit, he [Paul] proclaimed in his most polemic epistle the great principle: "In Jesus Christ neither circumcision availeth anything nor uncircumcision"—may we add, in the same spirit: Neither immersion nor pouring, neither episcopacy nor presbytery, neither Lutheranism nor Calvinism, neither Calvinism nor Arminianism, neither Romanism nor Protestantism, nor any other ism—availeth anything, but a new creature. And as many as walk according to this rule, peace be on them, and mercy, and upon the Israel of God.—*Dr. Philip Schaff.

Who's Who

FOR the purpose of identifying the leaders appearing in the illustrations of this volume, the following biographical sketches have been prepared. Some additional persons are also listed. The omission of a multitude of worthies is apparent, and is hereby admitted.

Addams, Jane, 1860–1935. Helped open Hull House, Chicago (1889), becoming chief resident. President Women's International League for Peace. President or leader in many national and international Christian ethical enterprises. Author. Shared Nobel Peace Prize in 1931. Congregationalist in latter part of her life.

Alexander, Archibald, 1772–1851. President Hampden-Sydney College, 1799–1807. Professor of Theology, Princeton Theological Seminary, 1812–1851.

Baker, Daniel, 1791–1857. Missionary to Texas, 1840. Founder of Austin College, 1849, and was its president in 1853. Promoter of public schools in the Southwest.

Baldwin, Matthias William, 1795–1866. Inventor, manufacturer, philanthropist.

Barnes, Albert, 1798–1870. Pastor, First Presbyterian Church, Philadelphia, 1830–1835, 1836–1870. Prominent in Old School–New School differences.

Beatty, Charles Clinton, 1715–1772. Theological education in Log College on the Neshaminy, 1739–1741. First Protestant minister to preach west of Alleghenies, at Fort Pitt, 1758. Again at same place in 1766. Chaplain to Colonial troops. Trustee College of New Jersey. Grandfather of Charles C. Beatty, preacher, educator, philanthropist, Western Theological Seminary and Washington and Jefferson College. The latter appears in the list of illustrations.

Beecher, Lyman, 1775–1863. Preacher, reformer, author. First president and professor of Lane Theological Seminary, 1832–1850.

Bell, Alexander Graham, 1847–1922. Inventor, scientist, educator, world citizen.

Benton, Thomas Hart, 1782–1858. U.S. Senator from Missouri, 1821–1851. Member U.S. Congress, 1853–1855.

Boudinot, Elias, 1740–1821. Revolutionary statesman. Trustee of College of New Jersey, 1772–1821. Member of Continental Congress, 1777, 1778, 1781–1784; president of the same, 1782; Secretary of Foreign Affairs under the same, 1783. Signer of Treaty of Peace with England. Member of U.S. Congress, 1789–1795. Presided in Nassau Hall when Washington was thanked for services. Helped finance American Revolution. Author.

Brackenridge, Hugh Henry, 1748–1816. Chaplain, Continental Army, 1777–1783. Member of Pennsylvania Assembly, 1786–1788. Judge, District Court of Pennsylvania, 1789–1799, and Supreme Court of Pennsylvania, 1799–1816. Founder of Pittsburgh *Gazette* and a founder of the University of Pittsburgh.

Briggs, Charles A., 1841–1913. Scholar, author, professor, Union Theological Seminary, New York City, 1874–1913. Suspended from Presbyterian ministry in 1893; this proved to be a discouraging factor relative to fearless, unbiased scholarship in American Presbyterianism.

Brown, Arthur Judson, 1856—. Secretary, Presbyterian U.S.A. Board of Foreign Missions, 1895–1929. Official in numerous national and international movements. Author of *One Hundred Years*, a history of the foreign missions of the Presbyterian Church.

Buchanan, James, 1791–1868. President of the United States, 1857–1861.

Buttrick, George A., 1892—. Pastor, Madison Avenue Presbyterian Church, New York City, since 1927. President, Federal Council of Churches. Author, editor, preacher. Chairman of the Board of Preachers and Plummer Professor of Christian Morals, Harvard University.

Caldwell, Eugene Craighead, 1856–1931. Professor, Austin Texas Theological Seminary, 1906–1914. Professor of Biblical exegesis, Union Theological Seminary, Richmond, 1915–1931.

Calvin, John, 1509–1564. Protestant Reformation leader. Its most influential theologian, educational theorist, and ethical reformer.

Carnegie, Andrew, 1835–1919. Inventor, manufacturer, philanthropist, world citizen. Never an active member of the Presbyterian Church. Born in Presbyterian home. Last rites, Presbyterian.

Cleveland, Stephen Grover, 1837–1908. President of the United States, 1885–1889, 1893–1897.

Coffin, Henry Sloane, 1877–1954. President, Union Theological Seminary, New York City, 1926–1945. Moderator, Presbyterian Church U.S.A. General Assembly, 1943. Author, preacher.

Compton, Elias, 1856–1938. On faculty of College of Wooster, Ohio, 1883–1928. Professor Philosophy, same, 1887–1928; dean, 1899–1921; acting president, 1919. Father of Arthur Holly, Karl Taylor, and Wilson M. Compton.

Corbett, Hunter, 1835–1920. Missionary in China, 1863–1905. Moderator, Presbyterian Church U.S.A. General Assembly, 1906. Author.

Davies, Samuel, 1723–1761. Preacher. Founder of Hanover Presbytery, 1755. President, College of New Jersey, 1759–1761.

Dickinson, Jonathan, 1688–1747. Preacher, leader in modified subscription to Westminster Standards. First president of College of New Jersey, 1747.

Doak, Samuel, 1749–1830. Faculty, Hampden-Sydney, 1776. Founder and first president of Washington College, Tenn., 1783–1818. Founder, later president, Tusculum College, Tenn., 1818.

Dodge, Cleveland, 1860–1926. Merchant, manufacturer, philanthropist. President, board of trustees, Robert College, Constantinople.

Dollar, Robert, 1844–1932. Steamship line owner. Philanthropist.

Dulles, John Foster, 1888——. Counselor to nations. Member of delegation for organization of United Nations. Negotiator of Japanese Peace Treaty, 1951. Leader in Federal Council and National Council of Churches. Secretary of State, 1953——.

Eagan, John J., 1870–1924. Chairman, board of trustees of Berry Schools. Philanthropist. Promoter of Christian interracial relations in the South.

Edwards, Jonathan, 1703–1758. Pastor, Northampton, Mass., 1729. Evangelist, preacher, author. President, College of New Jersey, 1757–1758. Though a Congregationalist, he was a Calvinist and greatly influenced Presbyterian thought.

Eisenhower, Dwight David, 1890——. Commander General Allied Powers, 1943. President Columbia University, 1948–1950. Supreme Commander Allied Powers of Europe, 1950–1952. President United States, 1953——.

Elliot, David, 1787–1874. Reviver and acting president of Washington College, Pa. Professor, Western Theological Seminary, Pittsburgh, 1836–1871. Moderator, Presbyterian Church General Assembly, 1837.

Erskine, Ebenezer, 1680–1754. Preacher, author. Leader in the formation of the Secession Church in Scotland. Principal forerunner of the United Presbyterian Churches in Scotland, Ireland, and America.

Ewing, James C. R., 1854–1925. Missionary to India, 1879–1922. Principal, Forman Christian College, Lahore, 1888–1918. Vice chancellor, Punjab University, 1910–1917.

Finney, Charles G., 1792–1875. Preacher, evangelist, reformer. Professor, Oberlin College, 1835–1875. Second president of the same, 1851–1866. Began a Presbyterian, transferred to the Congregational Church. Pastor, First Congregational Church, Oberlin, 1835–1872.

Gould, Helen (Shepard), 1868–1938. Philanthropist, Christian leader.

Graham, William, 1746–1788. Teacher in Augusta Academy, Mount Pleasant, Va., 1774. Founder and principal of Liberty Hall Academy (now Washington and Lee University), Lexington, Va., 1877.

Green, Ashbel, 1762–1848. President, Princeton College, 1812–1822. Director of Princeton Theological Seminary, 1812–1848. President of General Assembly Committee for Western Seminary, 1825—. President, board of trustees, Jefferson Medical College, 1826–1848.

Grosvenor, Gilbert Hovey, 1875—. Editor, *National Geographic Magazine*, 1903–1954. Author, explorer, geographer, scientist.

Gurley, Phineas, 1816–1868. Pastor of Abraham Lincoln, a regular attendant at services in the Second (now New York Avenue) Presbyterian Church, Washington, D.C. Moderator of General Assembly Presbyterian Church U.S.A., 1867.

Happer, Andrew P., 1818–1894. As an ordained clergyman and doctor of medicine, he performed a remarkable service as a missionary in Canton, China, 1844–1894.

Harrison, Benjamin, 1833–1901. United States Senator, 1881–1887. President of the United States, 1889–1893.

Hay, John Milton, 1838–1905. Poet, journalist, historian, diplomat. One of Lincoln's private secretaries. Secretary of State, 1898–1905.

Heinz, Henry John, 1844–1919. Packer, merchant, philanthropist. State and world Sunday School leader.

Higginbottom, Sam, 1874—. Missionary to India, 1903—. Moderator, Presbyterian Church U.S.A. General Assembly, 1939. Promoter of Christian missions through scientific agriculture.

Hodge, Archibald Alexander, 1823–1886. Author. Professor, Western Theological Seminary, 1864–1877; Princeton Theological Seminary, 1877–1886.

Hodge, Charles, 1797–1878. Member of the Faculty, Princeton Theological Seminary, 1820–1878. Editor of *Biblical Repertory and Princeton Review* 40 years. Author, *Constitutional History of the Presbyterian Church; Systematic Theology.* Father of Caspar Wistar and Archibald Alexander Hodge.

Hoge, Moses Drury, 1818–1899. Pastor, Second Presbyterian Church, Richmond, Va., 1845–1899. Moderator, Presbyterian Church U.S., 1875. Preacher, lecturer.

Holland, William J., 1848–1932. Zoologist, paleontologist, educator. Chancellor of Western University of Pennsylvania (now University of Pittsburgh), 1891–1901. Director, Carnegie Institution, 1898–1922.

Hoover, J. Edgar, 1895—. Director of the Federal Bureau of Investigation, Department of Justice of the United States, since 1924.

Horton, Mildred McAfee, 1900—. Dean of Women, Oberlin College, 1934–1936. President of Wellesley College, 1936–1949. Director of Women's U.S.N.R., 1942–1946. Prominent officer in Federal and National Councils of Churches. Now Congregationalist.

Jackson, Andrew, 1767–1845. Member of Constitutional Convention of Tennessee. President of the United States, 1829–1837.

Jackson, Samuel Macauley, 1851–1912. Philanthropist, church historian, author. Close collaborator with Philip Schaff (*q.v.*).

Jackson, Sheldon, 1834–1909. Missionary and pioneer in western United States and Alaska. Moderator, General Assembly Presbyterian Church U.S.A., 1897.

Jackson, Thomas Jonathan (Stonewall), 1824–1863. Beloved general in the Armies of the Confederacy, 1861–1863.

Jesup, Morris K., 1830–1908. Banker, philanthropist.

Jones, Charles Colcock, 1831–1893. Author, historian. Charles Bancroft termed him the "Macaulay of the South."

Kagawa, Toyohiko, 1888—. Notable preacher, evangelist, author, and sociologist in Japan and throughout the world. Emphasizes Christian brotherhood economics through cooperatives.

Kelso, James Anderson, 1873–1951. Theologian. Old Testament scholar. Acting president, 1908–1909, then president, 1909–1943, Western Theological Seminary.

Kendall, Henry, 1815–1892. Missions administrator. First secretary of New School Presbyterian Church Home Missions, 1861–1870. General Secretary Presbyterian Church U.S.A. Home Missions, 1870–1892.

Kerr, Hugh Thomson, 1871–1950. Preacher, author. President, Board of Christian Education, Presbyterian Church U.S.A., 1923–1941. Moderator, Presbyterian General Assembly U.S.A., 1930–1931. Notable radio ministry.

Ketler, Isaac, 1853–1915. Founder and president, Grove City College, Pa., 1876–1913. Author.

Knox, John, c. 1505–1572. Chief promoter of Protestant Reformation in Scotland. Preacher, author, historian.

Lapsley, Samuel N., 1866–1892. Pioneer missionary to Congo. Associated with W. H. Sheppard (*q.v.*).

Lindsley, Philip, 1786–1855. Vice president, College of New Jersey, 1817; acting president of same, 1823. Refusing several offers of college presidencies, became president of Cumberland College, 1825–1850, then professor in the New Albany (now McCormick) Theological Seminary, 1850–1855.

McCormick, Cyrus Hall, 1809–1884. Inventor, manufacturer, philanthropist.

McCormick, Samuel Black, 1858–1928. Educator. President, Coe College, Iowa, 1897–1904. Chancellor, University of Pittsburgh, 1904–1921.

McDowell, John, 1870–1937. Secretary, Board of National Missions, U.S.A., 1919—. Secretary, Committee on Social and Industrial Relations, 1930–1942. Moderator, Presbyterian Church U.S.A. General Assembly, 1933–1934.

McFarland, Amanda R., Home missionary, Presbyterian Church U.S.A. Outstanding service in western U.S. and in Alaska.

McFarland, Samuel Gamble, 1830–1897. Missionary in Siam. Commissioned by the king of Siam, he organized public education in Siam. Author of English-Siamese dictionary.

Mackay, John A., 1889—. Missions administrator. Educator, author. President, Princeton Theological Seminary. President, International

Missionary Council, 1947—. Moderator, Presbyterian Church U.S.A. General Assembly, 1953–1954. President of the World Alliance of the Reformed Churches.

McMillan, John, 1752–1833. A founder of Washington and Jefferson academies and colleges, Pa. Vice principal and professor of divinity, Jefferson Academy and College.

McNaugher, John, 1857–1947. President and professor, Pittsburgh (later Pittsburgh-Xenia) Theological Seminary U.P. Church, 1887–1945. Moderator, U.P. Church General Assembly. Author.

Makemie, Francis, c. 1658–1708. "Father of American Presbyterianism." Came to America, 1683. Moderator of first Presbytery, 1706. Author. Founder of churches. Extended religious liberty.

Martin, W. A. P., 1827–1916. Missionary to China. An organizer of the Imperial University, Peking, China, becoming its president in 1898. Author of many important works relative to China.

Mellon, Andrew William, 1855–1937. Industrialist, banker, statesman, philanthropist. Secretary, U.S. Treasury, 1921–1932. Ambassador to Great Britain, 1932–1933.

Moffat, James David, 1846–1916. President, Washington and Jefferson College, 1882–1915. Moderator, General Assembly Presbyterian Church U.S.A., 1905. Led in doctrinal changes in U.S.A. Church.

Moore, Walter W., 1857–1926. President, Union Theological Seminary, Richmond, Va., 1904–1926.

Morrison, William McCutchen, 1867–1918. Famous missionary to Belgian Congo, Africa, 1897–1918. Presbyterian Church U.S. Championed rights of Africans versus King Leopold.

Morse, Hermann Nelson, 1887—. General Secretary, Presbyterian U.S.A. Board of National Missions. Vice president, National Council of Churches. Moderator, Presbyterian Church U.S.A. General Assembly, 1952.

Mudge, Lewis Seymour, 1868–1945. Administrator, preacher, ecumenical leader. Stated Clerk, Presbyterian Church U.S.A. General Assembly, 1921–1938. Moderator of same, 1931–1932.

Nevin, John Williamson, 1803–1886. Professor, Western Theological Seminary, 1829–1840. Professor, Mercersburg Theological Seminary, 1840–1853. President, Marshall College, 1841–1853. President, Franklin and Marshall College, 1866–1876.

Palmer, Benjamin Morgan, 1818–1902. Professor, Columbia Theological Seminary, 1854—. First Moderator of the General Assembly of the Presbyterian Church U.S., 1864.

Pew, J. Howard, 1882–—. Industrialist, philanthropist. President, Board of Trustees, General Assembly Presbyterian Church U.S.A.

Plumer, William Swan, 1802–1880. Professor of Theology, Western Theological Seminary, 1854–1862. Professor, Columbia Theological Seminary, 1867–1880. Moderator, Old School General Assembly, 1838. Moderator, General Assembly of Presbyterian Church U.S., 1871.

Pressly, John T., 1795–1870. Professor, Allegheny Theological Seminary, 1831–1870. Pastor, First Church (Associate Reformed, then, 1858, U.P.), Allegheny, 1833–1870. Moderator, First General Assembly U.P. Church, 1858. Author.

Rice, David, 1733–1816. Father of Presbyterianism in Kentucky. Member, Kentucky Constitutional Convention, 1792.

Rice, John Holt, 1777–1831. Pastor of the First Presbyterian Church, Richmond, Virginia, 1812–1823. On the faculties of Hampden-Sydney and Union Theological Seminaries. In the latter at Richmond he was Professor of Theology, 1824–1831.

Riddle, Matthew Brown, 1836–1916. Professor, Western Theological Seminary, 1887–1911. Member of American Committee for Bible revision, 1871–—. Author.

Ruffner, Henry W., 1790–1861. President, Washington College, Va., 1836–1848. Author. Promoter of general education in Virginia.

Rush, Benjamin, 1745–1813. Member of Continental Congress, 1776–1777. Signer of Declaration of Independence, 1776. Surgeon General Continental Army, 1777; physician general, 1777–1778. Member of the Pennsylvania Constitutional Convention. Professor, University of Pennsylvania, 1769–1813. Appointed Treasurer of U.S. Mint, 1797–1813. Founder of Dickinson College, Pa.

Schaff, Philip, 1819–1893. Professor, Union Theological Seminary, New York City, 1870–1893. Probably foremost ecumenical scholar, leader, and author of the nineteenth century. Historian.

Severance, Louis Henry, 1838–1913. Capitalist, philanthropist. Generous supporter of foreign missions. Also of Oberlin College, Western Reserve University, and the College of Wooster.

Sheppard, William H., 1865–1926. Missionary to Belgian Congo from Presbyterian Church U.S., 1890–1910. Made courageous exposure of forced labor of Negroes in Congo, attracting world attention. Fellow of Royal Geographic Society.

Speer, Robert E., 1867–1947. Secretary, Presbyterian Church U.S.A. Board of Foreign Missions, 1891–1937. Author. Moderator, Presbyterian Church U.S.A., 1927. President of Federal Council of Churches. Leader of World Christian Assemblies.

Stelzle, Charles, 1869–1941. Founder, Labor Temple, New York City, 1910. Superintendent of Department of Church and Labor, Presbyterian Church U.S.A., 1903–1914.

Stimson, Henry Lewis, 1867–1950. Secretary of War, 1911–1913. Governor General, Philippine Islands, 1927–1929. Secretary of State, 1929–1933. Secretary of War, 1940–1945.

Stockton, Richard, 1730–1781. Lawyer, statesman. Member of Continental Congress, 1776–1781. Signer of Declaration of Independence.

Stockton, Robert Field, 1795–1866. Held naval offices. Active in annexation of Texas. Led in conquering California. U.S. Senator from New Jersey, 1851–1853.

Stowe, Harriet Beecher, 1811–1896. Author, humanitarian.

Swift, Elisha P., 1792–1865. Acting professor, Western Theological Seminary, 1827–1828. Preacher, author. Organizer of the Western Missionary Society, forerunner of the Presbyterian Church U.S.A. Board of Foreign Missions.

Talmage, T. De Witt, 1832–1902. Pastor, preacher, author, lecturer.

Tennent, Gilbert, 1703–1764. Preacher, evangelist. Trustee of College of New Jersey.

Tennent, William, 1673–1745. Founder and principal of the Log College on the Neshaminy, 1726–1746. A cut of this Log College appears in illustrations.

Thompson, R. E., 1844–1924. Author, church historian, scholar.

Thompson, William Oxley, 1855–1933. Educator. President, Miami University, Ohio, 1891–1899. President, Ohio State University, 1899–1925. Moderator, Presbyterian Church U.S.A. General Assembly, 1926.

Underwood, Horace Grant, 1859–1916. Missionary in Korea. Helped establish Chosen Union Christian College, Seoul. Author.

van Dyke, Henry, 1852–1933. Poet, preacher, author, diplomat. Professor, Princeton University. Moderator, General Assembly Presbyterian Church U.S.A., 1902. Minister to the Netherlands and Luxembourg.

Wanamaker, John, 1838–1922. Merchant, philanthropist, Sunday School leader. Postmaster General U.S., 1889–1893.

Warfield, Benjamin B., 1851–1921. Professor, Western Theological Seminary, 1879–1887. Professor, Princeton Theological Seminary, 1887–1921.

Watson, Charles R., 1873—. Corresponding Secretary, United Presbyterian Board of Foreign Missions, 1902–1916. President, American University of Cairo, Egypt, 1922—. Moderator of the U.P. General Assembly.

Westinghouse, George, 1846–1914. Inventor, industrialist, philanthropist.

Whitefield, George, 1714–1770. Preacher, evangelist. Influenced founding of University of Pennsylvania. Helped found Calvinist Methodist Church of Wales. This church now united in the United States with Presbyterian Church U.S.A.

Whitman, Marcus, 1802–1847. Physician, pioneer, missionary under American Board to Northwest. Presbyterians, New School, then in the American Board.

Wilson, John Leighton, 1809–1886. Missionary, Africa, 1833–1852. Secretary, Board of Foreign Missions Presbyterian Church, 1853–1861; Secretary, Board of Foreign Missions of Presbyterian Church U.S., 1861–1886.

Wilson, Woodrow, 1856–1924. Professor Princeton University, 1889—. President, Princeton University, 1902–1910. Governor of New Jersey, 1911–1913. President of United States, 1913–1921. A founder of the League of Nations.

Winsborough, Hallie Paxson, 1865–1940. A leading organizer of women's work in Presbyterian Church U.S. Executive secretary of same. Prominent officer in Home Missions and Interracial commissions in her church. Similar positions in the Federal Council of Churches. Led in movement to abolish lynching.

Witherspoon, John, 1723–1794. Member Continental Congress, 1776–1783. Signer of Declaration Independence, 1776. Member of the New Jersey Assembly and Senate, also of New Jersey Constitutional Convention. First Moderator of the General Assembly, 1789. President of College of New Jersey, 1768–1794.

Woodrow, James, 1828–1907. Professor of Natural Science and Revelation, Columbia Theological Seminary, 1861–1868. Professor of Science, University of South Carolina, 1869–1891; and president, 1891–1897.

Appendix

Educational Institutions in the United States and Foreign Lands ALSO Theological Seminaries in the United States Related to American Presbyterians

As indicated in Chapter VI, "The Founding of Educational Institutions," the Calvinists in America, by about the year 1835, had excelled all other groups in founding institutions of higher learning. These include Congregationalists, Anglicans, early Baptists, the Dutch and German Reformed, and the Presbyterians. Below, under various categories, are listed those institutions in connection with which the Presbyterians had either the whole, the chief, or a cooperative part in their founding.

I. COLLEGES AND UNIVERSITIES CONCERNING WHICH THE PRESBYTERIANS HAD AN IMPORTANT, IF NOT DOMINANT, PART IN FOUNDING

1746	Princeton University, Princeton, N.J.
1749	Washington and Lee University, Lexington, Va.
1787	The University of Pittsburgh, Pittsburgh, Pa.
1794	The University of Tennessee, Knoxville, Tenn.
1795	Union College, Schenectady, N.Y.
1804	Ohio University, Athens, Ohio
1809	Miami University, Oxford, Ohio
1820	Indiana University, Bloomington, Ind.
1826	Western Reserve University, Cleveland, Ohio
1831	New York University, New York, N.Y.
1833	University of Delaware, Newark, Del.
1835	Oglethorpe University, Oglethorpe University, Ga.

1846 University of Buffalo, Buffalo, N.Y.
1848 University of Wisconsin, Madison, Wis.
1853 Beaver College, Jenkintown, Pa.
1868 University of California, Berkeley, Calif.

II. INSTITUTIONS FOUNDED BY THE CONGREGATIONALISTS AND PRESBYTERIANS UNDER THE PLAN OF 1801

1829 Illinois College, Jacksonville, Ill., now Presbyterian U.S.A.
1837 Knox College, Galesburg, Ill., later Congregational
1846 Grinnell College, Grinnell, Iowa, later Congregational
1846 Beloit College, Beloit, Wis., later Congregational
1847 Rockford College, Rockford, Ill., later Congregational
1849 Pacific University, Forest Grove, Ore., later Congregational
1851 Ripon College, Ripon, Wis., later Congregational
1851 Milwaukee-Downer College, Milwaukee, Wis., later Congregational

III. INSTITUTIONS FOUNDED BY PRESBYTERIANS WHICH NOW HOLD AN AFFILIATED RELATION TO SOME PRESBYTERIAN DENOMINATION. THIS IMPLIES NEITHER LEGAL TIES NOR ECCLESIASTICAL CONTROL

1780 Washington and Jefferson College, Washington, Pa. (U.S.A.)
1794 Tusculum College, Greenville, Tenn. (U.S.A.)
1812 Hamilton College, Clinton, N.Y. (U.S.A.)
1827 Hanover College, Hanover, Ind. (U.S.A.)
1832 Wabash College, Crawfordsville, Ind. (U.S.A.)
1837 Blackburn Junior College, Carlinville, Ill. (U.S.A.)
1842 Mary Baldwin College, Staunton, Va. (U.S.)
1851 Coe College, Cedar Rapids, Iowa (U.S.A.)
1851 Westminster College, Fulton, Mo. (U.S.A.)
1853 Western College for Women, Oxford, Ohio (U.S.A.)
1854 Lincoln University, Lincoln University, Pa. (U.S.A.)
1855 Elmira College, Elmira, N.Y. (U.S.A.)
1875 Park College, Parkville, Mo. (U.S.A.)
1876 Grove City, Grove City, Pa. (U.S.A.)
1887 Occidental College, Los Angeles, Calif. (U.S.A.)
1889 Agnes Scott College, Decatur, Ga. (U.S.)

IV. INSTITUTIONS FOUNDED BY PRESBYTERIANS AND NOW CLOSELY
RELATED TO A PRESBYTERIAN DENOMINATION

1764	West Nottingham Academy, Colora, Md. (U.S.A.)
1776	Hampden-Sydney College, Hampden-Sydney, Va. (U.S.)
1819	Centre College, Danville, Ky. (U.S.)
1819	Maryville College, Maryville, Tenn. (U.S.A.)
1826	Lafayette College, Easton, Pa. (U.S.A.)
1827	Lindenwood, St. Charles, Mo. (U.S.A.)
1834	College of Ozarks, Clarksville, Ark. (U.S.A.)
1837	Davidson College, Davidson, N.C. (U.S.)
1837	Muskingum College, New Concord, Ohio (U.P.)
1839	Erskine College, Due West, S.C. (Ref. P.)
1842	Bethel College, McKenzie, Tenn. (Cumberland P.)
1842	Cumberland University, Lebanon, Tenn. (U.S.A.)
1846	Carrol College, Waukesha, Wis. (U.S.A.)
1848	Southwestern, Memphis, Tenn. (U.S.)
1848	Geneva College, Beaver Falls, Pa. (Ref. P.)
1849	Waynesburg College, Waynesburg, Pa. (U.S.A.)
1849	Austin College, Sherman, Tex. (U.S.)
1851	Westminster College, Fulton, Mo. (U.S.)
1852	University of Dubuque, Dubuque, Iowa (U.S.A.)
1852	Westminster College, New Wilmington, Pa. (U.P.)
1853	Monmouth College, Monmouth, Ill. (U.P.)
1857	Lake Forest College, Lake Forest, Ill. (U.S.A.)
1857	Queens College, Charlotte, N.C. (U.S.)
1866	The College of Wooster, Wooster, Ohio (U.S.A.)
1867	Lewis and Clark College, Portland, Ore. (U.S.A.)
1867	Johnson C. Smith University, Charlotte, N.C. (U.S.A.)
1867	King College, Bristol, Tenn. (U.S.)
1869	Trinity University, San Antonio, Texas (U.S.A.)
1869	Wilson College, Chambersburg, Pa. (U.S.A.)
1872	Arkansas College, Batesville, Ark. (U.S.)
1875	Parsons College, Fairfield, Ia. (U.S.A.)
1875	Knoxville College, Knoxville, Tenn. (U.P.)
1880	Presbyterian College, Clinton, S.C. (U.S.)
1882	Hastings College, Hastings, Neb. (U.S.A.)
1882	Emporia College, Emporia, Kan. (U.S.A.)
1883	Huron College, Huron, S.D. (U.S.A.)
1883	Tarkio College, Tarkio, Mo. (U.P.)

1883   Jamestown College, Jamestown, N.D. (U.S.A.)
1885   Macalester College, St. Paul, Minn. (U.S.A.)
1887   Sterling College, Sterling, Kansas (U.P.)
1888   Missouri Valley College, Marshall, Mo. (U.S.A.)
1890   Whitworth College, Spokane, Wash. (U.S.A.)
1891   Buena Vista College, Storm Lake, Ia. (U.S.A.)
1891   College of Idaho, Caldwell, Idaho (U.S.A.)
1894   University of Tulsa, Tulsa, Okla. (U.S.A.)
1894   Belhaven College, Jackson, Miss. (U.S.)
1896   Flora Macdonald College, Red Springs, N.C. (U.S.)
1901   James Millikin University, Decatur, Ill. (U.S.A.)
1903   Davis and Elkins College, Elkins, W. Va. (U.S.) (U.S.A.)
1916   Montreat College, Montreat, N.C. (U.S.)
1923   Intermountain Union, Polytechnic, Mont. (U.S.A.)

JUNIOR COLLEGES

1856   Lenox College, Hopkinson, Ia. (U.S.A.)
1856   Mitchell College, Statesville, N.C. (U.S.)
1857   Peace College, Raleigh, N.C. (U.S.)
1865   Lincoln Junior College, Lincoln, Ill. (U.S.A.)
1875   Westminster College, Salt Lake City, Utah (U.S.A.)
1883   Lees Junior College, Jackson, Ky. (U.S.)
1889   Pikeville College, Pikeville, Ky. (U.S.A.)
1900   Lees-McRae College, Banner Elk, N.C. (U.S.)
1929   Presbyterian Junior College for Men, Maxton, N.C. (U.S.)

V. INSTITUTIONS FOUNDED BY PRESBYTERIANS AND NOW RELATED TO OTHER DENOMINATIONS (See also II above)

1773   Dickinson College, Carlisle, Pa., now Methodist
1780   Transylvania College, Lexington, Ky., now Disciples of Christ
1815   Allegheny College, Meadville, Pa., now Methodist
1845   Adrian College, Adrian, Mich., now Methodist

VI. COLLEGES AND UNIVERSITIES, AND INSTITUTIONS OF HIGHER LEARNING, AND JUNIOR GRADE, FOUNDED, OR LARGELY FOUNDED, IN FOREIGN LANDS BY AMERICAN PRESBYTERIANS

1845   Hangchow Christian College, Hangchow, China (U.S.A., U.S.)

1850	Imperial University of China, Peking (U.S.A.)
1864	Cheeloo University (formerly Shantung Christian University) (U.S.A.)
1865	Assiut College, Assiut, Egypt (U.P.)
1866	Forman Christian College, Lahore, India (now affiliated with Punjab University) (U.S.A.)
1885	Severance Union Medical College, Seoul, Korea (U.S.A.)
1893	Gordon College, Rawalpindi, Pakistan (U.P.)
1897	Medical College, Miraj, West India (U.S.A.)
1898	Union Medical College, Pyengyang, Korea (U.S.A.)
1899	Hackett Medical College, Canton, China (U.S.A.)
1901	Silliman University, Dumaguete, P.I. (U.S.A.)
1902	Ewing Christian College, later Allahabad Christian College, Allahabad, India (U.S.A.)
1905	Chosen Christian College, Seoul, Korea (U.S.A.)
1907	Union Theological Seminary, Manila, P.I. (U.S.A. cooperating)
1910	Nanking University, Nanking, China (U.S.A. cooperating)
1910	American College for Girls, Cairo, Egypt (U.P.)
1913	Ginling College for Women, Nanking, China (U.S.A. cooperating)
1917	Yenching University, Peiping, China (U.S.A. cooperating)
1922	American University, Cairo, Egypt (U.P. cooperating)
1925	Teheran College, Teheran, Iran (U.S.A.)

VII. PRESBYTERIAN THEOLOGICAL SEMINARIES
Within the United States

Because of the distance from colleges and universities, American Presbyterianism, west of the Allegheny mountains, in the instance of two of its denominations began the training of ministers in Log Colleges or academies with the Reverends Joseph Smith and John McMillan for the Presbyterians and the Reverend John Anderson for the Associate (now United Presbyterian) Church. These beginnings, which continued in unbroken line until the General Assemblies, in each case, took over the sponsorship, are figured in establishing the founding dates given below. This is quite in accord with the accepted method of fixing the date for the founding of institutions, even though the name and sponsorship have changed. See, e.g., Chapter VII, note 20.

Name	Founded	Established by General Assembly	Present Location	Denomination
Western	1785	1825	Pittsburgh, Pa.	U.S.A.
Pittsburgh-Xenia	1794	1825 (by Synod)	Pittsburgh, Pa.	U.P.
Reformed (Old Light)	1810	1810 (by Synod)	Pittsburgh, Pa.	Ref. Pbn. Ch. (Old Light)
Princeton	1812	1812	Princeton, N.J.	U.S.A.
Union	1812	1812	Richmond, Va.	U.S.
Auburn	1818	1818	N.Y. City (with Union)	U.S.A.
Columbia	1828	1828	Decatur, Ga.	U.S.
Lane	1829	1829	Chicago, Ill. (with McCormick)	U.S.A.
McCormick	1829	1829	Chicago, Ill.	U.S.A.
Dubuque	1852	1852	Dubuque, Iowa	U.S.A.
Louisville	1853	1853	Louisville, Ky.	U.S., U.S.A.
Lincoln University	1866	1866	Lincoln University, Pa.	U.S.A.
Bloomfield	1869	1869	Bloomfield, N.J.	U.S.A.
San Francisco	1871	1871	San Anselmo, Calif.	U.S.A.
Austin	1902	1902	Austin, Tex.	U.S.

Notes

CHAPTER I *Origins*

1 A. Steele, *Chief of the Pilgrims: Life and Times of Elder William Brewster* (1857), pp. 376–378. Plymouth Court Records, I, 53–59. Brewster, a graduate of Cambridge, served as Secretary to Queen Elizabeth's Ambassador to the Netherlands in 1585 and was himself a publisher of many learned works, including those of Beza, Peter Martyr, Erasmus, Chrysostom, and Calvin.

2 The historian Livingston has given us a description of their plight and of their decision. See Alexander, *History of the Presbyterian Church in Ireland*, pp. 58–59. See also J. W. Reid, *History of the Presbyterian Church in Ireland* (1853), I, 191–194.

3 Taken from G. J. Slosser, *Christian Unity, Its History and Challenge* (London and New York, 1929). The graph "Presbyterian Family Connection" was constructed by H. C. Weber with Dr. Slosser's aid.

4 Charles A. Hanna, *The Scotch-Irish; or, The Scot in North Britain, North Ireland, and North America* (New York, 1902), II, 182.

5 John Calvin, *Institutes of the Christian Religion*, 1559 ed., Chaps. XXI–XXIII.

6 G. J. Slosser, *The History of the Westminster Assembly and Standards* (1943), pp. 29–30.

7 Herbert D. Foster, article "Calvinists and Education," with appended bibliography, in Monroe, *A Cyclopedia of Education*, Vols. I and II combined, pp. 499ff.

8 Calvin, *Institutes* IV. x. 1–12; IV. xx. 1–32. The manner in which these principles were applied must be drawn from Calvin's "Ordonnances" for the church's life in Geneva and from the theory as to the relation of church and state under Calvinistic influences here in America.

9 Edward Fisher, *The Marrow of Modern Divinity*, in two parts; 1830, the first American, revised from the eighth Scottish, edition. This book, very probably beyond all others, except the Bible, influenced the founding of the United Presbyterian Church of Scotland and indirectly the United Presbyterian Church of North America, causing the former to be the first of the Presbyterian churches of the world to adopt Arminianism and catholic-minded evangelism.

[10] See Chapter V, in which it is set forth that the Reformed Church in America continues a modified form of this same conviction.

[11] *Story of the Scottish Church* (London, 1875), pp. 470–471.

[12] Let it be remembered in connection with this statement that Presbyterian polity is here thought of as including bishops for the well-being (*bene esse*), never for the being (*esse*), of the church.

CHAPTER II   Beginnings in the North

[1] L. J. Trinterud, *The Forming of an American Tradition*, p. 15.

[2] T. C. Pears, *This American Wilderness*, p. 119, Stone Lectures for 1942.

[3] Cotton Mather, *Magnalia*, I, 74–75, 362.

[4] The Cambridge Platform, adopted in 1648, embodied several distinctive Presbyterian principles of polity. See Trinterud, *op. cit.*, p. 21.

[5] Charles A. Briggs, *American Presbyterianism* (New York, 1885), p. 97, and Appendix IV, where John Eliot's letter, written in 1650, is quoted in full.

[6] Mather, *op. cit.*, I, 80; also Paul McClurkin, Presbyterianism in Colonial New England, p. 6, a manuscript dissertation for an evaluation of Mather's statement in Library of Dept. of History, Witherspoon Bldg., Phila.

[7] Briggs, *op. cit.*, p. 100.

[8] E. H. Gillett, *History of the Presbyterian Church U.S.A.* (Philadelphia, 1864), I, 30.

[9] W. P. Finney, "Period of the Isolated Congregations and the General Presbytery," *Journal of the Department of History*, XV, 11, March, 1932.

[10] W. W. Sweet, *Religion in Colonial America* (New York, 1943), p. 259.

[11] Gillett, *op. cit.*, p. 20.

[12] *Records of the Presbyterian Church*, p. 9. On deposit in the Library of the Department of History, Witherspoon Bldg., Philadelphia.

[13] Charles A. Hanna, *The Scotch-Irish* . . . II, 2.

[14] Guy Klett, *Presbyterians in Colonial Pennsylvania*.

[15] Hanna, *op. cit.*, I, 76, records the names of the three lawyers: James Reigniere, David Jameson, and William Nicholl.

[16] *Journal of the Department of History* (1933), XV, 325.

[17] *Records of the Presbyterian Church*, p. 10; Minutes of Presbytery of Philadelphia, March 26, 1707.

[18] Alfred Nevin, *History of the Presbytery of Philadelphia and of Philadelphia Central* (Philadelphia, 1888), p. 7.

[19] Frederick W. Loetscher, "The Adopting Act," *Journal of the Presbyterian Historical Society*, XIII, 338–341.

[20] *Records of the Presbyterian Church*, p. 95.

[21] H. J. Ford, *The Scotch-Irish in America*, p. 265.

[22] *Ibid.*, p. 32.

[23] Typed Minutes of Donegal Presbytery, April, 1773; October, 1773; etc.

[24] L. E. Brynestad, "The Great Awakening in New England and the Middle Colonies," *Journal of the Presbyterian Historical Society*, XIV, 87.

25 Trinterud, *op. cit.*, p. 58.

26 A. Alexander, *Biographical Sketches of Log College*, p. 53.

27 Brynestad, *op. cit.*, p. 116. He quoted a letter written by Gilles, who heard Whitefield on the Jersey shore while speaking from the steps of the Philadelphia Court House on Market Street.

28 June 12, 1740.

29 Gilbert Tennent, *The Danger of an Unconverted Ministry* (Philadelphia, 1740), pp. 14ff. *Records of the Presbyterian Church*, pp. 159f. *et passim*.

30 Pears, "Colonial Education Among Presbyterians," *Journal of the Presbyterian Historical Society*, XXX, 117.

31 *Records of the Presbyterian Church*, p. 287.

CHAPTER III *Beginnings in the South*

1 Carl Bridenbaugh, *Myths and Realities* (Louisiana State University Press, Baton Rouge, 1952), p. vii.

2 George Maclaren Brydon, *Virginia's Mother Church* (Virginia Historical Society, Richmond, Va., 1947), I, 18.

3 In a letter written June 18, 1614, to William Gouge, minister of St. Anne's Blackfriar's Church in London, quoted by Brydon, *op. cit.*, I, 24, from Purches, *His Pilgrimes*, IV, 1770–1771.

4 William Waller Hening, *The Statutes at Large: Being a Collection of All the Laws of Virginia, from the First Session of the Legislature in the Year 1619*, I, 149 (quoted by Brydon, *op. cit.*, I, 88).

5 Brydon, *op. cit.*, I, 29.

6 Leonard J. Trinterud, *The Forming of an American Tradition* (The Westminster Press, Philadelphia, Pa., 1949), p. 34.

7 A section which remains a stronghold of Presbyterianism to the present.

8 Guion Griffis Johnson, *Ante-Bellum North Carolina: A Social History* (University of North Carolina Press, Chapel Hill, 1937), p. 349.

9 *Op. cit.*, p. 120.

10 *Ibid.*, p. 130.

11 George Howe, *History of the Presbyterian Church in South Carolina* (1870), I, 363.

12 Charles A. Hanna, *The Scotch-Irish* . . . I, 2.

13 *Records of the Presbyterian Church* (Presbyterian Board of Publication, Philadelphia, 1841), p. 103.

14 *Ibid.*, p. 141.

15 *Ibid.*, p. 145.

16 Wesley M. Gewehr, *The Great Awakening in Virginia, 1740–1790* (Duke University Press, Durham, N.C., 1931), p. 49n.

17 Quoted in William Henry Foote, *Sketches of Virginia* (1850), p. 128.

18 Brydon, *op. cit.*, I, 159–160.

19 *Memoirs of the Rev. David Rice*, p. 151.

20 Foote, *op. cit.*, p. 286.

21 *Ibid.*, pp. 287, 288, 290.

22 Foote, William Henry, *Sketches of North Carolina* (1846), p. 167.

23 *Op. cit.*, p. 106.

24 Quoted in William Henry Foote, *Sketches of Virginia*, p. 33.

25 W. L. Saunders, ed., *Colonial Records of North Carolina, 1765–1768*, VII, 252 (P. N. Hale, state printer, 1886–1890, Raleigh, N.C.).

26 McGeachy, Neill R., History of the Sugar Creek Church, N.C. (typed thesis, Union Theological Seminary, Richmond, Va., 1954).

CHAPTER IV   *The United Presbyterian Church*

1 Donald Fraser, *The Life and Diary of the Reverend Ebenezer Erskine*, A.M. (Edinburgh, 1831), p. 11.

2 *Ibid.*, p. 327.

3 Cf. Chap. I in this volume, pp. 14f.

4 R. D. Harper, *The Church Memorial* (Columbus, 1858), pp. 13, 14.

5 It should be pointed out, in all fairness, that just about every United Presbyterian who has written on this subject contended that the Marrowmen were innocent of the charges. It is, we believe, true that *they* were innocent, but the *book*, against which the charges were made, was guilty. The Marrowmen became guilty as unconscious accomplices.

6 James Brown Scouller, *A Manual of the United Presbyterian Church of North America, 1751–1887* (2nd ed., Pittsburgh, 1887), p. 15.

7 Fraser, *op. cit.*, p. 325.

8 Wilson, *A Defense of the Reformation Principles of the Church of Scotland*, in James Harper, *et al.*, *Lives of Ebenezer Erskine, William Wilson and Thomas Gillespie, Fathers of the United Presbyterian Church* (Edinburgh, 1849), p. 63.

9 Harper, *op. cit.*, p. 18.

10 Cf. *A Display of the Religious Principles of the Associate Synod of North America* (revised by the Associate Synod, 1813; 5th ed., Albany, 1828).

11 By the revision of 1925, three of the "five points of Calvinism" were eliminated; namely, (1) unconditional election either to salvation or damnation; (2) limited atonement, i.e., Christ died not for all but for the elect only; (3) irresistible grace, i.e., the elect will persevere because for them the grace of God is irresistible. The two points retained were: (1) total depravity (Article VIII); and, (2) the perseverance of the saints (Article XXIII, of the Security of Believers). Dr. Gerstner at the Symposium indicated that personally he is out of sympathy with such changes to Arminianism, the official doctrinal attitude of his church denomination.

12 In a doctoral thesis (University of Pittsburgh, 1947) with the subject *The United Presbyterian Church and Church Union*.

13 Harper, *op. cit.*, pp. 74, 75.

14 For convenient summaries of these official actions, cf. Ralph Wilson

Lindsay, *A Brief History of the United Presbyterian Church of North America* (Pittsburgh, n.d.), pp. 42f.; Harper, *op. cit.*, pp. 38f.; Scouller, *op. cit.*, pp. 29f.

[15] Article 14; cf. W. J. Reid, *United Presbyterianism* (Pittsburgh, 1881); Scouller, *op. cit.*, p. 89.

[16] William E. McCullough, "The United Presbyterian Church in America," in *The American Church of the Protestant Heritage*, ed. by V. Ferm (New York, 1953), p. 212.

[17] Scouller, *A Manual* . . . , p. 8.

[18] Cf. *ibid.*, p. 26.

[19] *A Display of . . . Religious Principles . . .* , p. 44.

[20] C. J. Williamson, "I Am a United Presbyterian," in McCullough, *op. cit.*, p. 217.

CHAPTER V   *The Reformed Presbyterian Church in America*

[1] Philip Schaff, *Creeds of Christendom*, I, 686–688.

[2] Written in 1687, by James Renwick.

[3] *A Renewal of the Covenants* . . . (n.p., 1748), p. 44.

[4] *Reformed Presbytery of Scotland: A Short Account of the Old Presbyterian Dissenters* (Falkirk, 1806), p. 10.

[5] The phrase is Samuel Blair's. L. J. Trinterud, *The Forming of an American Tradition* (Philadelphia, Westminster, 1949), p. 79.

[6] Donegal Presbytery Minutes, typescript in Presbyterian Historical Society. Ib, 304.

[7] *Ibid.*, Ib, 303, 304.

[8] *Ibid.*, Ib, 307.

[9] Alexander Craighead, *The Reasons of Mr. Alexander Craighead's Receding from the Present Judicatures of the Church* (Philadelphia, Benjamin Franklin, 1743), p. 31.

[10] *A Renewal of the Covenants*, 1743, published, with a preface, by W. M. Glasgow (Beaver Falls, Pa., 1895), p. 32.

[11] *Ibid.*, p. 33.

[12] William H. Foote, *Sketches of North Carolina* (New York, Robert Carter, 1846), pp. 183ff.

[13] The diary is in the possession of the Pittsburgh–Xenia Theological Seminary. See also William L. Fisk, Jr., "The Diary of John Cuthbertson, Missionary to the Covenanters of Colonial Pennsylvania," *Pennsylvania Magazine of History and Biography*, LXXIII (October, 1949), 441–458.

[14] Diary, July 31, 1754.

[15] William M. Glasgow, *History of the Reformed Presbyterian Church in America* (Baltimore, Hill and Harvey, 1888), p. 741.

[16] W. W. McKinney, *Early Pittsburgh Presbyterianism* (Pittsburgh, Gibson, 1938), p. 175.

[17] *Reformed Presbyterian*, X (1846–1847), 119.

[18] *Ibid.*, IX (1845–1846), 155.

[19] Minutes of Synod, 1847, in the *Covenanter*, II (July–August, 1847), 363ff.

[20] *Minutes of the Reformed Presbytery* (Pittsburgh, Bakewell & Matheny, 1874), p. 6.

[21] *Ibid.*, p. 18.

[22] MS Minutes of session, Second Church of the Covenanters, Philadelphia, *passim*.

[23] Glasgow, *op. cit.*, p. 268.

[24] MS Minutes of session, First Church of the Covenanters, Philadelphia, Nov. 25, 1835, *et passim*.

[25] *Minutes of the Reformed Presbytery, op. cit.*

[26] J. R. Wilson, *Prince Messiah's Claims to Dominion Over All Governments* . . . (Albany, 1832), p. 14.

[27] *Reformation Principles Exhibited* (New York, 1807), pp. 134, 136.

[28] *The Constitution of the Reformed Presbyterian Church* . . . (Pittsburgh, n.p., 1949), p. 204.

[29] A. McLeod, *A Scriptural View of the Character, Causes, and Ends of the Present War* (New York, Eastburn & Kirk, 1815), p. 15.

[30] From his unpublished diary, Nov. 9, 1839; March 21, 1840.

[31] *The Constitution of the Reformed Presbyterian Church*, p. 208.

[32] *Ibid.*, p. 209.

[33] An excellent study of this subject is D. R. Wilcox, The Reformed Presbyterian Church and the Antislavery Movement, an unpublished thesis, Colorado State College of Education, 1948. To it I am indebted for much of the material that follows.

[34] Minutes of Synod, in the *Covenanter*, IV (July, 1849), 358.

[35] *Extracts from the Minutes of the Synod of the Reformed Presbyterian Church* (n.p., n.d.), p. 134.

[36] *Congressional Globe*, Dec. 21, 1843; Feb. 19, 1844.

[37] Wilcox, *op. cit.*, p. 155.

[38] Minutes of Synod, *Reformed Presbyterian*, V (December and January, 1841, 1842), p. 324.

[39] Glasgow, *op. cit.*, p. 155.

CHAPTER VI *The Founding of Educational Institutions*

[1] W. W. Sweet, *Religion in Colonial America* (New York, Scribner's, 1942), Chap. VIII, "The Presbyterian Irish," pp. 245–270.

[2] For an account of the Hampden-Sydney and Washington college revivals see E. H. Gillett, *History of the Presbyterian Church in the United States of America*, 2 vols. (Philadelphia, 1864), I, 281–283.

[3] Charles E. Cuningham, *Timothy Dwight, 1752–1817: A Biography* (New York, 1942), especially Chap. IX, "The Conquest of Infidelity." See also Charles E. Keller, *The Second Great Awakening in Connecticut* (New Haven, 1942), Chap. III, "The Counter Reformation."

[4] For the details of the Presbyterian phase of the western revival, see W. W.

Sweet, *Religion on the American Frontier*, Vol. II, *The Presbyterians* (New York, 1936), Chap. IV, "Revivalism and Presbyterian Controversy," pp. 82–96.

⁵ Donald G. Tewksbury, *The Founding of American Colleges and Universities Before the Civil War, with Particular Reference to the Religious Influences Bearing Upon the College Movement* (New York, Teachers College, Columbia University, 1932), is a mine of accurate information relative to the great period of college founding in the United States.

⁶ Pittsburgh, University of Pittsburgh Press, 1952. See particularly Chap. V, "Education," pp. 80–100.

⁷ *University of Pittsburgh Bulletin*, "The Celebration of the One Hundred and Twenty-fifth Anniversary" (Pittsburgh, 1912), pp. 108, 111, 114.

⁸ New York, Columbia University Press, 1938. See also W. W. Sweet, *The Presbyterians*, pp. 74–75; C. E. Hix, Jr., The Conflict Between Presbyterians and Free-Thought in the South, 1776–1838 (Ph.D. thesis, University of Chicago, 1937).

⁹ D. G. Tewksbury, *The Founding of American Colleges and Universities*, p. 90, and numerous other references.

¹⁰ Charles A. Hanna, *The Scotch-Irish* . . . 2 vols. See also the map in Sweet, *The Presbyterians*, frontispiece; also Sweet, *Religion in Colonial America*, pp. 250–254.

¹¹ Tewksbury, *op. cit.*, p. 84.

¹² *Ibid.*, pp. 75–89.

¹³ M. H. Sonne, *op. cit.*

¹⁴ *University of Tennessee Record*, July, 1898, pp. 219ff., 267ff.

¹⁵ See Tewksbury, *op. cit.*, especially Chap. III, "The Founding of State Universities Before the Civil War," pp. 133–207. This chapter contains a wealth of pertinent facts on the part the churches played in founding early state institutions.

¹⁶ These facts may be found in W. W. Sweet, *Indiana Asbury-Depauw University, 1837–1937: A Hundred Years of Higher Education in the Middle West* (New York, 1937), pp. 25–30.

¹⁷ This was a major motive in the founding of Andover Seminary in 1808, Princeton Theological Seminary in 1812, Auburn Seminary in 1818, Union Theological Seminary in Virginia in 1824, and Union Seminary in New York, in 1836.

¹⁸ See S. J. M. Eaton, *History of the Presbytery of Erie, etc.* (New York, 1868), pp. 94–95; also Sweet, *The Presbyterians*, pp. 77–79; also Guthrie, *op. cit.*, pp. 74–76.

¹⁹ *Minutes of the General Assembly* (1825), pp. 267ff.

²⁰ Beginning in 1785 in a log cabin seminary in the yard of the Reverend Joseph Smith at Upper Buffalo, Pennsylvania, which institution gave itself exclusively to the preparation of men for the ministry, the seminary named "Western" by the General Assembly in 1825 descended through John McMillan's Academy, 1788–1792, which was merged into the Canonsburg (Pa.) Acad-

emy, 1792–1802, which, in the latter year, became Jefferson College. The first active trustees of Western in 1825 were, at the same time, trustees of Jefferson College.

[21] Other western Presbyterian seminaries founded during these years were the seminary in connection with Centre College founded in 1828; a seminary at Marysville, Tennessee, and another at Nashville. See the circular letter of Joshua L. Wilson, dated Cincinnati, Sept., 1822, on the subject of a theological seminary in the West (W. W. Sweet, *The Presbyterians*, pp. 590–591).

[22] Jesse Johnson, "Early Theological Education West of the Alleghanies," in *Papers of the American Society of Church History*, Second Series, V, 121–131. See further references in Sweet, *The Presbyterians*, pp. 79–81.

CHAPTER VII *Service in Founding and Preserving the Nation*

[1] See *Westminster Assembly Addresses*, W. H. Roberts, ed. (Philadelphia, 1898), p. 327.

[2] C. A. Hanna, *The Scotch-Irish . . . ,* II, 1–2.

[3] John Fiske, *Dutch and Quaker Colonies*.

[4] P. 78. Copyright, 1944, by Harper & Brothers. Used by permission.

[5] A. N. Addleman, Early Presbyterianism in Westmoreland County, Ph.D. thesis, University of Pittsburgh; C. A. Briggs, *American Presbyterianism: Its Origin and Early History*, pp. 344–347.

[6] *Records of the Presbyterian Church in the U.S.A.* (1904), Appendix.

[7] George P. Hays, *Presbyterians* (1892), p. 106.

[8] *Ibid.*, p. 107.

[9] J. R. Sizoo, article in *Journal of the Presbyterian Historical Society*, XV, 56. See also Biography of Thomas Polk, *Dictionary of American Biography*; *Dictionary of American History* (1940), III, 368. Here the Mecklenburg Resolves and the so-called Declaration of Independence are discussed.

[10] H. J. Ford, *The Scotch-Irish in America*, pp. 466–468; also Appendix E, pp. 583–587.

[11] Also cited by W. W. Sweet, *The Story of Religion in America*, p. 178.

[12] Thomas Smyth, "Presbyterianism, the Revolution and the Declaration of Independence," pp. 32ff. (pamphlet).

[13] Sizoo, *op. cit.*, XV, 57.

[14] Briggs, *op. cit.*, p. 354.

[15] *Records of the Synod*, p. 499.

[16] The influence of Presbyterianism or of Presbyterians in the formation and adoption of the U.S. Constitution is impossible of accurate appraisal. In the Constitutional Convention of 1787, there were: 1 Methodist, 2 Quakers, 2 Roman Catholics, 19 Episcopalians, 8 Congregationalists, and 7 Presbyterians. Prior to the adoption of the First Amendment to the Constitution, the Presbyterians in the various states led in opposition to ratification owing to their fear of the Anglican Church becoming established here.

Dr. Lefferts A. Loetscher has compiled the following special bibliography on Presbyterians and the Revolution:

1. C. Inglis and E. B. O'Callaghan, eds., *The Documentary History of the State of New York* III (Albany, 1850), 1047–1066.

2. John Witherspoon, *Works* (Albany, 1850).

3. *Records of the Presbyterian Church in the U.S.A.* (Philadelphia, 1904), pp. 464–469, 472, 481.

CHAPTER VIII   *Missionary Expansion at Home*

1 William Warren Sweet, *Religion in Colonial America* (1942), p. 251.

2 *Records of the Presbyterian Church in the United States of America* (1841), p. 454, and Samuel Miller, *Memoirs of Rev. John Rodgers, D.D.* (1813), p. 200.

3 P. 474.

4 P. 954. Copyright 1953, Harper & Brothers, N.Y. Quoted by permission.

5 *Op. cit.*, p. 1229.

6 P. 172. Copyright, rev. ed., 1944, Harper & Brothers, N.Y. Quoted by permission.

7 P. 230.

8 *The Story of Religion in America* (1950), p. 198.

9 Robert Baird, in *State and Prospects of Religion in America*, p. 24, estimated that in 1800 the Presbyterian Church had 300 ministers, 500 churches, and 40,000 members.

10 P. 160.

11 *Minutes of Standing Committee*, p. 177.

12 *Journal of the Presbyterian Historical Society*, March, 1948, p. 43.

13 P. 51.

14 P. 485.

15 See Chap. VI. Although Lane Theological Seminary is now consolidated with McCormick, and Union and Auburn are not officially connected with the Presbyterian Church, yet for many years these seminaries were an active part of the church and are therefore here included.

16 See Chap. VI. See also the Appendix.

17 From transcript at San Francisco Theological Seminary.

CHAPTER IX   *Serving Overseas*

Fully to document this chapter would result in a thin margin of text at the top of hundreds of footnotes. Even to list all the titles employed in gathering the data which have been assembled would unduly prolong these pages. We must, however, venture to select and list the more useful books.

Foremost must be an official history by a secretary emeritus of the Board of Foreign Missions of the Presbyterian Church in the U.S.A.:

A. J. Brown, *One Hundred Years: A History of the Foreign Missionary Work of the Presbyterian Church in the U.S.A., with Some Account of Countries, Peoples and the Policies and Problems of Modern Missions.* New York, 1937, pp. 1140.

On Latin America see:

E. Braga and K. G. Grubb, *The Republic of Brazil: A Survey of the Religious Situation.* London, 1932, p. 184.

S. R. Gammon, *The Evangelical Invasion of Brazil; or a Half-Century of Evangelical Missions in the Land of the Southern Cross.* Richmond, 1910, pp. 179.

J. C. Porter, *An Open Door in Brazil: Being a Brief Survey of the Mission Work Carried on in Brazil Since 1869 by the Presbyterian Church in the United States.* Richmond, 1925, pp. 235.

W. A. Ross, *Sunrise in Aztec Land: Being an Account of the Mission Work That Has Been Carried on in Mexico Since 1874 by the Presbyterian Church in the United States.* Richmond, 1922, pp. 244.

W. R. Wheeler, *et al., Modern Missions in Chile and Brazil.* Philadelphia, 1926, pp. 173ff.

On Africa see:

R. D. Bedinger, *Triumphs of the Gospel in the Belgian Congo.* Richmond, n.d., pp. 218.

W. H. Sheppard, *Presbyterian Pioneers in Congo.* Richmond, n.d., pp. 157.

W. R. Wheeler, *The Words of God in an African Forest: The Story of an American Mission in West Africa.* New York, 1931, pp. 318.

On the Near East see:

A. Watson, *The American Mission in Egypt, 1854 to 1896.* Pittsburgh, 1904, pp. 487.

C. R. Watson, *Egypt and the Christian Crusade.* Philadelphia, 1907, pp. 288.

Various authors, *A Century of Mission Work in Iran (Persia).* Beirut, pp. 171.

On India see:

A. Gordon, *Our India Mission: A Thirty Years' History of the India Mission of the United Presbyterian Church of North America Together with Personal Reminiscences.* Philadelphia, 1888, pp. 516.

Historical Sketches of the India Missions of the Presbyterian Church in the United States of America. Allahabad, 1886, pp. iv, 182, iv.

Survey of the Evangelistic Work of the Punjab Mission of the Presbyterian Church in the U.S.A. 1929 (prepared by order of the India Council), pp. vii, 239.

On Thailand see:

G. B. McFarland, ed., *Historical Sketch of Protestant Missions in Siam, 1828–1928.* Bangkok, 1928, pp. xvii, 386.

On the Philippines see:

J. B. Rodgers, *Forty Years in the Philippines: A History of the Philippine*

Mission of the Presbyterian Church in the United States of America. New York, 1940, pp. viii, 205.

On China see:

J. R. E. Craighead, *Hunter Corbett: Fifty-six Years a Missionary in China.* New York, 1921, pp. 224.

D. W. Fisher, *Calvin Wilson Mateer, Forty-five Years a Missionary in Shantung, China.* London, 1911, pp. 342.

K. S. Latourette, *A History of Christian Missions in China.* New York, 1929, pp. xii, 930.

H. S. C. Nevius, *The Life of John Livingstone Nevius.* Chicago, 1895, pp. 476.

S. I. Woodbridge, *Fifty Years in China.* Richmond, 1919, pp. 231.

On Korea see:

C. A. Clark, *The Korean Church and the Nevius Methods.* New York, 1930, pp. 278.

L. G. Paik, *The History of Protestant Missions in Korea, 1832–1910.* Pyeng Yang, 1929, pp. v, 438, xiii.

On Japan see:

O. Carey, *A History of Christianity in Japan.* New York, 2 vols., 1909.

W. E. Griffis, *Hepburn of Japan.* Philadelphia, 1913, pp. ix, 238.

CHAPTER X *Wrestling with Human Values: The Slavery Years*

1 *The American Nation,* ed. A. B. Hart, Vol. 16, Chapters 4–5.

2 Writings of Thomas Jefferson. See Malone, *Jefferson and His Times,* pp. 264f.

3 Session Records of Presbyterian Church of Norwich, Ohio, on file at Wooster. See Records of New School Synod of Cincinnati for similar case of Wm. Graham, also on file at Wooster.

4 Letter in writer's possession.

5 This claim has been made both for the German Reformed Church of Germantown, Pa., now the Market Square Presbyterian, and for the Germantown Friends' Meeting. The year was 1688.

6 *Minutes of Synod of New York and Philadelphia,* 1787, p. 3.

7 *Minutes of General Assembly,* 1795, pp. 103–104.

8 *Minutes of General Assembly,* 1815, 1818.

9 Publications of Ohio Archaeological and Historical Society, IV, 44–63. See also *The American Nation,* ed. Hart, Vol. 16, *passim.*

10 The American Tract Society, in reprinting several English books and tracts, carefully deleted all references to slavery. From the Presbyterian Hymnal of 1834, Stanza 4 of Hymn 363 was deleted, because it referred to Negro slavery. Legacies to our Board of Foreign Missions were more than once paid from proceeds of sale of slaves. See *American Missionary Magazine,* Oct., 1857, p. 224, and *Free Presbyterian* for March 10, 1852.

[11] *Minutes of General Assembly*, 1845.

[12] These were James Robertson, Adam B. Gilleland, James McKean, Samuel E. Hibben, M. C. Williams, John C. Eastman, John D. Whitham, Ezekiel Miller.

[13] See Records of presbyteries of Chillicothe, New Lisbon, Coshocton, St. Clairsville, etc.

[14] See Chapter VIII, p. 175.

[15] *Minutes of New School General Assembly*, 1839.

[16] *Minutes of New School General Assembly*, 1846.

[17] Rankin, *Letters on Slavery* (1826), his letter to Presbytery of Chillicothe, 1836, and Records of Presbytery of Chillicothe.

[18] *Minutes of New School General Assembly*, 1849.

[19] *Minutes of New School Synod of Cincinnati*, 1846, 1847.

[20] Rankin, "History of the Free Presbyterian Church," published serially in the *Free Presbyterian*. See issue of Feb. 25, 1857.

[21] *Life and Writings of Joseph Gordon.*

[22] *Minutes of Presbytery of St. Clairsville*, I, 251–257, 281–282.

[23] Wilson, *Presbyterian Historical Almanac*, 1858, 1860.

[24] *Minutes of Free Presbytery of Mahoning*, Vol. 1, and Rankin, "History of the Free Presbyterian Church."

[25] *Minutes of Free Presbytery of Mahoning*, Vol. 1.

[26] See various pronouncements in minutes of these bodies between 1820 and 1860.

[27] The *Presbyterian* (Philadelphia) and the *Princeton Theological Review* contain articles in this tenor from Charles Hodge and Samuel Miller. See also the action of the Richmond Convention of Pro-Slavery Presbyterians in 1857.

[28] Frequent references in the *Free Presbyterian*. See especially the issue of June 27, 1855.

CHAPTER XI *Events and Trends—Early Nineteenth Century*

[1] W. W. Sweet, *Religion on the American Frontier*, Vol. II, *The Presbyterians*, *1783–1840*. Here by maps and text this expansion is clearly set forth. Very extended bibliography.

[2] B. W. McDonald, *History of the Cumberland Presbyterian Church*; Minutes of the General Assembly 1807, 1808, 1809, 1814; pp. 10ff. *et passim.*

[3] McDonald, *op. cit.*, pp. 82ff.

[4] See this volume, pp. 260–261.

[5] *Minutes of the General Assembly*, 1794, 1801, 1837, 1869, 1870. See also: Isaac V. Brown, *Historical Vindication of the Abrogation of the Plan of Union*, *1855*, pp. 32ff.; Z. Crocker, *The Catastrophe of the Presbyterian Church*, *1832*; S. J. Baird, *A History of the New School.*

[6] An affirmation designed to safeguard the unity and liberty of the Presbyterian Church in the United States of America with all the signatures and the

Note Supplementary, May 5, 1924 (The Jacobs Press, Auburn, New York).

[7] J. W. Nevin, *The Mystical Presence*, p. 53.

[8] *Ibid.*, p. 3.

[9] *Ibid.*, p. 107.

[10] *Ibid.*, p. 106n.

[11] *Ibid.*, p. 109.

[12] *Ibid.*, p. 74n.

[13] *Ibid.*, p. 98n.

[14] Charles Hodge, "Doctrine of the Reformed Church on the Lord's Supper," *Biblical Repertory and Princeton Review* (1848), p. 251.

[15] *Ibid.*

[16] *Ibid.*, p. 252.

[17] J. H. A. Ebrard, *Das Dogma von Heiligen Abendmahl und seine Geschichte.* Nevin had received the first volume in time to incorporate certain references to it in his *The Mystical Presence.*

[18] Alexander Barclay, *The Protestant Doctrine of the Lord's Supper* (Glasgow, 1927). Cf. Barclay 134 with Nevin 475, 188–198 with 487–496, 280–284 with 506, 510, 107–111 with 464–466 and footnote on 467, 117 with 473. Mr. Robert Clemmer called my attention to this relation.

[19] "The Reformed Doctrine of the Lord's Supper," *Mercersburg Review*, 1850, p. 523.

CHAPTER XII   *Some Events and Trends Since 1869*

[1] *Minutes of the General Assembly of the Presbyterian Church in the U.S.A.* (hereafter cited as G.A. *Mins.*), 1907, p. 261.

[2] *Ibid.*, 1874, p. 94; 1906, p. 245.

[3] *Ibid.*, 1876, p. 94; 1889, pp. 63–64.

[4] *Ibid.*, 1886, p. 122; 1896, pp. 58–65; 1898, p. 140.

[5] *Ibid.*, 1895, p. 145; 1898, p. 153.

[6] Cf., e.g., *Presbyterian Quarterly and Princeton Review*, VI (1877), 719–744.

[7] Cf. C. Hodge, in *Biblical Repertory and Princeton Review*, XLVIII (1871); A. T. Pierson, in *Presbyterian Review*, I (1880).

[8] Cf. L. A. Loetscher, "Presbyterians and Political Reform in Philadelphia from 1870 to 1917," in *Journal of the Presbyterian Historical Society*, XXIII (1945), 2–18, 119–136; W. A. Brown, *A Teacher and His Times* (New York, 1940), p. 136.

[9] G.A. *Mins.*, 1896, p. 159; 1897, p. 32; 1898, pp. 50, 61; 1899, p. 65.

[10] Cf. G.A. *Mins.*, 1898, p. 66; *Presbyterian and Reformed Review*, IX (1898), p. 710; *Presbyterian*, June 8, 1898, p. 32.

[11] G.A. *Mins.*, 1899, p. 129; 1902, p. 119.

[12] *Ibid.*, 1870, p. 131; 1878, p. 42; 1881, p. 536; 1907, p. 137.

[13] Cf. D. Moore to J. Maclean, Aug. 25, 1876; S. H. Kellogg to J. Maclean, Feb. 9, 1882, in the John Maclean Papers, Princeton University Library.

14 *G.A. Mins.,* 1881, p. 548; 1882, p. 57.

15 *Ibid.,* 1871, p. 5; 1879, pp. 622–633.

16 See Chap. I, p. 13, and Chap. IV, p. 91. See *G.A. Mins.* for May 27, 1904; May 26, 1906; and for 1912, pp. 209ff. On Nov. 6, 1911, the U.S. Supreme Court fully sanctioned the legality of the change. Thus the insertion of the phrase "in harmony with," while not implying that no doctrinal change had been made, did indicate that a church denomination remains the same denomination when, by its own legal processes, it changes its system of doctrine. See Gaius J. Slosser, *History of the Westminster Assembly and Standards* (1943), pp. 20–24.

17 *G.A. Mins.,* 1903, p. 113; 1905, pp. 165–174.

18 In *American Presbyterian Review,* N.S., II (1870), 305–306; cf. also C. A. Aiken, in *Presbyterian Quarterly and Princeton Review,* N.S., I (1872), 26–27.

19 In . . . *History* . . . *Documents of* . . . *Sixth General Conference of the Evangelical Alliance* (New York, 1874), pp. 139ff.

20 *G.A. Mins.,* 1873, pp. 557–558; 1876, pp. 22, 50.

21 Cf. also *ibid.,* 1890, pp. 103–104.

22 Cf. *Form of Government,* Chap. X, Sec. XIV.

23 *G.A. Mins.,* 1903, pp. 90–91, 147; 1904, pp. 120ff.

Bibliography

SOURCE BOOKS

The sources consulted in the preparation of this volume are indicated in part in the footnotes. Excellent bibliographies may be found in the following:

Jackson, Samuel M., A Bibliography of American Church History, 1820–1893. Vol. III of the American Church History Series. New York, 1894.

Latourette, Kenneth S., History of the Expansion of Christianity, 7 vols. New York, 1943.

Schaff, Philip, History of the Christian Church, 7 vols., especially Vols. VI and VII. 1895.

Slosser, G. J., The History of the Westminster Assembly and Standards. Pittsburgh, 1943.

Sweet, W. W., Indiana Asbury-Depauw University, 1837–1937: A Hundred Years of Higher Education in the West. New York, 1937.

———, Religion in Colonial America. New York, 1943.

———, Religion on the American Frontier. Vol. II, The Presbyterians, 1783–1840. New York, 1936.

———, The Story of Religion in America. New York, 1950.

Trinterud, L. J., The Forming of an American Tradition: A Re-examination of Colonial Presbyterianism. Philadelphia, 1949.

GENERAL BIBLIOGRAPHY

Many of the persons mentioned in the narrative or listed in the Who's Who of this volume are, or were, themselves authors or were the subjects for authors. In the notes for Chapter IX, source books for the history of the foreign missions program are included. The various educational institutions, for the most part, can and will furnish books or pamphlets telling of their history and background.

The as yet unpublished manuscripts containing the records of the various Presbyterian judicatories have been examined as necessary. There is no point in relisting them here as far as most readers are concerned. The books listed below may be called the "veterans" that are to be found in well stocked libraries.

Briggs, Charles A., *American Presbyterianism: Its Origin and Early History*.

Brown, A. J., *One Hundred Years*. A history of Presbyterian U.S.A. foreign missions.

Dictionary of American Biography.

Dictionary of National Biography.

Drury, Clifford M., *H. H. Spalding*.

————, *Marcus Whitman*.

————, *Presbyterian Panorama*. A history of Presbyterian U.S.A. home missions.

Elliot, David, *Life of Elisha McCurdy*.

Finley, John H., *The Coming of the Scot*.

Fleming, J. R., *The Burning Bush*.

Ford, H. J., *The Scotch-Irish in America*.

Gibbons, Herbert A., *John Wanamaker*. 2 vols.

Gillett, E. H., *History of the Presbyterian Church U.S.A.*

Glasgow, W. M., *Cyclopedic Manual of the U.P. Church*.

Grimm, Harold J., *The Reformation Era*.

Guthrie, Dwight R., *John McMillan*.

Hanna, C. A., *The Scotch-Irish; or, the Scot in North Britain, North Ireland, and North America*. 2 vols.

Hanzsche, W. T., *The Presbyterians*.

————, *Forgotten Heroes*.

Hodge, Charles, *Constitutional History of the Presbyterian Church*.

Klett, Guy S., *Presbyterians in Colonial Pennsylvania*.

Knox, John, *The Works of John Knox*, ed. David Laing, 6 vols.

Latourette, K. S., *A History of Christianity*.

Lindsay, T. M., *The History of the Reformation*. 2 vols.

Loetscher, L. A., *A Brief History of Presbyterianism*.

McKinney, W. W., *Early Pittsburgh Presbyterianism*.

Mackinnon, James, *John Calvin*.

McNaugher, John, *Theological Education in the U.P. Church*.

Mitchell, A. F., *The Westminster Assembly.*

———, *The Minutes of the Westminster Assembly.*

Moffatt, James, *The Presbyterian Churches.*

Ogilvie, J. N., *The Presbyterian Churches of Christendom.*

Posey, W. Brownlow, *Presbyterianism in the Old South West.*

Reed, Edith, *Woodrow Wilson.*

Reid, J. W., *History of the Presbyterian Church in Ireland.* 2 vols.

Robertson, H. M., *Rise of Economic Individualism.*

Rouse, Ruth and Neill, Stephen Charles, *A History of the Ecumenical Movement.*

Schaff, Philip, *History of the Christian Church.* 7 vols.

———, *Creeds of Christendom*, Vols. I and III.

Scouller, J. B., *A Manual of the United Presbyterian Church.*

Slosser, Gaius Jackson, *Christian Unity, Its History and Challenge in All Communions in All Lands.*

Smith, Joseph, *Old Redstone.*

———, *History of Jefferson College.*

Sprague, W. B., *Annals of the American Pulpit.*

Tawney, R. H., *Religion and the Rise of Capitalism.* Corrected by H. M. Robertson.

Tewksbury, Donald G., *The Founding of American Colleges and Universities.*

Thompson, R. E., *A History of the Presbyterian Churches in the United States.*

Vander Velde, L. G., *The Presbyterian Churches and the Federal Union 1861–1869.*

Weber, Max, *The Protestant Ethic and the Spirit of Capitalism.* Corrected by H. M. Robertson.

Who's Who in America.

Who Was Who in America.

Woods, David W., *John Witherspoon.*

Zenos, Andrew C., *Presbyterianism in America.*

Index

Also consult "Who's Who," pp. 292-301, and the list of educational institutions in the Appendix, pp. 302-307.

Abélard, 14
Abernethy, John, 13
Abolition, Abolitionists, 219 ff.
Academies, 54, 140 f.
Accomac County, 62
Act for the Establishment of Religious Freedom in Virginia, 133
Adams, John Q., 124
Adopting Act (1729), 41 f.
Africa, West, missions, 195
Agricultural Missions Foundations, 203
Alaska, missions, 252
Albemarle County, Va., 70
Alison, Francis, 54, 106
Alliance of the Reformed Churches, 265, 286
American Board of Commissioners for Foreign Missions, 175, 192 ff.
American Home Missionary Society, 176
American Presbyterianism, three early groups of, 1 f.
Anderson, John, 96
Andrews, Jedediah, 33, 44
Apostolic Succession, 23 f.
Arminianism: in the adopted standards of various Presbyterian churches, 260 f.; in churches in Scotland and Ulster, 14 f.; espoused by Ebenezer Erskine, 14 ff.; in Marrow of Modern Divinity, 14 f.
Associate Reformed Church, 96
Augusta Academy, 84
Awakening, Great. See Great Awakening

Awakening, Second Great. See Great Awakening, Second

Back Country, Shenandoah Valley, 65 f.
Bacon, L. W., quoted, 170
Bancroft, George, quoted, 151
Baptists, 138 f., 169, 178 ff., 199, 235
Bay Psalm Book, 20
Beecher, Lyman, 135, 148
Belfast Society, 13
Bishop, the, 22 f.
Black, John, 70
Blackburn, Gideon, 173
Book of Sports, The, 18
Boston, Mass., 43
Boston, Thomas, 89
Brainerd, David, 130 f.
Brewster, William, 2
Bridenbaugh, Carl, 60
Briggs, Charles A., 3
Brown, William A., 206 f.
Browning, Robert, quoted, 192

Caldwell, Frank H., quoted, 271 ff.
Caldwell, Pastor, Springfield, N.J., 159
Calvin, John, 127 ff. See under Calvinism
Calvinism: defined, 8 f.; fundamental principles of, 153; its influence, 127 ff., 143 f., 151 ff.; its principal emphases and teaching, 10 ff.; its modification, 235 ff.
Cameron, Richard, 102, 104 f.
Cameronians, 107 ff.
Canonsburg, Pa., 148

Canonsburg Academy, 140, 148
Carolina Society, 63 f.
Carolinas, Western, 76 f.
Cartwright, Thomas, 17
Catechisms: Heidelberg, 11; Larger, 11, 18; Shorter, 11, 18
Character contributions, 24 f.
Chesapeake Society, 60 ff.
China, Church of Christ in, 207
Christ, sovereignty of, in Constitution, 119 ff.
Christian Endeavor Society, 253
Christy, Wayne, 91, 98
Church and sacraments, 238 ff.
Church and state, 132 ff., 257
Colleges, church, factors in founding, 122 ff., 132 ff., 143 f.
College of New Jersey, 1, 12, 54 f., 75, 90, 128 ff., 135 f.
Committee on Cooperation in Latin America, 206
Communion, closed, 91 f.
Confession of Faith, Westminster, 11, 17 f., 41 f., 63, 68, 72, 257, 259 ff.
Confessional Statement of 1925 of the U.P. Church, 91
Constitution, Federal, influence on, 162, 315, note 16
Continental Congress, First, 35
Contributions of Presbyterians in the South, 80 ff.
Cornbury, Governor, 36 f.
Cosmopolitanism, 3
Covenanter Church. *See* Reformed Presbyterian Church
Covenanting, 108, 118 ff., 126
Covenants, Doctrines of, 17
Craig, John, 70, 83 f., 103
Craighead, Alexander, 77, 82, 105 ff.
Craighead, Thomas, 135, 141
Cumberland Presbyterian Church, 179, 235
Cuthbertson, John, 95, 109 f.

Dartmouth College case, 134
Davies, Samuel, 73 f., 79 f., 140
Declaratory Statement, 1902–1903, 260 f.
Denton, Richard, 31

Dickinson, Jonathan 2, 40, 47
Doak, Samuel, 135
Doctrinal changes, 235 ff., 259 ff.
Doctrines brought to America, 10 f.
Dodd, Thaddeus, 140
Doughty, Francis, 31
Dwight, Timothy, 135, 184

Eagle's Wing, ship, 2
Economics and slavery, 216 ff.
Ecumenical participation, 264 ff.
Educated ministry. *See* Ministry, educated
Education: founding of institutions for, 122 ff., 132 ff., 143 f., 302 ff.; and theological seminaries, 146 ff., 180 ff.; why notable contributions to, 127 ff.
Edwards, Jonathan, 46 f., 130
Election Day sermons, 156
Eliot, John, 1
Eliot, T. S., quoted, 284
Episcopacy, 22 f., 155
Erskine, Ebenezer, 14 ff., 87 ff., 92
Evans, David, 39
Ewing, J. C. R., 202

Federal Constitution, 162, 315, note 16
Federal theology, 17
Finley, Samuel, 71, 73
Finney, Charles G., 235
First Presbytery in America, 2 f., 32 ff., 62, 165, 167
Fisher, Edward, 14
Fisher, James, 15
Forman Christian College, 202
Free Presbyterian Church in America, 214 ff., 230 ff.
Frelinghuysen, Theodore J., 47
Frontier challenges, 136 ff.
Froude, James, quoted, 7

General Assembly: organization and first meeting, 58 f., 168; pronouncement relative to slavery, of 1795, 218 f.; of 1818, 220
Gewehr, W. M., quoted, 80
God, His sovereignty, 119 ff.

Graham, William, 83
Graphs of Scottish, Ulster, and American Presbyterianism, 4 f.
Great Awakening, 1725–1745, 1, 12, 45 ff.
Great Awakening, Second, 1796–1835, 134 ff.
Green, Ashbel, 220, 226
Groups in American Presbyterianism prior to 1787, 1 ff.
Guthrie, Dwight R., 140

Hampden-Sydney College, 83 f.
Hampton, John, 33
Hanna, C. A., quoted, 152
Hanover revival, 71 f.
Hay-stack prayer-meeting, 192
Hempstead, L.I., 31
Hite, Joist, 66 f.
Hodge, Charles, 245 ff.

Independence, American, factors promoting, 154 ff.
India, North, United Church of, 208
India, South, United Church of, 207
Ireland, northern, 5 ff.

Jackson, Sheldon, 184 ff., 252
Japan, Church of Christ in, 207
Jefferson College, 140, 148, 314, note 20

Kendall, Henry, 252

Latourette, Kenneth Scott, quoted, 169 f.
Lay patronage, 7 f.
Liberty Hall, 82, 84
Lincoln, Abraham, 125
Lindsley, Philip, 135, 141
Log College, 1, 12, 47 f., 54, 128 ff., 139 f.
Log College of Guilford County, N.C., 84

McCormick Theological Seminary, 151 f.; Appendix, 306 f.
M'Crie, Thomas, 16 f.
McGready, James, 135 f.

Mackay, John A., 195, 207; quoted, 279 ff.
Mackenzie College, 202
Maclean, John, quoted, 130 f.
McLeod, Alexander, 115, 122 f.
McMillan, John, 135, 140
McNaugher, John, 101
McNish, George, 33, 35
Makemie, Francis, 32 f., 35 f., 61 f., 165
Manokin Church, 32
Marrow of Modern Divinity, and Marrowism, 14 ff., 88 ff.
Maryland, beginnings in, 62
Mather, Cotton, 29
Mayflower, ship, 2
Mecklenburg Convention and Resolves, 83, 157 f.
Mecklenburg County, N.C., 82
Mercersburg Controversy, 238 ff.
Methodists, 138, 145 f., 169, 178 ff., 199 f., 235
Migration, across the Atlantic, 7 f., 27 f., 42 ff., 53, 64 f., 66 f., 105 f., 142 f., 152, 166, 169; westward, 172 ff., 234 ff.
Mills, Samuel J., 192
Ministry, educated, 55 ff., 143 f., 179 f.
Missions abroad, 191 ff.; union enterprises, 205 ff. For colleges and universities *see* pp. 305 f.
Missions at home, 165 ff., 173
Missions, Board of, 173
Missions, Board of Foreign, 173 *et passim*
Missions, earliest beginnings, 45, 166 ff.
Missions, expansion retarded, 178 ff.
Missions, philosophy and methods of, 175 ff., 198 ff., 237
Missions, Standing Committee of, 1802, 172 f., 175
Moderatism, 14 f.
Moncrief, Alexander, 15
Morton, Andrew, quoted, 82

Nation, service in founding and preserving, 150 ff.

National Covenant, 103
National Reform Association, 125 f.
Negroes, 74 f., 210 ff. *See also* Slavery
Nevin, John W., 239 ff.
New England Primer, 11
New Jersey, College of. *See* College of New Jersey
New School, attitudes of, toward slavery, 223 ff.
New School–Old School division, 1837–1870, 176 ff., 182 ff., 193 f.
New Side–Old Side division, 1741–1758, 12, 50 ff., 55, 70 f., 237
New Testament presbyterianism, 22 f.
Nineteenth century, events and trends in early, 234 ff.; trends in late, 251
North, beginnings in, 27 ff.
North Carolina, beginnings in, 64 f.
Northern Ireland, 5 ff.
Nottingham Academy, 254
Nottingham Sermon, Gilbert Tennent, 51 f.

Ohio Valley, 28
Old School–New School Schism, 1837–1870. *See under* New School
Old Side–New Side Schism, 1741–1758. *See under* New Side
Old Testament Church, 22
Origins, 1 ff.

Paik, George L., 204
Parkhurst, Charles H., 256
Pennsylvania Gazette, quoted, 50
Philadelphia, First Presbyterian Church of, 33
Philippines, United Evangelical Church of, 207 f.
Pierson, Arthur T., and Delavan, 193 f.
Pierson, John, 40
Pitts Creek Church, 32
Pittsburgh, Pa., First Presbyterian Church of, 158
Pittsburgh, University of, 140 f.
Pittsburgh-Xenia Theological Seminary, 100
Plan of Union of 1801, 138, 174 ff., 177, 193, 236 ff.

Presbyterian growth, 1800–1830, 177
Presbyterianism through the centuries, 21 ff.
Presbyterians, English, 13
Presbyteries: Abingdon (Ky.), 78; Allegheny, 223; Associate of the Reformed and United Presbyterian churches, 2, 34, 95; Athens, 238; Beaver, 223; Boston, 43; Central Ohio, Free, 229; Cincinnati, Free, 229; Cleveland, 238; Coshocton, 227; Donegal, 42, 45, 69 f.; East, Me., 43; East Jersey, 42; Erie, 238; First in the U.S.A., 2 f., 32 ff., 62, 165, 167; Grafton, 43; Grand River, 238; Hanover, 78; Hillsboro or Highland, 228, 229; Illinois, Free, 229; Iowa, Northwest, Free, 229; Laggan, Ireland, 32; Lexington, 71, 78; Londonderry, 43; Long Island, 31, 39, 42; Mahoning, Free, 228 f.; Meadville, 238; Montana, 185; New Brunswick, 42, 52, 55 f.; New Castle, 39, 53; New Lisbon, 222 f., 235; New York, 42, 53; Orange, 78, 79; Philadelphia, 39, 185; Portage, 238; Redstone, 28, 58, 78; Reformed, of the Associate Church, 2 f.; Ripley, Free, 227, 229; Ripley, New School, 242; Salem, 43; San Francisco, 184; San Joaquin, 187; Snow Hill, 39; South Carolina, 78 f.; Transylvania, 78; Trumbull, 238
Pressly, John T., 91
Price, Frank W., 205
Princeton Theological Seminary, 240. *See also* Theological institutions, and Appendix, 306-307
Princeton University, 1, 54 f., 128 ff.
Protestant beginnings in northern Ireland, 5 ff.
Psalmody: in America, 92; its origins, 19 f.
Psalter: Geneva, 19 f.; Tate and Brady, 20
Puritans: in New England, 1, 165; presbyterially inclined, 29
Puritan strictness, 24 f.

Reformed Presbyterian Church, 5, 102 ff., 104 f.; educational institutions, 113 ff.; foreign missions, 110 ff.; maintenance of identity, 114 ff.; politics, 121 f.; practice of covenanting, 118 ff., 126; religious journals, 115; slavery, 122 ff.; society meeting, 116 ff.; sovereignty of Christ in the Constitution, 119 ff.
Reformed Presbytery, First, 110 f.
Remonstrants of Dort, 261 f.
Revolutionary War, 151 ff., 158 ff., 316
Rice, David, 135, 141
"Road Ahead," 285 ff.
Robinson, William, 72 f.
Roosevelt, Theodore, 139
Rous, Francis, version of the Psalms, 19 f.
Rush, Benjamin, 160

Sabbatarianism, 17 f.
Salem, Mass., 1
San Francisco Theological Seminary, 181, 306 f.
Saybrook Platform, 1, 29
Schaff, Philip, 3, 103, 239 ff., quoted, 291
"Scotch-Irish," 5 f.
Scottish Confession of Faith (1560), 2, 12
Scouller, J. B., quoted, 96
Secession in Scotland, 90
Serving Overseas, 191 ff.
Silliman University, 202
Slavery, 93 f., 122 ff., 210 ff.; background facts, 212 ff.; economics of the problem of, 216 ff.; New School Assembly attitudes toward, 223 f.; reversal of attitudes in the South toward, 220 ff.
Smith, Samuel B., 135
Smyth, Thomas, quoted, 159
Snow Hill Church, 32
Sociological and spiritual service, 163 f., 254 ff.
Solemn League and Covenant, 86, 103
South, beginnings in, 60 ff.
South Carolina, 67 f.

Southampton, L.I., 30
Southold, L.I., 30
Spalding, Henry, 183 f.
Speer, Robert E., 194 ff., 206, 252
Spring, Gardiner, quoted, 173
Stelzle, Charles, 255
Stobo, Archibald, 63 f.
Stowe, Harriet Beecher, 148 f.
Strictness in godly character, 24 f.
Subscription to the Westminster Standards, 3, 41
Sunday schools, 253
Sweet, William W., quoted, 170, 171, 178
Synods: Associate Reformed, 96; California, 181; the Carolinas, 78; Cincinnati, 227; Cincinnati, Free, 227 f.; Colorado, 185; First, 62, 167; Illinois, 181; Kentucky, 179, 235; New Jersey, 181; New York, 53, 70, 156, 185; New York and Philadelphia, 58, 77, 156 f., 167, 181; Ohio, 148, 181; Pennsylvania, 181; Perth and Sterling, 14 f.; Philadelphia, 39 ff., 69 f., 156; Pittsburgh, 148, 179, 197; Ulster, 13; Utah, 187; Virginia, 78

Talbot, ship, 1
Tate and Brady Psalter, 196
Tennent, Gilbert, 47 f., 57 f., 70, 128 f.
Tennent, William, Sr., 47 f., 70, 128 f.
Test Act of 1704, 6 f.
Thailand, Church of Christ in, 207
Theological institutions, 146 ff., 180 ff.; Auburn, 147; Lane, 148 f.; Princeton, 147; Western, 147 ff. *See also* Appendix, 306-307
"Today and Tomorrow," 267 ff.
Trueblood, Elton, quoted, 153 f.

Ulster: persecutions in, 6 ff., 8 f., 18 f., 142 f., 152 f.; Protestant beginnings in, 511
Ulster Plantation, 6 ff., 13
Ulster-Scotch, 1-8, 155

United Presbyterians, 86 ff.; abandonment of much of Calvinism by, 91, 93; colleges of, 100; ecumenical attitude of, 101; exclusiveness of, 16 f., 91 f.; foreign missions of, 99; inner development of, 89 ff.; marrowism in background of, 14 ff., 91 f.; outer development of, 94 ff.; particular emphases of, 91 ff.; statistics of growth of, 99; union activities of, 98 f.; union of 1858 of, 94, 97 f.

Van Dusen, Henry P., 207
van Dyke, Henry, quoted, 37 f.
von Ranke, Leopold, quoted, 151

Wanamaker, John, 255
Washington and Jefferson College, 140 f., 148, 314, note 20
Washington and Lee University, 84, 135
Watson, Charles R., 195, 202
Watts, Isaac, 21, 159
Welsh, Robert, 215
Western Foreign Missionary Society, 176

Western Missionary Society, 176
Western Theological Seminary, 140, 148, 240 f., 314, note 20. *See also* Appendix, 306-307; Theological institutions
Westminster Standards, 3, 11 ff.; amendments to, 260 ff.; not purely Calvinistic, 12 f.
Whitaker, Alexander, 1, 61
Whitaker, William, 2
Whitefield, George, 48 f., 130
Whitman, Marcus, 183 f., 190
"Who's Who," 292 ff.
Wicomico Church, 32
Wilder, Robert P., 194, 206
Wilder, Royal G., 193 f., 194
Willey, Samuel, 184
Witherspoon, John, 58, 155, 156 f., 160, 168
Wordsworth, William, quoted, 25
World Council of Churches, 206 ff.

Yale, 40, 46, 128 f., 130 f.
Young, John, 30

Zwingli, Huldreich, 9, 246 f.